Enterprise Architecture for Digital Business

Enterprise Architecture for Digital Business
Integrated Transformation Strategies

Tushar K. Hazra
Bhuvan Unhelkar

CRC Press
Taylor & Francis Group
Boca Raton London New York

CRC Press is an imprint of the
Taylor & Francis Group, an **informa** business
AN AUERBACH BOOK

First edition published 2021
by CRC Press
6000 Broken Sound Parkway NW, Suite 300, Boca Raton, FL 33487-2742

and by CRC Press
2 Park Square, Milton Park, Abingdon, Oxon, OX14 4RN

© 2021 Taylor & Francis Group, LLC

CRC Press is an imprint of Taylor & Francis Group, LLC

ISBN: 978-1-498-72788-4 (hbk)
ISBN: 978-0-367-55718-8 (pbk)
ISBN: 978-1-315-12040-9 (ebk)

Typeset in Times
by codeMantra

To my beloved Mom – without you I mean nothing
and to the loving memories of my dad [TH]

To Naman & Monika [BU]

Contents

PART A   Setting the Context for Digital Business

PART B   The Digital Enterprise Architecture Life Cycle

PART C   *Leveraging the Value of Digital Enterprise Architecture*

List of Figures

List of Tables

Foreword

Today, it is almost impossible to find a mid- or large-size enterprise that isn't undergoing some sort of digital transformation. Not only is it happening in large businesses, but even small businesses are embracing digitization. This is an interesting phenomena considering the fact that it has been only five years since Digital Transformation (DT) entered the mainstream of the Enterprise Architecture (EA) discipline. While the costs of transformation efforts are coming down, the main reason for DT efforts is the resultant value to the customer going up.

I've dedicated the last ten-plus years of my professional career to enterprise transformations globally and have seen many businesses struggle with how to transform efficiently and cost effectively. Organizations undergoing DT have to avoid the trap of either being too canonical, such that the transformation's architecture starts with a solid theoretical foundation but becomes an implementation nightmare, or starting the transformation in an ad hoc manner, leading to skyrocketing costs and a lack of time for formal design. Both these options result in a negative economic impact to the business and severe dissatisfaction for customers.

Tushar and Bhuvan wrote this book, *Enterprise Architecture for Digital Business*, to help you avoid those situations by balancing a thorough and practical approach that could save you headaches, frustration, time, and rework. The authors did a fine job of bringing together various and, at times, disparate topics in a practical way to demonstrate how an enterprise can transform to a digital business.

In addition, as a Lean Agile executive coach, I find it very appropriate that this book deals with Digital Business in the context of business agility. Agility is a cornerstone of business success and digital technologies and digitized business processes play a key roles in achieving it. Most importantly, though, as my decades of experience working in the industry tell me, the key purpose of this entire exercise is more than just digital business or business agility. The ultimate goal is the enhancement and provisioning of customer value while also increasing financial success (in a for-profit business) or achieving its mission (in a government office or a not-for-profit organization). Efforts that don't enhance the value a business provides to the external or internal customer are a complete waste.

The book you are holding in your hand is an excellent and honest effort by the authors to ensure that your enterprise's path to digitization is as productive as it can be. To sum it all up, even though this book is about EA itself, I am delighted to observe that it is more about how EA can help in enhancing the capabilities of the enterprise so that it achieves its ultimate goal – customer value.

I compliment the authors on their work. And I wish you, the reader of this book, the very best in your digitization efforts – whether you are in private industry, in a government body or, like me, running a consulting practice.

Masa K. Maeda, PhD
Lean Agile executive coach and
enterprise transformation expert
Founder and principal consultant
Valueinnova LLC
Lehi, Utah, USA

Dr. Masa K. Maeda is a Lean-Agile enterprise transformation coach and trainer, and a program/product manager. He has undertaken digital transformations, training, and management at companies from Fortune 500 to start-ups in 15 countries around the world. He has successfully applied his multidisciplinary background and experience to bring about fundamental changes in the way enterprises in many different industries operate in the new digital economy. He is a:

- Certified Kanban Mentor/Leader/Methodologist/Coach/Trainer
- Certified Scrum Trainer/Product Owner/Scrum Master/Agile Expert
- Certified XSCALE Business Agility

Preface

This book approaches the vast topic of Enterprise Architecture (EA) from a futuristic viewpoint. While there is substantial literature on EA already published over the last decade, this book approaches it from a business transformation viewpoint. EA is treated as a framework that can be used to understand where the business is today and what it should do in order to transform into a digital business. That is the theme of this book.

A key differentiator of this book is the integrated transformation approach that capitalizes on the EA of the organization. Instead of limiting EA to its contemporary technical dimension, this book integrates the technologies, business, frameworks, people, quality, and governance of the organization in order to create a future-ready business. Thus, this book further dives into the techno-business aspects of Big Data, Mobile, and Cloud that form the basis for digital business transformation strategies.

The authors' combined experience of working in the EA space provide practical hands-on advice to professionals on digital transformations, especially in globally dispersed medium to large organizations. Furthermore, consulting companies and individuals will also find this a valuable addition to their bookshelf in terms of practical insights and guidance that we ourselves have gleaned as practitioners. The case studies in this book are based on our experiences and, as such, provide a useful, real world angle to the topic of EA for future digital businesses.

An EA is the technical fabric of the enterprise and transcends technology to move into business spaces. Therefore, it needs to be discussed in an integrated, holistic manner. Only such an approach can provide the necessary basis for a transformation that readies the enterprise for the myriad business and technological challenges it will invariably face. For example, Big Data, Mobile, and Cloud Computing are all highly disruptive technologies that require a fine balance between their business and technical aspects. This book focuses on preparing an organization for the impact of that.

Following are the important questions addressed in this book:

- What are the key considerations of a business in the digital world? What should these businesses expect – technically – in the next 3 to 5 years that will impact them?
- How can EA be used to shape the direction for medium to large organizations?
- What are the potential risks of disruptive technologies to those businesses unprepared for technology-driven change?
- What needs to be done to a current EA to prepare it for a future EA?
- What are the issues and challenges with regard to governance, risk, and compliance when disruptive technologies hit an organization?
- How can EA plug the gap between technology and business that results from changes to either of them?

This is a *practical* book that is based on our experiences as well as our investigations and research into the changing face of EA. Thus, although this book can be used by a practice leader or a manager, its basis is in solid theory and research. This book contains numerous examples, case studies, diagrams, tables, and discussion topics that provide value to readers. The challenges outlined in this book and the proposed approaches to solving them are all derived from the authors' practical experiences in the industry.

READERS

There are diverse categories of readers who will likely find this book interesting, as it covers crucial practical aspects and is underpinned by theory. More specifically, this book is aimed at the following audience:

   a. An enterprise architect responsible for the creation and maintenance of an organization's EA and its application in digital transformation
   b. A senior manager/decision maker who wants to prepare for changes brought about by Big Data, Mobile, and Cloud technologies
   c. An academic who wants to introduce a practical graduate course dealing with the impact technologies can have on digitizing businesses
   d. A researcher who is exploring the various opportunities and challenges of EA
   e. A person in charge of governance, risk, and compliance at an organization

This book covers not only traditional EA fundamentals, but also integrated transformation roadmaps and their implementation. The advantage of this book lies in its practical aspects.

HOW TO USE THE BOOK (CHAPTER SUMMARIES)

MAPPING BOOK TO A WORKSHOP

The material in this book is presentable in varying formats. These include:

   • A two-day practical training course or a workshop that can be delivered in public or in-house (customized) format to industrial participants
   • A one-semester, 13-week, graduate-level course
   • A distance-learning format wherein the physical book is still required by the students, but the assessments, case studies, etc., are based online.

Acknowledgements

Abbass Ghanbary
Abhay Saxena
Amit Tiwary
Andy Lyman
Anurag Agarwal
Asim Chauhan
Aurilla Aurelie Arntzen
Bhargav Bhatt
Bharti Trivedi
Bryan Lambe
Bryan Messer
Carlos Mantilla
Colleen Berish
David Sanders
Geoff Hummer
Gerardo S. Reyna Camano
Girish Nair
Haydar Jawad
James Wendland
Javed Matin
Jose Romero
Josh Baker
Keith Sherringham
Liz Yannoni
M.N. Sharif

Malcolm Slovin
Masa K. Maeda
Milind Barve
Mohammed Maharmeh
Naman Jain
Prince Sounderarajan
Ram Govindu
Reenie Askew
Robert Pillar
S.D. Pradhan
Sami Albana
San Murugesan
Sanjeev Sharma
Sanjiv Kumar
Sonia Schmitt
Steve Blais
Steve Plante
Sunita Lodwig
Suresh Paryani
Tad Gonsalves
Trivikrama (T.V.) Rao
Vivek Eshwarappa
Walied Askarzai
Warren Adkins
Yi-Chen Lan

FAMILY

This book is dedicated to my parents – especially my mother who passed away just when it was to be submitted for publication. I remain eternally grateful for her blessings and encouragement of me over my life. Rest in peace, Mom!

Tushar K. Hazra

Thanks to my family for their support and good wishes: Asha (wife), Sonki (daughter), Keshav (son), Chinar (sister-in-law), and our dog, Benji. This book is dedicated to a fine young man who is a strategic thinker and an entrepreneur with deep interests in application of technologies to business (in particular education business) – and his better half!

Bhuvan Unhelkar

Authors

Tushar K. Hazra is an executive-level Enterprise Architect with over twenty years of experience. He is a successful and recognized thought leader, actively involved in the digital transformation of organizations, and in architecting and implementing every stage of enterprise-level business solutions, from facilitation of strategy, blueprint, roadmap, and strategic initiative planning to business solution delivery.

As Principal of EpitomiOne, Dr. Hazra has been actively involved in designing, developing, and delivering mission-critical, patient-centric, innovative, and cost-effective IT solutions across the US federal, state, and local government agencies, as well as in private healthcare organizations (payers and providers). Tushar has a proven track record in aligning IT with business goals through planning, prioritization, and implementation.

During his professional career, Tushar has demonstrated C-Level executive partnership, technical thought leadership, program management, P&L responsibility, and health IT system engineering domain expertise. He has successfully leveraged emerging technologies such as social media, Cloud Computing, Big Data analytics, Internet of Things, and Mobile Computing.

His key accomplishments include:

- Aligned healthcare IT strategies with business objectives while assisting VA and DoD (IPO) executives to make informed decisions with their technology investments
- Established EA practice at a state government quasi-agency – defined the target architecture model, set of standards, governance structure and processes, and performance metrics to assess the efficiency of the entire IT organization
- Led the strategic IT initiatives prioritization for a federal healthcare organization, as SOA and Web Strategy Practice Director of a consulting firm: helped define a multiyear implementation roadmap for technology initiatives aligned with potential business growth
- Led the EA efforts for a large healthcare insurance provider for the eligibility, enrollment, and claim processing components and reengineered its business operations while complying with Affordable Care Act mandates
- Defined the target operating model to enable transformation of core business processes, as Enterprise Architect at a global healthcare delivery firm; defined the Business Domain model and mapped technology capabilities to optimize application portfolio and reduce operational costs; key solution areas included improvement of operational efficiency and governance, risk management and compliance
- Developed and led large-scale architecture strategy and systems integration programs with major corporate enterprises in the healthcare, financial services, insurance, retail, and supply chain industries

Dr. Bhuvan Unhelkar (BE, MDBA, MSc, PhD, FACS) has extensive strategic and hands-on professional experience in the Information and Communication Technologies (ICT) industry. He is a full professor and lead faculty of IT at the University of South Florida, at their Sarasota-Manatee campus. He is the founder of and consultant at *MethodScience* and *PlatiFi*. He is also an adjunct professor at Western Sydney University, Australia, and an honorary professor at Amity University, India. His current industrial research interests include AI and ML in business optimization, Big Data and business value, and business analysis in the context of Agile. Dr. Unhelkar holds a Certificate-IV in TAA and TAE, Professional Scrum Master – I, SAFe (Scaled Agile Framework for Enterprise) Leader, and is a Certified Business Analysis Professional® (CBAP of the IIBA).

Dr. Unhelkar's areas of expertise include:

- Big Data Strategies: *BDFAB* – with an emphasis on applying Big Data technologies and analytics to generate business value
- Artificial Intelligence & Business Optimization
- Agile Processes: *CAMS* – practical application of composite Agile to real-life business challenges not limited to software projects
- Business Analysis & Requirements Modeling: Use Cases, BPMN, and BABOK – helping organizations upskill and apply skills in practice
- Software Engineering: UML, Object Modeling – includes undertaking large-scale software modeling exercises for solutions development
- Corporate Agile Development – upskilling teams and applying Agile techniques to real-life projects and practice
- Quality Assurance & Testing – with a focus on prevention rather than traditional detection
- Collaborative Web Services: SOA, Cloud – upgrading EAs based on services including developing Analytics-as-a-Service
- Mobile Business and Green IT – with the goal of creating and maintaining sustainable business operations

His industry experience includes banking, finance, insurance, government, and telecommunications where he develops and applies industry-specific process maps, business transformation approaches, capability enhancement, and quality strategies.

Dr. Unhelkar has authored numerous executive reports, journal articles, and 22 books with internationally reputed publishers including *Outcome Driven Business Architecture* (Taylor & Francis/CRC Press, USA, 2019), *Software Engineering with UML* (Taylor and Francis/CRC Press, USA, 2018), and *Big Data Strategies for Agile Business* (Taylor & Francis/CRC Press, USA, 2017). *Cutter Consortium* executive reports (Boston, USA) including *Psychology of Agile, Agile Business Analysis, Collaborative Business & Enterprise Agility, Avoiding Method Friction and Agile in Practice-a Composite Approach*. He is also passionate about coaching senior executives; training, re-skilling, and mentoring IT and business professionals; forming Centers of Excellence, and creating assessment frameworks (SFIA-based) to support corporate change initiatives.

Dr. Unhelkar is an engaging presenter, delivering keynotes, training seminars, and workshops that combine real-life examples based on his experience with audience participation and Q&A sessions. These industrial training courses, seminars, and workshops add significant value to the participants and their sponsoring organizations as they are based on practical experience and a hands-on approach, and are accompanied by ROI metrics. Consistently rated highly by participants, the seminars and workshops have been delivered globally to business executives and IT professionals in Australia, USA, Canada, the UK, China, India, Sri Lanka, New Zealand, and Singapore. Dr. Unhelkar is the winner of the IT Writer Award (2010), Consensus IT Professional Award (2006), and Computerworld Object Developer Award (1995). He also chaired the Business Analysis Specialism Group of the Australian Computer Society.

Dr. Unhelkar earned his PhD in the area of "object orientation" from the University of Technology, Sydney. His teaching career spans both the undergraduate and master's levels, wherein he has designed and delivered courses including Global Information Systems, Agile Method Engineering, Object Oriented Analysis and Design, Business Process Reengineering, and New Technology Alignment in Australia, USA, China, and India. Online courses designed and delivered include the Australian Computer Society's distance education program, the M.S. University of Baroda (India) Master's program, and, currently, Program Design with the UML and Mobile App Development at the University of South Florida Sarasota-Manatee, USA.

At Western Sydney University, he supervised seven successful PhD candidates, and published research papers and case studies.

Professional affiliations include:

- Fellow of the Australian Computer Society, Australia; elected to this prestigious membership grade in 2002 for distinguished contribution to the field of ICT
- IEEE Senior Member, Tampa Chapter, USA
- Life member of the Computer Society of India (CSI), India
- Life member of Baroda Management Association (BMA), India
- Member of Society for Design and Process Science (SDPS), USA
- Rotarian (Past President) at Sarasota Sunrise Club, USA; Past President – Rotary Club in St. Ives, Sydney, Australia (Paul Harris Fellow; AG)
- Discovery Volunteer at NSW Parks and Wildlife, Australia
- Previous TiE Mentor, Australia

Previous books by Dr. B. Unhelkar, published by CRC Press (Taylor & Francis):

Unhelkar, B., (1999), *After the Y2K Fireworks: Business and Technology Strategies*, CRC Press, Boca Raton, FL, USA; July 1999; Total pages: 421. Foreword by Richard T. Due, Alberta, Canada

Unhelkar, B., (2013), *The Art of Agile Practice: A Composite Approach for Projects and Organizations,* CRC Press, (Taylor & Francis Group /an Auerbach Book), Boca Raton, FL, USA. Authored ISBN 9781439851180, Foreword Steve Blais, USA

Tiwary, A., and Unhelkar, B., (2018), *Outcome Driven Business Architecture,* CRC Press, (Taylor & Francis Group /an Auerbach Book), Boca Raton, FL, USA. Co-Authored

Unhelkar, B., (2018), *Software Engineering with UML,* CRC Press, (Taylor & Francis Group /an Auerbach Book), Boca Raton, FL, USA. Authored, Foreword Scott Ambler. ISBN 978-1-138–29743-2

Unhelkar, B., (2018), *Big Data Strategies for Agile Business,* CRC Press, (Taylor & Francis Group/an Auerbach Book), Boca Raton, FL, USA. Authored ISBN: 978-1-498–72438-8 (Hardback), Foreword Prof. James Curran, USFSM, FL, USA

Part A

Setting the Context for Digital Business

1 Digital Business, Enterprise Architecture, and the Transformation Imperative

SUMMARY

This chapter presents an overview of digital business and introduces arguments for the transformation imperative. The evolution of digital business, its elements, their relationships, and how they have emerged over the past decade provide the necessary background for the transformation imperative. Digital Transformation (DT) is discussed here keeping digital technologies and the fundamentals of Enterprise Architecture (EA) in perspective. The complexities and challenges of digital business enterprise are ideally handled by the EA discipline. EA supports digital strategic planning by bringing business and IT viewpoints together. Security, privacy, and managing governance, risk, and compliance in the digital age are important considerations. Recognizing, developing, and establishing DT initiatives require exploration of emerging technology trends. The technologies of Cloud Computing, the Internet of Things (IoT), Artificial Intelligence (AI), Machine Learning (ML), and Big Data Analytics are all considered in terms of their potential impact on digital business. Finally, the nexus between EA and Business Architecture is discussed from the DT viewpoint.

WHAT IS DIGITAL BUSINESS?

Digital business is the norm of today – not just an exception nor simply an extension. It is almost impossible to imagine a business that is not digital in some shape or form. Starting with the ubiquitous website and simple mobile apps through to bookkeeping, accounting, trading, and compliance, all businesses utilize digital technologies today. Therefore, digital business has become a continuous evolution of the current format into an automating, optimizing, and collaborating phenomena for the digital world. This evolution or transition from where the company is today to a fully digitized business of the future requires a thorough understanding of the structure and dynamics of the current organization. Digital Transformation (DT) needs to be considered in a strategic, holistic, and consistent manner. Piecemeal transformation of a company into a digital business does not provide the necessary advantage. The possibility

3

of a half-baked transformation creating friction and challenges in the business are too
high. Therefore, strategic consideration and investment in DT is an imperative for all
businesses today. Furthermore, given the complexity of the initiative – it revamps
the entire business – DT also includes strategies for change management with due
consideration given to the shift in the organizational culture. Thus, DT is not merely
a technology issue; it includes business and human concerns alike.

An understanding of what "digital" means is an important starting point for DT.
This meaning, however, has a wide range and can differ from one perspective to
another. For example, digital can mean going paperless or automating processes
through to data analytics, process optimization, and the use of Artificial Intelligence
(AI) in decision-making. Data storage, processing, and communications technologies are coupled with business processes and people in order to accomplish successful DT. Needless to say, such a dramatic change often requires leadership to envision
the challenges and benefits of digitization, while keeping multiple facets of the organization aligned with its current operating environment.

Figure 1.1 summarizes what is meant by digital business and DT. On the left is
the current business that may use basic digital technologies. The business leadership
wonders, "What will the transformed digital business look like?" Some leaders may
also wonder, "Why transform at all?" The reason for undertaking DT is explained by
the characteristics of the new business:

- Data related to all business functions is collected, stored, and secured,
  ensuring that the business is able to gather a wide variety and large amount
  of data that they may not have otherwise.

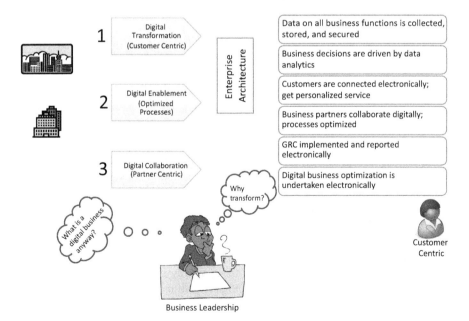

FIGURE 1.1 Digitizing the business.

- Business decisions are driven by Data Analytics rather than by the intuition of the senior-most decision makers of the organization. Such scientific method reduces biases in decisions.
- Customers are connected electronically with the business, enabling them to operate at any time of the day or night and at any location (especially when mobility compliments electronic connectivity). Customers are also able to receive personalized service as the digital business is able to precisely identify their needs and provide for it.
- Other firms collaborate digitally with the business, enabling a wider expansion of offerings and providing opportunities to capitalize on the needs of the partner company's customers. Collaborations on electronic/mobile platforms also enable process optimization.
- Digitizing records makes it easier for businesses to adhere to Governance-Risk-Compliance mandates, than if they were managed on paper. Storing the records and reporting them electronically to legal and audit authorities simplifies business processes and provides clear audit trails.
- All business functions are optimized through digital technologies – including sales, marketing, inventory, accounting, and human resources.

Figure 1.1 further shows that DT includes Digital Enablement (of processes) and Digital Collaboration (with partners). Enterprise Architecture (EA) is the conduit of successful DT as it establishes the foundation for consistent enablement and develops a standardized framework for seamless collaboration.

DIGITIZATION LANDSCAPE AND OPPORTUNITIES

Digital business can range from a simple website through to entire global digital companies such as Amazon, Apple, and Google. Examining a business critically from a DT viewpoint leads to the following questions being asked up front by the business leaders:

- What opportunities does DT bring to the business?
- Will digitization enhance the user experience for both consumers and employees?
- Will digitalization enable enterprise agility?
- What are the efforts and corresponding risks in DT?
- What are key criteria to ensure successful change management?
- Which digital business processes will be automated and which will be optimized?
- How will digitization impact sustainability?
- How does digital technology enhance communication and collaboration amongst business partners?
- How will digitization ensure compliance?
- Which system solutions will transition to the Cloud?
- Where will the data be stored (data privacy and security)?
- How will data be provided to business functions?

- What is the role of EA in undertaking DT?
- How will the success of DT be measured (metrics/KPIs)?
- Is DT a technology initiative?

Starting with the answer to the last question, DT is driven by data and associated technologies but it is *not* a technology initiative. Undertaking DT is a strategic business decision driven by the changes to and the availability of technologies. A brief review of the landscape of technologies and how they have impacted businesses is shown in Figure 1.2.

Figure 1.2 summarizes "System Solutions Technologies" and "Communications Technologies." Both types have incrementally spawned the federated digital era that has enabled digital business today.

Part A of Figure 1.2 presents the technologies that enable increasingly sophisticated digital services:

- **Object Oriented Technologies** were a major revolution in solutions development technologies as they enabled faster time-to-market for IT solutions and, through the application of encapsulation, higher quality.
- **Component Based Technologies** encapsulated a group of objects in design, implementation, and execution, leading to an even faster time-to-market for the IT solution. These technologies were not as nimble as the Object-Oriented ones due to larger-sized components, leading to challenges in maintenance and operation.
- **Service Oriented Technologies** enabled offering of components over the internet, making it easier and faster for solutions to be developed using the services created by other providers in real time. Service Oriented Architecture (SOA) changed the landscape of providing solutions from component-based, single-site to a collaborative suite of services.
- **Big Data,** and data in general, made it possible for businesses to collect information they could not earlier and store it for processing. Big Data and

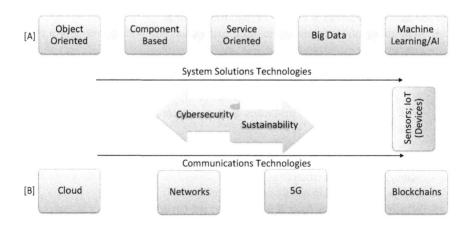

FIGURE 1.2 Landscape of technology-based federated digital era.

Analytics develop a comprehensive view of different master data management elements (e.g., customers, products).

- **Machine Learning (ML)** enabled businesses to undertake data-driven decision-making. This is so because ML/AI makes it possible to derive insights from Big Data. ML capabilities (e.g., process mining) can extend enterprise systems' capabilities.

Part B of Figure 1.2 presents the technologies that enable increasingly sophisticated digital communications.

- **Cloud – and Associated Storages** – was a game changer for the digitization landscape as it eliminated the administration and management of routine data functions from the business and shifted it elsewhere, leaving the business to focus on its core competencies.
- **Networks**, local and global, played a crucial role in the digitization of a business by providing connectivity.
- **5G and Mobile** made it possible to shift analytics and processing from a fixed location to being completely location-independent.
- **Blockchains** offered another game-changing opportunity for digital business by providing a high level of veracity of data and analytics. This is due to blockchains' potential to provide highly secured and validated data – especially after integration with existing enterprise systems. Blockchain technology also impacts the governance of information stored in enterprise systems.
- **Sensors – Internet of Things (IoT) and Internet of Everything (IoE)** – enabled collection of data with or without specific input from users. A number of IoT sensors collect massive amount of data associated with the business and/or the government and make it available for processing.
- **Cybersecurity** and **Sustainability** are the two important underlying architectural considerations in the overall landscape of digital era technologies.

CONTEMPORARY DIGITAL TECHNOLOGIES AND THEIR IMPACT ON DIGITAL TRANSFORMATION

Emerging digital technologies are significant and need to be understood from an architectural viewpoint. Table 1.1 summarizes these emerging technologies and also lists their potential impact on business agility.

These technologies are affected by the way an architecture is construed and used. For example, an architecture can facilitate controlled iterations, incorporating new ways of organizing technology components and understanding limitations of existing technical parameters. An architecture can provide the basis for the planning, storage, and processing capacities of the organization.

The maturity of an organization in terms of its data and applications can also be ascertained through an architecture. Thus, an approach to increase existing capabilities of an organization can be created before introducing new technologies. An architecture also provides a method to absorb and integrate new technologies with existing ones in a secure manner.

TABLE 1.1

Contemporary Digital Technologies and Their Impact on Digital Transformation

Digital Technology	Description	Digital Transformation Consideration
IoT (Internet of Things) IoE (Internet of Everything). IoT can be personal or industrial.	Enables non-stop sourcing of data – typically from individual users and their devices (e.g., a GPS) – resulting in high velocity and volume.	Data can be used for immediate decision-making (e.g., change the route while following a GPS navigation) – opening up opportunities for agility in business processes.
Cloud Computing	Storing and sharing of data independent of its source – based on IaaS, PaaS, and now AaaS. Typical Cloud-based Hadoop installations can ingest vast amounts of data and store it at a very cheap price.	Facilitates interfacing with additional data lakes (collaborations) that feed vast reference data and improved insights in decision-making (e.g., weather data in GPS). Cloud also enables creation of a Lean, Agile front-end in a business process, resulting in opportunities, particularly for small and medium enterprises.
Presentation technologies	Providing analytical results in many different formats and on varying devices in order to suit the needs of a variety of users. This presentation, usually called "visualization," also includes audio (voice) clues and machine sensors (vibrates). Holographic projections are set to come into play with high bandwidth availability.	Enabling user to choose the style of visuals depending on the context (location, time); also using audio (voice message) and sensors (vibrate) to suit the user, adding to the flexibility of usage and process agility. Increases opportunity for users with certain limitations of visuals (including, for example, when driving a vehicle).
Semantic Web	MapReduce and associated algorithms embedded in software tools are used to create new semantics between large pods of internal and external data. Ingestion of machine data in Big Data analytics is also facilitated by Semantic Web as it enables assignment of meaning to that data.	Flexibility and cross-functionality in development and usage of Big Data. "Sensing" can be non-visual and machine generated when incorporated in business processes without human intervention. This results in the agility of business processes
Data stores (NoSQL)	NoSQL (Key-Values, Document, Columnar, and Graphics) are the types of data stores that can accept semi- and unstructured data that are characteristic of Big Data.	These technologies, characterized by rapid access (in Memory Computing), provide significant dynamicity in decision-making, resulting in business agility.
5G	Location-independent (mobile) high-speed connectivity.	Digitizing mobile business processes and enabling mobile collaboration.
Blockchains	Security of data and analytics through blocks.	Providing innovative digitization in business processes.

EVOLUTION OF ARCHITECTURES IN ORGANIZATIONS

In addition to the discussion on the federated digital era, it is also important to consider how digital evolution has impacted corresponding architectures. Figure 1.3 depicts these major technological trends and the subsequent evolution of architectures. Starting with monolithic architecture corresponding to Mainframe Computing, the evolution into client-server (distributed) architectures, service-based architectures, and – more recently – Cloud-based architectures occurs.[1,2,3] These architectures provide stability for digital technologies in the business. Each of these architectures is also responsible for providing opportunities for careful change in the business on its digital quest. Digital business is, thus, based on these architectures. From Mainframe Computing to PC Computing, the transition was about system architecture; with PC Computing to Network Computing, the transition was about distributed and network architectures. The transition and the associated disruption from Network Computing to Cloud Computing over the internet and Grid Computing phases is the mainstay of contemporary digital business. The degree of disruption and the complexities of EAs continue to grow. Therefore, no DT can succeed without due consideration to EAs.

DIGITAL TRANSFORMATION IMPERATIVE

DT is a fundamental change in the business in order to meet personalized customer demand, independent of time and space. The ever increasing expectations of customers are fulfilled through digitizing businesses. DT integrates data-driven decision-making with all areas of any business model. The structure and dynamics of the organization undergo change during the incorporation of data-driven decision-making. Processes and people also undergo changes during DT! It is a risky, long-term, iterative, and incremental exercise that requires a strategic approach to change.

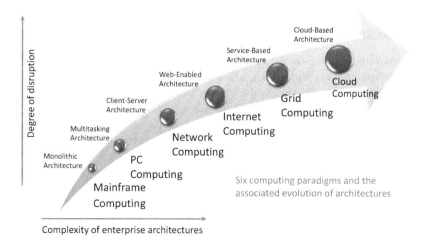

FIGURE 1.3 Evolution of architectures corresponding to the shift in computing paradigms.

The measure of success of DT is in the increased value it brings to customers:

- A seamless user experience, as the customer does not go from "department to department" in order to receive the goods or services.
- Agility in decision-making by the business enables the customer to make changes to his/her needs without being penalized for it.
- The data-driven digitization of business processes that enables their optimization which, in turn, reduces overall costs and time required to provide service to a customer.
- The integration of analytics, AI, and ML in decision-making provides "fine granular" analytics that reflect the personalized needs of the customer.
- The adoption of the Cloud by a digital business, enabling a customer to access his/her data from anywhere and at any time.
- Electronic collaboration with all stakeholders and the ongoing formation of digital partnerships that lead to wider offerings for the customer and a greater number of choices.
- Changes to organizational culture that produce decisions with less biases and more pinpointed satisfaction of customer needs.
- Strategic and holistic approaches to cybersecurity that reassure the customer of the safety and security of their data.

Risks are inevitable in DT and must be addressed for the journey to be successful. The DT effort can span multiple projects, not all of which will have favorable outcomes. Therefore, it is important to approach DT goals through the building of capabilities rather than only through projects (Chapter 5). A holistic and strategic view of DT is a necessity (discussed in detail in Chapter 3).

Agility plays a crucial role in DT (Chapter 7). The goal is to learn and adjust by looking at the strategic impact (e.g., revenue growth, lifetime customer value, time-to-market), operational impact (e.g., productivity improvements, scale, operational efficiencies), and cost impact.

CHALLENGES AND RISKS IN DIGITAL TRANSFORMATION

DT is risky mainly because such transformation usually happens when the business is already operational. While a digital business is aligned with customer needs and is aimed at providing personalized customer value, that value in itself may not be easy to define. Therefore, in every DT effort, customer expectations need formal management. The changes to the structure and dynamics of the organization – while in operation – are complex, requiring a stable reference point. Such a "base" or "foundation" of stability is provided by the EA.

Figure 1.4 highlights five key areas of a business that need attention during the DT process. They are:

- **People** – their biases in decision-making; their lack of skills in being part of data-driven processes; and their concerns for their own employability with the advent of data-driven decision-making.

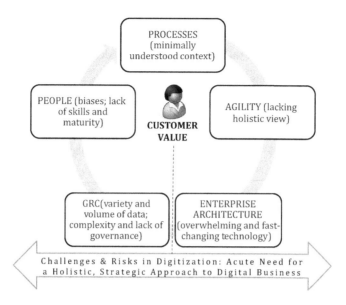

FIGURE 1.4   Challenges and risks in digital business.

- **Processes** – especially as they are embedded with data analytics.
- **Agility** – the organization may not be prepared for holistic business agility and may be only interested in software project agility.
- **EA** – overwhelming and fast-changing technologies require EA to provide a stable reference point.
- **Governance, Compliance, Risk Control** – this can be challenging if the volume and complexity of data is not understood and there is lack of structure around the processes.

Following is a further expansion of the challenges often encountered while embarking upon digital business transformation:

- **IT Strategy and Architecture are No Longer in Tune with Current Business Drivers, Strategies, or Requirements** – due to acquisitions and business expansion decisions, the business vision and goals change; as a result, there can be a need to integrate ready-made software solutions rather than to develop them from scratch. The EA has to change in order to accommodate changes to business drivers.
- **Tightly Coupled, Isolated, or Disparate Business Processes and Inefficient Information Sharing Across the Organization** – this is the result of isolated efforts to support different business clients with custom application development and management services. The concerns are to identify reusable IT assets, application components, and business services that can be assembled and managed efficiently to address similar business needs of multiple business functions.

- **Lack of Collaboration in Developing Common or Shared Services** – organizations fail to identify reusable IT assets, application components, and business services that can jointly address identical needs of multiple functions – as they often have no common understanding for each of these operations. Lack of prior channels for communication or collaboration can make it difficult to establish a common ground for "shared responsibility."
- **Efficiency of Services Supporting Business Operations** – the lack of consistent standards or a cohesive approach to developing information, application, and technology architectures puts the interoperability of data and services to the test.

Some of the above-mentioned challenges, issues, and concerns are complex and have no easy resolution. Most of these are reviewed periodically during DT and external help is sought, if needed.

ARCHITECTURE AND BUSINESS ORGANIZATIONS

The architecture of an organization represents its fundamental structure. This structure is heavily dependent on the systems, databases, and applications of the company. Therefore, "architecture" in the context of this discussion relates to the technical aspects of the enterprise.

The IEEE (2007) defines architecture as the "the fundamental organization of a system, embodied in its components, their relationships to each other and the environment, and the principles governing its design and evolution." Conceptually, these elements of IT are not new. However, these IT elements are becoming increasingly complex as they encompass multiple systems and databases across many different functions of the enterprise.[4,5]

Earlier, Figure 1.3 discussed the evolution of architectures with an organization. There are a number of architectures that play a role in DT. They include:

- **Business Architecture** – this presents business process flows, with business drivers and existing technical imperatives as two vital inputs. The use of business architectures is helpful in discussing the big picture with senior leadership teams and executives, and are useful in obtaining their approval. Moreover, these models are helpful in the event of necessary changes (i.e., reengineering, automation, or other modifications) to certain business processes while transitioning the existing EAs to collaborative ones. Current processes provide the context of existing business architecture and the capture of operational aspects of the existing EA.
- **Infrastructure Architecture** – provides an inventory of physical communication networks and associated management elements such as hubs, routers, and switches.
- **Technical Architecture** – presents a list of previously adopted technologies, tools, and techniques built in-house or by third parties. Technical architecture usually extends to application and integration architectures, although in reality they influence and refine the overall collaborative EA.

- **Information Architecture** – organizes the information that various business applications across the enterprise need or use while servicing user information-exchange needs.
- **Application Architecture** – identifies various business applications and services in terms of component models and captures frameworks and architectural patterns used in building them.
- **Integration Architecture** – focuses on integration technologies such as brokers, adapters, and connectors that are used as information exchange mechanisms to connect various business applications for the enterprise.
- **Data Architecture** – deals with the approach to data, Big Data, and its volume and velocity.
- **Science Architecture** – deals with the provisioning of web-services, micro-services, and knowledge services.
- **Operations Architecture** – details the operational view of hosting business applications. Naturally, it includes hardware, software, operating systems, platforms, and environments used to deploy the entire existing EA. In practice, application and operations architectures facilitate the deployment of the collaborative EA during the final stage of development.
- **Implementation Architecture** – elaborates on actual implementation of business applications using technologies adopted by the enterprise as they are listed in the technical architecture.

Business processes represent the behavior of an organization. Architecture also shows the relationships of technologies and systems to business processes. A comprehensive architecture describes the way in which people and processes relate to and consume technologies.

Figure 1.5 shows the four key things an architecture does in a digital business:

- **Connect** – devices, people, data – mostly starts at the application level.
- **Communicate** – networks, analytics – starts at the communication network level.

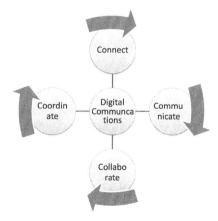

FIGURE 1.5 Architecture in the digital communications era.

- **Collaborate** – business partners, customers – starts at business and functional level.
- **Coordinate** – processes for optimization – starts at the user and system level.

BIG DATA AND ARTIFICIAL INTELLIGENCE

Big Data analytics and AI add to the complexity and challenges of an architecture. The Big Data space includes a suite of technologies that enable sourcing of data (from devices and machines, external data stores, and human data entry); its storage (locally; on servers; and, increasingly, on the Cloud); processing (analytical algorithms and tools); and display (visualization and user interface designs). Architecture in the AI space includes data and the basis for utilizing that data through ML and its variations (e.g., supervised and unsupervised learnings). Furthermore, architecture also encompasses the way in which these technologies interrelate. Big Data analytics is not made up of "standalone" software components with a clean Application Programming Interface (API); instead, they are embedded with a collection of algorithms – typically coded in Python or "R" – or another analytical package in separate business processes. This creates challenges of integration, maintenance, verification, and security across enterprise systems, applications, and databases.

Interspersed with the intricacies of quality (veracity), Big Data technologies and analytics are subject to further controlling parameters of volume, velocity, and variety. For example, analytics require integration between existing structured (relational) data and incoming unstructured data. These characteristics of Big Data start creating qualitative differences in technical management of solutions as compared to traditional, structured data. The size and frequencies of inputs and outputs of data, their relationships with external sources, the levels of granularity of desired analytics, and security and privacy aspects are all considered together within the technical architecture of the enterprise.

Achieving technical homogeneity of the systems, applications, and databases is a balancing act that is important to reduce the risks in transformation and also to provide business value. This balancing act between new technology adoption and its resultant value to the business is a challenge that is intensified by Big Data.[6] For example, Big Data comprises a substantial amount of data that is not generated and owned by the enterprise. Instead, large external data sets are purchased, hired, interfaced (when made openly available by governments[7]), or simply referenced as part of the analytics. The assorted and unstructured nature of data and its sources in Big Data present challenges that require careful modeling, mapping, reviews, experimentation, and iterations under the existing architectural umbrella of the organization.

DATA FRICTION

Another challenge presented by Big Data technologies is the generation of minute incoming data points. These data points need to be continuously ingested and synchronized with current data made up of the existing enterprise's structured and unstructured data. The relationships between existing and new data, and existing and new analytical applications, as well as the interfaces between large swaths of in-house and third-party data and services, have the potential to generate substantial "friction." Examples of friction in data within an architecture include duplications (presenting multiple sources for the same data), inconsistencies, and a resultant fragmented view of a single entity to a user. Friction in architectural elements can also result in security and privacy breaches, and misuse of data.

An example of architectural friction is the possible development of futile analytics and applications. An example of a system friction in operation is a Customer Relationship Management (CRM) system not providing the necessary user experience (performance) when another Enterprise Resource Planning (ERP) system is executing in the background. The end result of such friction is wrong decision-making and a subsequent loss of business agility.

Reviewing and experimenting with advancing technologies within and outside the Big Data domain helps understand their capabilities and also the potential for friction.

ENTERPRISE ARCHITECTURE IN DIGITAL TRANSFORMATION

ARCHITECTING FOR BUSINESS TRANSFORMATION

How does a business focus on transformation from an architectural perspective? Figure 1.6 represents a comprehensive approach for architecting to achieve success with business transformation:

"Coalition" with respect to an EA and the IoT expresses alliance or synergy – as shown in Figure 1.6. While EA and the IoT are distinct disciplines, there is an inherent synergy between them that is important in formulating a DT strategy. This synergy originates from the fact that each discipline supports digital strategies for disruptive business operations. They also support each other in the way they deliver value to an enterprise. EA is used to formulate the blueprint and road map for the transformation initiative. EA is also the basis for a collaborative enterprise. The IoT primarily represents devices, applications, and services using the principles and standards that EA formalizes – therefore creating a connected enterprise. Collectively, the EA and the IoT coalition offers a foundation for the DT journey of an enterprise, as shown in Figure 1.6.

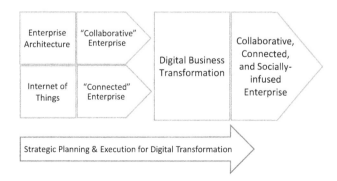

FIGURE 1.6 Enterprise Architecture for Digital Transformation.

EA in DT is not an elaborate "big picture" view comprising blueprints and multiyear road maps for strategic business modernization. Instead, EA embraces highly collaborative architectural approaches that are swift, lean, agile, and scalable. Such approaches are innovation-led and can be effective when embarking upon DT. The IoT adds a new dimension to business-to-consumer engagement. DT combines the innovation and connectivity of an organization with its ability to coordinate and implement the transformation and possible disruption. DT is the strategic change that helps enterprises leverage their capabilities (people, process, and technology) while establishing mechanisms for ongoing improvement in customer value.

EA instills principles and guidelines for using standards, adaptable frameworks, and the concepts of flexible interoperability and security in an enterprise. The IoT can benefit from many of these forward-thinking EA principles and guidelines. Together EA and the IoT can deliver business value to an enterprise effectively, efficiently, and, most importantly, in a timely manner. For example, an EA team with a global financial services company decided on a set of technology standards, platforms, and network protocols for the entire enterprise. When solution developers from internal IT and outsourcing partners started implementing IoT devices, they realized the benefits of using EA guidelines and principles, as well as the standards stipulated by the EA team. The EA team collaborated with the solution developers to provide proof of concept or prototypes that other solution developers in the enterprise could leverage to expedite the IoT implementation. Overall, this approach helped the company significantly reduce its timeline to deliver three new IoT device–based business capabilities.

The synergy between EA and the IoT spans all phases of DT, from ideation and value creation to the value realization of connected digital assets. EA provides a flexible and collaborative approach to integrating applications, services, and devices in an enterprise-wide network. The IoT can use the same approach, frameworks, and standards that EA offers while integrating with the enterprise. While this point is similar to the first one, the emphasis here is on the use of EA and the IoT in the context of DT. In fact, it is not necessary that all IT assets be digital and they don't necessarily all change during DT. Hence, frameworks and standards must make room for the integration of legacy systems and those applications that may not use digital assets. With the synergy between EA and the IoT, the EA team for a retail supply chain established an architectural framework that allowed the integration of old and new Point of Sale systems with inventory and order entry systems – some involving RFID sensor readers and mainframe-based systems. The company utilized the framework to design and develop interim solutions while cultivating the use of emerging technology solutions (including the IoT).

The primary focus for EA and the IoT today is data analytics and how data needs to be ingested, processed, analyzed, disseminated, and subsequently used by data scientists or decision makers. Emerging technology trends such as Social Computing, Cloud Computing, Mobility, and Big Data add key benefits to the coalition of EA and the IoT. For example, the Cloud can facilitate the connection of IoT devices. Big Data analytics can help professionals observe the behavior of customers using IoT devices. For one healthcare services delivery organization, the EA and IoT coalition expanded to bring emerging technology trends in to develop a platform that could support patients and physicians alike, offering a world-class patient experience and supporting patient self-management throughout the care continuum.

The EA is the overall architecture of the organization that applies to its entirety. Due to the holistic nature of EA, success in adoption of newer technologies is possible on when it is done in the context of the organization's EA. EA is understood primarily at a technical level and is "inward facing". According to a Gartner definition, EA "is the process of translating business vision and strategy into effective enterprise change by creating, communicating and improving the key principles and models that describe the enterprise's future state and enable its evolution."[8]

An EA comprises networks, applications, databases, interfaces, and security. The EA has progressed from being a "standalone, silo components toward components integrated at an enterprise level, and this is now evolving to address enterprise-to-enterprise integration and even broader considerations about environmental and social architectural integration."[9]

A key motivation to develop and use an EA in DT is that it helps ease the introduction of Big Data technologies into the mix of existing systems. An EA helps synchronize the networks, databases, analytics, business processes, and presentation layers of an enterprise.

An EA can be considered a mechanism to facilitate controlled introduction of Big Data that may be allowed to disrupt but not destroy the existing technical setup of the enterprise. Thus, while EA provides the structure for technologies, the ease of introducing Big Data technologies paves the path for business agility. For example, through an EA a business analyst can question the purpose for collecting new data and ensure that it relates to business objectives. An EA can focus the attention of a senior decision maker on partnering agreements that result in collaborations and data exchange. Referencing an EA can bring together the security expert and the data analyst to talk about the security risks in sourcing data; and an EA can provide common ground for a user experience analyst to talk to a solutions developer on a visualization (e.g., where to represent the results – in a bar or pie chart).

At the development level, the EA enables a solutions developer and a data architect to work together to understand the capabilities of data and the best way to use it for an analytical application. For example, understanding the business context in which data analytics will be used helps in writing a MapReduce algorithm within the operational limitations of a Hadoop data store. While the specifics of each Big Data technology can vary, an understanding of how it fits into the overall scheme of an organization mitigates the risks associated with its introduction. Technology adoptions with reference to EA tend to have less friction during their operation than standalone introductions without due consideration to the EA. Attention to the aforementioned technical layers of an EA has been key to the smooth introduction of new technologies.[10] In fact, an EA works to align technical elements with strategic objectives and the business' vision.[11] Smooth introduction and functioning of Big Data technologies is vital, as it paves the path for agility in business decision-making.

The robustness of an EA helps avoid piecemeal and random introduction of technology. An EA provides a strategic context for the adoption of new technologies and the evolution of existing ICT systems. EA is the basis of the correct balance between ICT efficiency and business innovation.

EA as a Transformational Framework

EA provides the basis for a comprehensive transformational framework used in DT. Figure 1.7 shows the basis for such a framework, highlighting "agile," "lean," and "adaptive" as its hallmarks. Improving quality and responsiveness, enhancing customer outreach, and increasing employee and business partnership through engagement are the characteristics of a digital business supported by the transformational framework shown in Figure 1.7. More formal EA frameworks (e.g., Zachman and TOGAF, discussed in Chapter 2) are used in the background to develop digital capabilities for business strategies. An EA also helps minimize the disruption of established operations.

The transformational framework enables identification of key business functions and their enterprise-level objectives. Organizational maturity requires robust business-IT collaboration that is driven within a well-thought-out governance structure and a clearly defined vision. Business units drive and prioritize business process transformation (reengineering or improvement) initiatives. The transformation framework helps capture and articulate its impact on application, information, and technology architectures to maximize the benefits for business process transformation. EA governs business more than IT. There is a shift in roles and responsibilities for the EA. Hence, it is important that they be clearly defined and the accountabilities be well understood by the professionals involved.

Following are the advantages resulting from the use of EA in DT:

- Aligning business processes or components identified as part of the digital business strategy, vision, and objectives or potential business operation goals, and tracking them to improve system performance and efficiency.
- Making continuous and consistent process improvements using industry standards, recognized architectural frameworks, and full life cycle process maturity models along with a consistent measurement program.

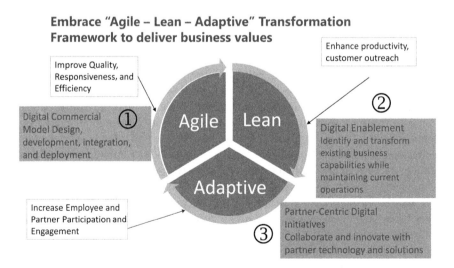

Embrace "Agile – Lean – Adaptive" Transformation Framework to deliver business values

Enhance productivity, customer outreach

Improve Quality, Responsiveness, and Efficiency

Digital Commercial Model Design, development, integration, and deployment ①

Agile   Lean

②

Digital Enablement Identify and transform existing business capabilities while maintaining current operations

Adaptive

Increase Employee and Partner Participation and Engagement

Partner-Centric Digital Initiatives ③ Collaborate and innovate with partner technology and solutions

FIGURE 1.7   The transformational framework foundation.

- Demonstrating business value (ROI) of DT efforts that cross boundaries, change how a company goes to market, and often fundamentally reshape interactions with customers and employees.[12]
- Applying governance and risk management processes to reconcile the capability of the organization in collaborating, coordinating, and delivering business.
- Employing a measurement program to monitor and manage the progress of DT in achieving its goals and objectives at each stage, and also in meeting the expectations of sponsors, customers, and stakeholders.
- Availability of a commonly understood suite of standards and an existing architectural framework that can be used to develop the next iteration of the enterprise solution, incorporating Big Data technologies and databases.
- Flexibility to decide on the "make or buy" aspects of Big Data tools, software solutions, and packages, as it may not always be prudent to develop a full solution from scratch.
- Reduced operational friction by facilitating interoperability amongst enterprise systems and networks. This in turn helps embed Big Data analytics within existing and running business processes.
- Improved understanding of existing technologies and systems within the organization to enable Agile experimentation (i.e., creation of prototypes and the iterative evolution of solutions) with models of Big Data solutions. This agility also reduces the development time of a solution to fit within a shortening window of opportunity.
- An enterprise-wide holistic view of the requirements of the enterprise from a "business process" viewpoint. This forms the basis for 360° unified customer view of their needs and enables the positioning of Big Data solutions.
- Development and application of a common and robust security policy that not only applies to all systems of the enterprise but also to the externally sourced Big Data and associated interfaces. This application is vital for IoT devices and the ingestion of their data for analytics.
- Risk reduction by sharing and utilizing previous architectural experiences within and outside the organization that provide basis for interfacing and integration of Big Data.
- Simplification of the otherwise complex application development through the use of architectural layers (discussed later in this chapter) that help in scoping the development and, later, putting the solutions together.
- Reduction in development time and enhancing the ability for rapid production of analytical software applications due to use and reuse of components and frameworks.
- The opportunity to interface with data suites on the Cloud, creating a sound basis for "Self-Serve Analytics" that enable users to configure their own analytics.
- Provision for future growth in technologies and analytics of Big Data in response to the needs of the business.

- Understanding the overall scope of work to position the place of outsourcing in developing and maintaining solutions. The amount of outsourcing undertaken is a delicate balancing act that requires careful study of the existing EA and the places where new technology will be introduced.

EA is a mechanism to absorb elements from Big Data technologies, tools, and projects. The configuration of machine-human interactions, as well as machine-machine interactions, requires the backdrop of an EA. The EA needs to accommodate these as semantic (meaningful) interactions between devices.

The risk in giving importance to an EA is that it can get equated to digital business. EA and digital business are two entities, with the former supporting the latter. However, the EA is not the main goal of DT, and neither is digitizing the business. Enhancing customer value is at the core of DT.

INTERNET OF THINGS, INTERNET OF EVERYTHING, AND DIGITAL BUSINESS

Cloud Computing, Visualizations, Semantic Web, and NoSQL are some of the technologies mentioned earlier in Table 1.1 that are associated with Big Data. An important part of these technologies, and a major contributor to the volume and velocity of Big Data, is the IoT.[13] The ubiquitous nature of the IoT (daily use devices ranging from wearables like watches to road navigation apps, fridges, and air conditioning) and its devices' ability to generate and transmit data over the internet make them integral to the discussion on Big Data. While the size of IoT devices is being miniaturized – down to a button on a shirt – their volumes, speeds, battery power, and update frequencies are all on the rise. The IoT, through its self-learning (programming), self-propagating, self-transmitting, and self-fixing abilities, is the key "feeder" of Big Data (see the sidebar for the IoT suite).

The IoE is a wider representation of the IoT and it acknowledges the role of people, processes, data, services, etc.[14] The IoT and IoE comprise devices that are closely interconnected with each other and that feed high volume and high velocity data, with or without human intervention, to back-end stores on the Cloud. Since these devices may not be limited by organizational boundaries – especially as a device may get used for personal as well as work activities[15] – their implementation and deployment need to occur with strong reference to the EA.

Since the IoE generates and senses incoming data, sensors fall under the IoT. These "sensing" devices may use visual or non-visual cues in decision-making. An EA provides the basis for visualizations to work across multiple IoT devices.

ENTERPRISE ARCHITECTURE AND BUSINESS ARCHITECTURE

There is yet another form of architecture that is worth mentioning in the EA discussion. That is, the architecture focusing on business outcomes as the basis for project initiatives within an organization. This "external facing" architecture reduces gaps between desired business outcomes and activities aimed at achieving them.

It is called the "Business Architecture" (BA).[16] The BA is a mechanism to ensure that all new initiatives and projects are undertaken to ensure well-defined business outcomes.[17] The EA coupled with the BA also holds the promise of going beyond the enterprise and understanding the national and social ecosystem in which the organization exists and operates. For example, the EA provides the starting point for Big Data governance that results in satisfying security, privacy and compliance needs of individuals, society and government.[18]

The BA represents a visual model of the enterprise in the context of its functions – primarily focusing on "what" the business does and "how" it executes its functional capabilities. The Object Management Group (OMG) defines BA as "the structure of the enterprise in terms of its governance structure, business processes, and business information. In defining the structure of the enterprise, business architecture considers customers, finances, and the ever-changing market to align strategic goals and objectives with decisions regarding products and services; partners and suppliers; organization; capabilities; and key initiatives."

The BA helps align the processes inherent to a business with its drivers including strategy, goals, and objectives. Outcome Driven Business Architecture (ODBA)[19] helps align strategies with capabilities. Business models are enhanced to leverage the mission of the company along with other architectural domain models.

A business-driven architecture forms the core of an integrated business and IT transformation across the enterprise. The BA consists of business process models, business capability matrix, concept of operations, and a maturity model, in addition to a self-assessment process to evaluate the level of maturity for each business process and to prepare for future modifications. In practice the BA gradually evolves, matures, and adds a significant value to the entire enterprise as a key component of its EA and beyond.[20]

Business-driven architecture, or business system architecture, dates back to the early days of EA planning.[21] The Open Group Architecture Framework (TOGAF),[22] the Zachman Framework,[23] and Federal Enterprise Architecture Framework (FEAF)[24] offer substantial information to help professionals get started with their BA initiatives.

BA has been rapidly becoming a mainstream concept in the industry. Over the past few years, many large and complex enterprises across the private and public sectors have already started to embrace its core concepts. For most of these business organizations, BA plays a significant role in defining the primary value proposition for the EA. It instills the foundation for building a mature and robust enterprise.

The BA plays a significant role as a driving force of the EA; there is a substantial nexus between the two. Standardization efforts establish modeling languages and notations in BA. However, the availability of tools for modeling as well as building the business architecture remains challenging.

The EA is a prime element in facilitating strategic planning for digital business. It is business driven – it helps business and IT leaders in their strategic planning – and customer focused – it places customer needs at the center of the business transformation. The BA is a formal link between strategy and results.[25]

The EA is critical to business and IT alignment. It influences business strategy and data-driven business processes. A well-governed and mature enterprise utilizes EA for effective alignment of strategies and capabilities.

BA AS A BUSINESS FUNCTION

BA is recognized as a business discipline, with value streams or chains, business models, strategic planning, and operational efficiencies. It includes IT as well as business and organization architectures. It is business driven and is called upon during the decision-making process, as it deals with the company's logic, technology, operation, and strategy. Therefore, a BA deals with the enterprise's DT portfolio that directly impacts investments and strategic and tactical decisions to drive operational efficiency. A BA requires stakeholders, owners, and investors to provide the blueprint of operations, to describe the IT assets, to provide proof of regulatory compliance, to map costs and profits on various operations, and to align business and IT strategies. A BA can handle regulatory requirements for publicly listed companies as well as the public sector.

BA DRIVES AGILITY IN BUSINESS

A BA is geared towards designing the business in a way that achieves desired outcomes. This helps professionals merge strategy and associated technology to drive results. Mergers, acquisitions, and outsourcing activities are also driven by the BA (ITO/BPO, SaaS, and ASP) and create nimble and Agile enterprises. BA leverages enabler technologies like Cloud Computing and Data Virtualization to drive towards utility models that provide an on-demand backbone for an Agile enterprise. A BA takes into account business strategy and requirements in order to drive directly the operational constructs that can leverage on-demand, architecturally coherent, cost-effective and "ready-when-needed" utility models.

EMERGING BA STANDARDS THAT SUPPORT COMMON BUSINESS GOALS

BA frameworks define a common standard and approach for the business world. For example, BA drives SOA as the target architecture and technology, rather than invoking shared services. The lack of universal BA standards has been a challenge that has hurt DT – but this is changing as businesses realize the value and as best practices are refined and gravitate towards common approach that is accepted across business and IT communities. Today, emerging standards are already being accepted more broadly. Experts are currently also leveraging several standard frameworks to suit BA needs. Existing standards and commonly available frameworks can provide support to a BA. A set of consistent, cohesive tools and standards are emerging as the BA field matures and supports DT.

DISCUSSION TOPICS

1. How would one characterize digital business in this 2020 decade? (*hint – more collaborative than competitive; focused on customer value*)
2. Why is DT an imperative? And what will happen if organizations do not undertake formal DT on a continuous basis?

3. What are the key challenges and risks *your* organization faces if it proceeds with formal DT?
4. What is the role of EA in handling the challenges and risks of DT?
5. Why should a digital business be considered an Agile business?
6. Discuss critically the transformation framework outlined in Figure 1.7 in terms of its applicability in your transformation initiative.
7. As a consultant, you are asked to present to the senior management/business decision makers the role of EA together with Business Architecture. Outline your approach in a succinct manner.
8. Why is the role of an enterprise architect so important for today's digital business?

NOTES

1 Hazra, T., and Unhelkar, B., (2015), "Cloud-analytics for digital business: A practical EA perspective in the age of big data." *SDPSnet Conference* (1–5 November, 2015. Dallas, TX). Proceedings published in the USA by 2015 Society for Design and Process Science. (www.sdpsnet.org).
2 Hazra, T., and Unhelkar, B. "Leveraging EA to Incorporate Emerging Technology Trends for Digital Transformation", *Cutter IT Journal*, (theme - Disruption and Emergence: What Do They Mean for Enterprise Architecture?), Vol. 29, No. 2, pp. 10–16, February 2016.
3 Hazra, T. K., (2012), *Cloud Architecture: Leveraging Strategies, Blueprints, and Roadmaps — What's Different Today?* Cutter, (Cutter Advisor), Boston, MA.
4 IEEE Standards Association. "IEEE Std 1471-2000. IEEE Recommended Practice for Architectural Description of Software-Intensive Systems", July 2007.
5 Unhelkar, B., (2018), *Big Data Strategies for Agile Business,* CRC Press, (Taylor & Francis Group/an Auerbach Book), Boca Raton, FL ISBN: 978-1-498-72438-8 (Hardback).
6 Bauer, M., and Quinn, P., Cutter IT Journal, Posted February 23, 2016 in Business & Enterprise Architecture, Data Analytics & Digital Technologies Cutter IT Journal.
7 Open Data movement in US, UK and Australia (the latter supported by the Australian Computer Society).
8 Lapkin A., Gartner Defines the term 'Enterprise Architecture', Gartner Research July 2006.
9 Dooley, B. "Analytics by the Footprint" Cutter Executive Update Posted August 3, 2015 in Business Technology & Digital Transformation Strategies, *Data Analytics & Digital Technologies*, Vol. 15, No.11, www.cutter.com.
10 Unhelkar, B. "Transitioning to a Mobile Enterprise: A Three-Dimensional Framework." *Cutter IT Journal*, Vol. 18, No. 8, August 2005.
11 Based on McGovern, J., Ambler, S., Stevens, M., and Sharan, V., (2004), *A Practical Guide to Enterprise Architecture,* Prentice Hall PTR, Upper Saddle River, NJ, United States.
12 https://enterprisersproject.com/tags/digital-transformation accessed 25 March, 2020.
13 The Global Standards Initiative on Internet of Things (IoT-GSI) http://www.itu.int/en/ITU-T/gsi/iot/Pages/default.aspx accessed 27 October, 2016.
14 See. For example, http://ioeassessment.cisco.com/learn/ioe-faq.
15 "BYOD" – Bring Your Own Device policy wherein staff can bring their own hand-held device (e.g., iPad, cell phone, laptop) to work and use it as an access mechanism for the enterprise data and applications sitting on the organization's Cloud.

16 Note: The profession of business analysis (and requirements modeling) is also represented by BA but the two are different.

17 See Tiwary, A., and Unhelkar, B., (2018), *Outcome Driven Business Architecture,* CRC Press, (Taylor & Francis Group /an Auerbach Book), Boca Raton, FL. Co-Authored.

18 Unhelkar, B., (2018), *Big Data Strategies for Agile Business,* CRC Press, (Taylor & Francis Group/an Auerbach Book), Boca Raton, FL. ISBN: 978-1-498-72438-8 (Hardback).

19 Tiwary, A., and Unhelkar, B., (2018), *Outcome Driven Business Architecture,* CRC Press, (Taylor & Francis Group /an Auerbach Book), Boca Raton, FL.

20 Ibid. Co-Authored.

21 Spewak, S. H., and Hill, S. C., (1993), *Enterprise Architecture Planning – Developing a Blueprint for Data, Applications, and Technology,* QED Publishing Group, Boston, USA.

22 https://www.opengroup.org/togaf.

23 http://www.zachman.com.

24 Federal Enterprise Architecture Framework (FEAF).

25 Whittle R., and Myrick C. B., (2004), *Enterprise Business Architecture – The Formal Link Between Strategy and Results* (2016) e-Book; CRC Press, Boca Raton, FL p. 31.

2 Enterprise Architecture and Services Orientation in Digital Transformation

SUMMARY

Enterprise Architecture (EA) is a transformational framework that provides the building blocks for successful digital business transformation. This chapter discusses the elements, structure, and positioning of such an EA framework. An EA framework helps understand the technologies, their impact on processes, and, consequently, the risks associated with Digital Transformation (DT). Services – including web services, analytical services, and knowledge worker services – are important capabilities in DT. These services and their interrelationships are crucial in DT. The EA transformation framework is created with reference to known and robust frameworks such as TOGAF and Zachman. Cloud, Big Data Analytics, Machine Learning and Mobility technologies and their impact on DT are discussed. The EA life cycle and its alignment with business is presented. Finally, the important roles of agility and change management in digital business are introduced.

ENTERPRISE ARCHITECTURE AS A TRANSFORMATIONAL FRAMEWORK

Enterprise Architecture (EA) contains the blueprint for the technologies and processes of a business, including its data, analytics, processes, networks, and the hardware and sensors associated with it. The term "enterprise" implies a high-level, strategic view of the organization and its management mechanism, while the term "architecture" implies a structured framework for the analysis, planning, and development of resources.[1] EA is the practice of analyzing, designing, planning, and implementing enterprise-level capabilities that help a business achieve its goals.[2]

The EA framework brings together people, processes, data, and technology, and sets rules for their relationships. Thus, EA is necessarily holistic. EA provides a common language and best practices for the organization. EA also enables process optimization by making business processes more efficient, effective, and reliable.

An EA and its associated technologies need to provide business value. The complexity of technologies and systems is such that organizations require a holistic, long-term strategic approach to provide continuous alignment of technologies within businesses. This is what EA provides as the business transforms; it lays out the foundation upon which new services or applications are built. Therefore, the EA becomes invaluable in Digital Transformation (DT).

EA is ideally poised to be a transformational framework that provides the building blocks for successful digital business transformation. EA enables an understanding of the technologies and risks associated with transforming businesses. Services – including web services, analytical services, and knowledge worker services – are integral to DT. The key capabilities of services and their relationships is discussed as part of the EA framework for DT.

Holistic EA strategies encompass the entire organization. EA enables and supports DT. EA has three different business, technology, and transformation perspectives. EA iteratively impacts and, in turn, is impacted by the goals of DT – essentially following an Agile process. EA brings together business and technology. As a result, a significant alignment of projects with business goals takes place.

The principles of the EA discipline, its charter, and its governing rules form the basis of its robustness. This is crucial and essential to DT. Developing and aligning EA principles consistently and comprehensively throughout its life cycle reduces the risks in DT.

EA intersects with Service-Oriented Architecture (SOA). Services are modules of business or application functionality with exposed interfaces, invoked through messages. SOA is uniquely connected to the concepts behind EA and Business Process Management (BPM) initiatives, where each of the three provide a set of building blocks for information sharing (see Figure 2.1).

The EA-BPM-SOA connection offers both strategic and tactical synergies across the entire enterprise. Strategically, it delivers business and IT alignment. EA guides and facilitates implementation of strategies and monitors their compliance across the enterprise. Tactically, the connection builds up operational flexibility and effectiveness. BPM offers the improvement of business processes and SOA transitions appropriate business processes and functions for reusable and

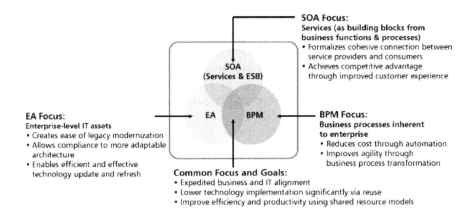

FIGURE 2.1   The BPM, EA, and SOA connection.

modular services. EA offers the ability to connect IT assets with processes and services, and capitalizes on this connection to deliver effective business solutions. Service adoption is a crucial interim phase in an EA-based implementation – both from the business and the technical perspective. The business perspective is the key driver of the inception of SOA, as argued by Marks & Bell: "SOA is a conceptual business architecture where business functionality or application logic is made available to SOA users or consumers as shared, reusable services on an IT network".[3]

The EA, BPM, and SOA each play a distinct role. Together, they serve common goals for establishing a collaborative and transformational enterprise, while also doing the following:

Recognizing Business Needs for Information Sharing
> DT determines needs early and gets the business involved from the beginning to identify candidate business processes from the BPM and IT assets of the EA that can be leveraged as services in SOA. As a result, they obtain timely buy-ins, adequate collaborations, and effective interactions, as well as compliance, to resolve relevant issues, challenges, and associated risks.

Understanding the Concepts Behind a Business Service
> A business service must be granular enough to encapsulate a business function that directly or indirectly relates to the operations of an enterprise. It is decoupled enough to serve a purpose of its own without depending completely on another service or business application. It should have at least one set of interfaces to interact with other services or business applications. A successful SOA usually focuses on identifying a small number of services with coarse granularity and loose coupling for implementation. Both EA and BPM help analyze business application components and associated processes to identify appropriate business service candidates. Over time, the identified services are modified or refined based on their priorities to serve business needs.

Readying the Organization for Information Sharing
> Companies typically start with assessing existing investments on technology, process, and people, and also put a set of governance principles, policies, and procedures in place. In many cases, companies with prior experience in EA and BPM initiatives employ existing management guidelines while embarking on SOA initiatives. It is also important to acknowledge the learning curve for the teams in the initiative and understand the complexity of adopting a new set of consistent processes and technologies. Since it is essential to pick the right candidates for a potential SOA transition, many companies choose only one or two major business applications or functions and roll out an enterprise service bus (ESB) to ensure the infrastructure supports their initiatives.

All business benefits that a company can achieve from pursuing DT depend on their ability to decompose their business processes (from BPM) and to encapsulate application functions (from EA) as services. Major benefits of the EA-BPM-SOA connection in the context of DT are:

- **Productivity Gain** – Rationalizing existing business processes, applications, and functions achieves this, as do consolidating redundancies and modernizing legacy systems. Many companies initially set metrics to measure productivity gain in EA and BPM initiatives and subsequently transition these metrics to manage SOA initiatives.
- **Operational Efficiency** – Increased business value delivery accomplishes this. Services can enhance responsiveness for practitioners or systems by allowing consumers to reach out to critical business functions faster. This benefit addresses the ability to serve multiple business needs (via reuse) and also to connect and collaborate with multiple services using flexible service-level agreements (SLAs).
- **Ease of Information Access** – The use of standardized technologies, techniques, and processes achieves this benefit. For most companies, the basic principles of EA and BPM focus on ease of information access. The SOA adds value to information access by managing the granularity, coupling, and interfaces of the services, and by reducing interdependencies among them. For many companies, reusing services adds to the ease of information access, as practitioners extend the services to effectively deploy or roll out "replicable" solutions across the enterprise.
- **Cost Reduction** – SOA adds to cost reduction via reuse. Practitioners start with a small number of services to reduce initial investments and to leverage lessons learned effectively. Cost reduction is common for most business and IT practitioners involved in enterprise-level integration initiatives and is prevalent in all efforts to share information.
- **Customer Satisfaction** – Serving prioritized and often critical business needs foster this benefit. Many companies meet their customers' expectations using open industry-standard technology solutions for EA and BPM initiatives. This approach applies equally well in porting services from one platform/language of implementation or environment to another, without affecting external interfaces or functions of the service in use.
- **Faster Time-to-Market** – By using investments in standard technologies, tools, frameworks, and techniques, as well as by leveraging expert human resources, companies can achieve this benefit. The financial component of investments made during EA and BPM initiatives is amortized over time and is typically recognized in budgetary considerations. The time spent and lessons learned from investments enable practitioners to create a transition path for transforming existing business functionalities to newly developed or acquired services.

ENTERPRISE ARCHITECTURE IN DIGITAL TRANSFORMATION

EA offers support for redesigns and reorganization, especially during major organizational changes, mergers, or acquisitions. EA brings discipline to an organization by standardizing and consolidating processes for more consistency. It helps businesses navigate complex IT structures and makes IT more accessible to other business units. EA is also used in system development, IT management and decision-making, and IT risk management to eliminate errors, system failures, and security breaches. Thus, EA plays a crucial role in DT.

As an organization undergoes DT, the EA facilitates the following:

- Collaboration between IT and business units that provides opportunities for the business to establish and promote its digital business goals and prioritize investments.
- An evaluation of existing architecture against DT that enables IT to assess and procure technology.

The EA also provides a comprehensive view of IT architecture to all business units beyond the IT function and enables benchmarking of digital technologies to compare results.

The EA establishes principles and guidelines for incorporating technologically significant components into the digital enterprise. The EA also provides overarching governance and handles multiple stakeholders, including sponsors, customers, partners, technologists, policy makers, and security and privacy personnel.

EA as a discipline has a responsibility to facilitate changing the mindset or culture of the enterprise. This is often a time consuming process that requires a multi-disciplinary approach (e.g. psycho-sociology) and comes with a price tag. Selecting the right resources and experts, and choosing a right set of technologies, can drive the impact and benefits of EA significantly in the DT of an enterprise.[4] One such key resource is the enterprise architect. The work carried out in developing and maintaining the EA framework is the responsibility of the enterprise architect, which is a specialist role highly valued during DT. The enterprise architect understands business structures and processes and how to align them with digital business strategic goals. They ensure the agility and quality of processes by modelling, testing, and deploying them. They need technical – as well as people – skills as they have to deal with both business and technology stakeholders. Communication, critical thinking, and leadership are vital skills expected of enterprise architects, in addition to them having a proper understanding of SOAs, Cloud Computing, solutions architecture, Big Data analytics, and cybersecurity.

Enterprise Architecture Elements and Digital Transformation

Figure 2.2 shows the significant elements of EA. These are the basis for the strategic role of EA in DT.

As also shown in Figure 2.2, the EA approach in DT is a middle-out one. This implies EA not only taking input from the enterprise strategy but also feeding back into it, and providing valuable input into technical architectural domains and operations. This iterative approach is characteristic of business agility. In this approach, EA starts by influencing a small, project-specific solution architecture. Once successful, enterprise architects then influence business and IT leaders to help align IT strategy and planning with the business. In addition, enterprise architects also help enforce the

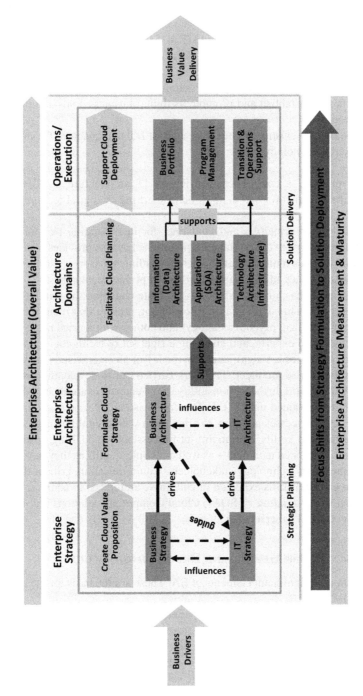

FIGURE 2.2   Enterprise Architecture elements and Digital Transformation.

principles and guidelines developed from the initial effort, as well as share the lessons learned and best practices captured with enterprise-wide project teams.

Incorporation of the Cloud in DT is an important example of how EA can help strategically. During the development of architecture domains for a digitally transforming enterprise, the architects can take input from the organization's EA and map Cloud architecture elements directly into three layers: service layer, resource abstraction and control layer, and physical resource layer.[5] The Cloud is a key technology embraced in DT because of its ability to enable enterprise agility. Big Data, Mobility, and social media are the other vital trends that leverage EA in DT.

Following are some of the direct impact from EA enabling the incorporation of emerging technology trends within strategies for DT:

CAPTURING THE TECHNOLOGY BASELINE

This provides an excellent starting point for encompassing the long-term IT strategies of an organization. The baseline itself can be further modified and expanded, based on business objectives, but the starting point for the organization needs to be spelled out. For example, the EA team of a mid-sized healthcare delivery business prepared an inventory of its existing IT assets to determine its readiness to embark upon DT. The EA team engaged its business stakeholders to support the development of a technology baseline, which formed the basis of the business case for funding needs.

EXPLORING THE CONSTRAINTS AND RISKS UP FRONT

EA offers invaluable information on the constraints, risks, and issues associated (i.e., in security and privacy) with emerging technology trends that impact strategic business objectives. For example, Big Data has risks associated with its use. The EA team experiments with the implementation of Big Data and analytics, including how data can be secured or protected across the enterprise in similar situations. Thus, the limitations of analytics and the risks of back-end data storage are exposed up front.

INFLUENCING BUSINESS OBJECTIVES

EA tempers leaders' business visions with technical facts and corresponding limitations. Therefore, EA as a discipline can effectively influence strategic vision as well as refine the business goals and objectives of an enterprise. For example, the EA team in a financial services company helped the office of the CIO define and refine its DT strategy to include a key business area that ultimately better leveraged the digital assets of the organization.

AUTOMATING BROKEN OR DISPARATE BUSINESS PROCESSES

An EA involves addressing challenges resulting from proliferation of disconnected business processes. This is particularly true of manual processes that can be very difficult to integrate with IT solutions. For example, the EA team of the aforementioned healthcare delivery firm helped the business and IT teams work together to identify processes related to staff scheduling that either needed to be automated or transformed before pursuing DT. This reengineering saved the company time and money in development and integration of applications that could be deployed on multiple devices. It also helped eliminate redundant business activities (e.g., use of whiteboards on walls to assist in staff scheduling) by providing opportunities for efficient technical solutions.

EMBRACING EMERGING TECHNOLOGIES

EA enables organizations to capitalize on emerging technologies by incorporating them into the technical architecture, as well as mapping them to business objectives. For example, the EA team for the healthcare delivery business realized the potential of Big Data and how the resulting analytics could help personalize the needs of the patient. Thus, the patient experience and behavior was carefully analyzed using Big Data. EA ensures that business goals are addressed in the process of embracing existing – and emerging – technologies.

CAPITALIZING ON THE OPERATING MODEL OF THE BUSINESS

EA identifies and documents the core operating model of an organization from a systems and applications perspective, while also considering a potential disruption of operations. For example, another healthcare delivery business' EA team was tasked to improve operational efficiency while considering all channels available to enhance patient–physician interaction. The EA team, in collaboration with physicians and business teams, mapped out the operating models and exposed potential channels for use.

Using standard architectural frameworks (discussed next) enables enterprise architects to understand the business, information, systems, and technologies and their relationship. Various models and their views, based on the framework, are created to help business functions and IT communicate and collaborate. At times, predefined frameworks can result in architectures that are not Agile. At other times, some crucial practices can be missing (e.g., TOGAF, the framework describe next, doesn't really explain the use of patterns, how to actually customize, create, or use a set of integrated architecture frameworks, how to use separation of concerns and deconstruction, or the use of strategic vectors and enterprise patterns to develop sustainable architectural evolution). These are all necessary elements in order to address disruption and transformational change. As a result, EA during DT need not be an exact replica of a predefined framework.

TOGAF AND ZACHMAN EA FRAMEWORKS

The Zachman[6] framework and The Open Group Architecture Framework (TOGAF)[7] are two highly popular EA standards. Both are helpful in Big Data adoption. Big Data Framework for Agile Business (BDFAB) uses a variation of these architectures in mapping new Big Data technologies with the existing layers of an enterprise.

TOGAF prescribes four layers of architecture to be used in the EA development – business, information, applications, and technology.

TOGAF as a *meta*-architecture is made up of two parts: the Architecture Development Method (ADM) and the Enterprise Continuum. As its name suggests, the ADM provides guidelines on creating architecture. The Continuum describes how an organization can move or transit itself from where it is to where it wants to be.

Zachman Framework is another popular EA structure whose columns describe the modeling blocks of an enterprise: data (what), process (how), network (where), people (who), time (when), and motivation (why).

Federal Enterprise Architecture Framework (FEAF) was introduced in 1996 as a response to the Clinger-Cohen Act, which introduced mandates for IT effectiveness in federal agencies. It was designed for the U.S. government, but can also be applied to private companies that want to use it.

Gartner established best practices for Enterprise Architecture Planning (EAP) and adapted them into the company's general consulting practices after acquiring The Meta Group in 2005. While it is not an individual framework, CompTIA recognizes it as a "practical" methodology that focuses on business outcomes with "few explicit steps or components."

These are just four of the most commonly referenced and recognized EA methodologies, but others exist. For example, there's the European Space Agency Architectural Framework (ESAAF), the Ministry of Defence Architecture Framework (MODAF), and the SAP Enterprise Architecture Framework. These are specifically targeted at individual industries or products, servicing a more niche market than the more generalized EA methodologies listed above.

EA creates a technology-business iteration and feedback mechanism that provides the basis for a road map for transition to an Agile digital enterprise. Iterations and increments help business and IT work together, share lessons, and improve the quality of service – resulting in a successful DT that improves the value provided to the customer and enhances their satisfaction.

There are two main aspects of software architecture as a design plan: a blueprint of a system and an abstraction to help manage the complexity of a system.[8]

Software architecture is also a conceptual framework that defines a set of components, the relationship among them, and the interfaces through which they interact.[9]

ENTERPRISE ARCHITECTURE'S TECHNOLOGY STACK

LAYERS OF THE ENTERPRISE TECHNOLOGY STACK

A variation of the EA in Figure 2.3 shows the complexity and relationships between key technological layers of an organization. The EA is representative of all existing and incoming technologies. Figure 2.3 shows five key technology layers interspersed with the security layer. They comprise the communication, storage, sources (analytics and ML), processes, and presentation (visualization) layers.

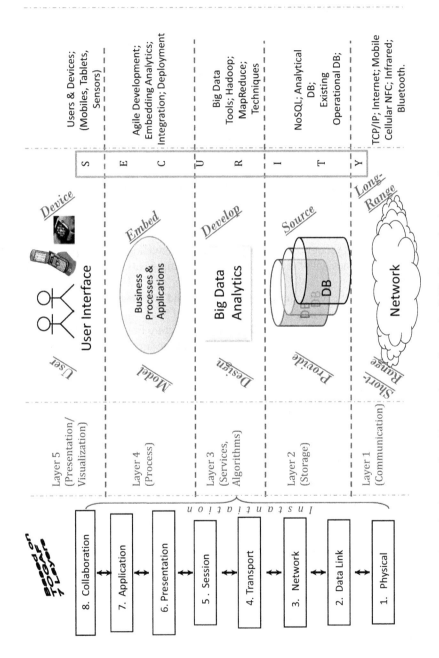

FIGURE 2.3   The enterprise technology stack and its mapping to (improvised) Big Data technology stack.

Study of these layers provides the architectural basis for applications and solutions during DT. Each layer of this enterprise technology stack is elaborated on below. This discussion also includes the application of principles and guidelines relating to solutions development, including the security layer. The convergence between all layers of this architecture is important for a smooth DT.

The customized EA shown in Figure 2.3 also roughly maps with seven layers of TOGAF.

The solutions development platform resulting from this convergence of architectural layers provides the basis for deriving multiple analytical solutions and services. Reusability and quality are also enhanced as a result of keeping the layers of the technology stack in mind while developing solutions.

A brief discussion of each of the layers follows:

LAYER 1: COMMUNICATIONS (NETWORKS AND INFRASTRUCTURE)

The base of Figure 2.3 shows the communications or network layer of the EA. This is the base, or Layer 1, of the architecture. Layer 1 is instantiated from the corresponding physical, network, and transport layers of the TOGAF framework. Starting with TCP/IP at the base, network technologies, interoperability, and Cloud form part of this layer. The network architecture includes the stack of networks and programmable interfaces as well. Various communications network standards and protocols form part of this layer.

All digital solutions depend on this layer for communications. This is because of the fact that Social media and Mobile (SoMo) is integral to provide and present data in Big Data solutions. Tightly integrated IoT devices in particular need to use this layer for communications. Cloud-based back-end infrastructure is part of this layer.

LAYER 2: DATA STORAGE (SQL AND NoSQL)

Contents and their storage form the second layer of this EA. Big Data technologies allow vast quantities of data to be stored across a distributed cluster. Layer 2 deals with the 3Vs (Volume, Velocity, Variety) of Big Data storage – high volume, high speed, and many different varieties of data. Data is typically stored in native Hadoop and also in sophisticated NoSQL databases.

An important architectural decision to make in this layer is arriving at the right mix of existing structured data and the new, incoming Big Data. The speed of access and the quality of content are influenced by decisions taken at this storage level. Technical decisions involve balance, speed, and quality, which can sometimes have opposing priorities. For example, data mirroring enables redundancy and improved reliability, but it may have a negative effect on the speed of access.

The Cloud infrastructure mentioned in the previous layer provides the basis for storing data on the Cloud in this layer. Analytics (part of the next layer) is facilitated by the sourcing of contents and their secured storage here.

Data storage needs to cater to data integrity. Multiple, real-time data updates occurring simultaneously from a suite of mobile users and devices can create challenges to data integrity and the ensuing analytics. The "randomness" of mobile user connections and the changing needs of analytics, depending on the context (specific location and time), add to the complexity of data storage approaches. The moment users change their location, the location-specific information (e.g. the location itself) of the source changes.

Applications and analytics based on location-specific information need to be able to not only handle the conflicts resulting from multiple updates but also identify in the first place that there is a conflict, even if the source of the data is at two different places. The sporadic nature of data inputs and the need to integrate them with existing data is a major challenge of this layer. One way of handling this is to produce a database architecture that is based on *progressive* storage and retrieval of data as the application executes. This ensures that data is stored incrementally and that processing can resume from where the disconnection has occurred. Integration and reliability of data is improved with incremental storages.

Layer 2 corresponds roughly with the "instantiation of the data link" layer of the TOGAF framework.

Layer 3: Analytics and Services (Machine Learning)

The Big Data analytics layer comprising services and algorithms is complex – it contains multiple layers or abstractions. This is so because this analytical layer has to pull together data from multiple sources established in the previous layer and enable analytics for the applications seeking those data and analytics.

The data sources are themselves a mash of structured data and unstructured or semi-structured Big Data. Avoiding data duplication and inconsistency – while keeping replication, security, and privacy of data in mind – only adds to the challenge. Therefore, the analytical layer is made up of "pre-fabricated" analytics that "anticipate" the needs of users and preempt some part of the analytics. These analytical patterns form a layer of abstraction above the data layer that can be used in self-serve analytics.

For example, a medical doctor looking for potential cases of Covid-19 needs to combine third-party provided semi-structured data on global cases and the path they are travelling, with the local (perhaps in-house) structured data on cases reported in the last month or quarter. A pre-fabricated trend plot on the existing structured data of previous reported cases gives this doctor (doing self-serve analytics) an indication of the number of potential cases to expect in the coming weeks. Lack of pre-fabrication in the Big Data analytics layer in Figure 2.3 would mean the doctor has to start an analytical project with elaborate requirements and design from scratch. The integration process of such a solution would also involve significant complexity because of data variations and lack of pre-fabricated analytics.

The services in this level contribute towards establishing this third Big Data Analytics architectural layer in Figure 2.3. Operational services and shared services (particularly data management) are major contributions to the services layer. These interface across different types of devices, applications, and databases by creating and using a common, standardized suite of protocols.

The primary task of this layer is to bring together, or gel, the various services or parts of analytical applications. Ultimately the top layer (customers) are able to benefit from a well-construed suite of services – as they can create and configure their own services, based on the pre-fabricated services made available.

LAYER 4: BUSINESS PROCESSES AND APPLICATIONS

Business processes supported by Big Data analytics, their systems, and their applications are represented in the fourth layer of Figure 2.3. Layer 4 includes the business processes and the models for collaborative web services with embedded analytics in them. Enablers, solutions providers, and application developers work in this layer. For example, product marketing, new service design, and billing applications are created and configured in this layer with the help of the Big Data analytics developed in the previous layer. Layer 4 corresponds to the 7th (application) layer of the TOGAF framework.

An important role of this layer is to enable a holistic process-oriented application of Big Data analytics. This layer *dissuades* the business from "attaching" devices at the end of existing business processes.[10] Instead a model is created and stepped through to ensure analytics are embedded within each activity of the process.

Interfaces provide a common mechanism for otherwise diverse applications to interact easily with each other. The previous layers of data storage and analytics also require interfaces. Interfaces at the application layer are able to connect and interact with networks and middleware of other applications that are required for the overall deployment of a system.

Connectivity is not a single homogenous process. With mobile enabled business processes, there is a need to connect-disconnect-reconnect at various steps of the application execution. This connectivity is required either to get some information or to authenticate parts of the transaction. Application layers handle connectivity requirements at key points in the process.

Big Data-based analytical applications will have mobility embedded in them. Therefore, these new applications designs will have to consider different types of users, their locations, and their needs for "self-service." For example, in a hospital environment, in addition to considering the networks, databases, and analytical algorithms, these Big Data-based applications will have to provide different levels of access to patients and various staff members, such as physicians, administrators, and nurses. The system will have to support physicians at various locations – whether they are in a clinic, at the hospital, making house calls, or at home themselves. The architecture and design of these applications need to keep the users' actual "workflow" in mind. The interfaces between existing and new data storages and the actual application for hospital management will have to consider access to those data related to clinical activities – such as patient history, reviews, details of physical exams, prescriptions and notes, and results of diagnostic tests – together with large volumes of unstructured and semi-structured data, like public health records, movement of diseases across the population, and trends based on patient demographics. These details need to be made available in real time to the doctor and the patient, keeping the security of transactions and the privacy of users in mind.

LAYER 5: PRESENTATIONS AND VISUALIZATION (USER INTERFACES) AND IoT DEVICES

The fifth and top layer of the EA shown in Figure 2.3 is the presentation layer. Layer 5 includes all aspects of presentation, including devices, user interfaces, and navigations. Layer 5 corresponds with the sixth layer, also called "the presentation layer," of the TOGAF framework. The devices in this layer include mobile phones, PDAs, as well as "wearable" IoT devices, GPS-enabled navigation systems, smart buttons, machine sensors, and laptops and desktops.

The devices and their user interfaces are major considerations in this layer. User Interface (UI) challenges are more than just graphic design obstacles – they need to consider the context of usage[11] for each business process supporting the visuals. UI designs identify the purpose of the presentation, the type of user that is going to use the interface and the decision-making process.

Visuals are a part of the overall strategy for presentation – which, in case of smart handheld devices, also include the ability to record and play audio cues, as well as and machine sensors (e.g., vibrate functions). The principles of usability discussed by Constantine and Lockwood[12] apply to these presentation designs and visualizations. The presentation layer also needs to deal with the social aspect of usability and privacy. The technical design in this presentation layer uses APIs to display and receive information from mobile user interfaces, and connect that information to the mobile applications and underlying content management systems.

SECURITY ARCHITECTURE (ALL LAYERS)

There are two parts to this discussion: the security of digital business and security enhancements due to digital technologies. The security of services, analytics, and applications is similar to the way all other applications are secured. Security because of digital technologies, however, is dimensionally different. Security, especially in the mobile usage of Big Data, includes a wide variety of technologies, including authentication, cryptography, secure communications, and secure mobile payment methods. This is especially crucial as communication through wireless and mobile networks is more vulnerable to attack than through wired networks.

Security challenges in Big Data usage include losses of confidentiality, integrity, and availability. The security architecture applies to all layers of the EA, as shown in Figure 2.3. Each of the five layers has its own security requirement. For example, network and application security measures need to be considered together when developing and using Big Data solutions. Big Data technologies based on Hadoop are yet to mature and, therefore, lack security features available in relational databases. For example, Hadoop offers a single point of access to its vast data storage. Therefore, once an access point is breached, so is the rest of the data. Security and compliance requirements of Big Data applications in production are the highest priority in any architectural work.

Data security includes that of machine sensors (IoT), network connections, devices, and their Cloud connections. These devices connect to the network, provide sensor information, and execute business processes. Currently, there aren't sufficient security standards and protocols for IoT devices. Furthermore, the ability to access and upgrade the security on these IoT devices is limited. While growing relationship between the IoT and Big Data pose security risks, the same relationship also has the potential of providing valuable security insights for the network.

Monitoring and detecting security issues before they occur is important for digital business. Big Data enhances security due to use of analytics in Big Data-enabled applications. Some of the security aspects of Big Data-enabled applications are as follows:

- Enables monitoring and analysis of vast data sets in their entirety (as against partial monitoring of data).
- Enables analysis of varied data types, especially unstructured data (e.g., SoMo, machine sensors, visuals and machine generated).
- Faster processing speed results in increased ability to handle velocity that can enable real-time monitoring and processing of streaming data generally associated with international money laundering.
- Server log data analysis is also frequently employed. Server logs are records pertaining to network operations. Hadoop provides a platform that can handle the massive volume of logs generated by network operations – analysis that can help forensics analysts in determining if a breach has occurred, where it originated, and possibly how.

SERVICES ORIENTED ARCHITECTURE

The concept of SOAs was introduced earlier in this chapter. SOA is a business-driven EA practice, requiring a clear understanding of how it creates and interacts with processes.

- It allows practitioners to reflect on the following questions: Where is SOA heading? What are the true benefits or promises of SOA for CIOs and other business and IT practitioners?
- It helps business and IT professionals review the challenges, issues, and risks they are experiencing today when embarking upon their initial SOA initiatives.
- It presents a clear picture of the current connections between the SOA, BPM, and EA worlds, from the CIO's and business and IT leaders' perspectives (including the evolution and maturities of the associated standards).
- It assists business and technology teams in revealing some of the prospects of SOA as it stands in the present, as well as in near-term future initiatives (long-term future may be too speculative in this rapidly changing technology space).
- It offers a reality check for what is up-and-coming with next-generation enterprise initiatives beyond SOA.
- It is a mainstream approach. SOA has been turning into the fabric of every complex enterprise. The practicality of business-driven service enablement has become its key delivery point.
- It embraces web technology and its practical benefits. The combination of SOA and portals enable organizations to implement DT initiatives much faster, as it creates a community of service users through social networks.
- The ultimate push of SOA and DT is the collaborative enterprise. As technology evolves, standards mature, and established architectural frameworks gain popularity and momentum in use, SOA will lead the business to achieving consensus-driven, collaborative, and customer-oriented business goals effectively.

Organizational, behavioral, and cultural issues contribute to challenges in deploying business-driven SOA successfully in an enterprise (mostly in medium-sized and large companies). These issues are usually interrelated and can shape the ability of an enterprise to adopt, as well as adapt to, SOA for information sharing. Organizational issues arise during integration of "silos" or disparate departments. Behavioral issues are observed in collaboration efforts where practitioners and their business functions share a number of IT resources. Cultural issues are primarily related to compliance in using tools, standards, and organizational or enterprise policies. From an EA standpoint, it is essential for business and IT practitioners to recognize the rapidly changing nature of their business first. Once business drivers are articulated, they can focus on current as well as future business processes and functions to make the case for SOA initiatives. Subsequently, cross-functional organizations must address the abovementioned issues, along with identified and prioritized candidate business processes and functions.

SOAs leverage services for information sharing. The primary objective is to guide business and IT teams in making informed decisions that will enable DT initiatives. Here, the stage is set for creating business-driven services and establishing SOA as an architectural approach. The practical concepts behind SOA are clarified and elaborated on, as are the various stages involved in adopting it. Finally, formulating a comprehensive architectural approach to building business-driven services as well as a road map for SOA are discussed.

"SERVICE" IN SOA

The business and IT communities have long been familiar with the concept of a "service." The model of "client" and "server" in client-server computing is a logical starting point for this matter. During the past two or three decades, the concept of client-server has evolved through phases of multitier, object-oriented, and component-based development, transforming into service-oriented computing.

Service orientation is a viable option for integrating business applications at the enterprise level. It enables practitioners to focus on business first without depending on technology decisions, in order to share information across multiple applications. In an SOA model, service providers create a set of services and publish them in a registry, and consumers can choose a service from one or multiple providers as long as they can discover and identify the services.

A service broker registers services from providers and helps consumers locate and bind with the desired one. In a business-first approach, practitioners can take advantage of the three basic features of a service: modularity, granularity, and loose coupling. Modularity or the ability to "plug and play" allows consumers to use or reuse services easily. The granularity of a service helps practitioners capitalize on the abstraction of a business function. Loose coupling separates services from each other – and enables practitioners to concentrate on service interfaces. This approach ultimately adds value toward achieving goals such as reuse and agility.

"Service" is an act of performing a set of work or duties for another person. This definition relates to exchanging or sharing information between two or more entities that can be human beings or business systems manipulating information for humans. Communities of people with similar business interests or professionals involved in similar fields of practice can exchange services.

In the business world, sharing information is nothing new. Collaboration and innovation are the most commonly known concepts used by the global workforce in information sharing. Most activities related to these concepts have influenced the creation of services and applications. Hence, SOA offers a prospect for businesses to discover and interact with each other while sharing or exchanging information through services.

SERVICES LANDSCAPE

There are number of different service types that play a role in DT. Each service type contributes to the digitization effort of the business. Services typically plug into business processes. Modularized services enable "plug and play" within business processes, enabling "Adaptiveness" and "Responsiveness" – thereby rendering the business Agile.

A basic understanding of the SOA landscape is most helpful in DT. This landscape must encompass advanced internet-based technologies and approaches that relate to information sharing and that are founded on or connected with various aspects of SOA. For example, Semantic Web/Semantic EA, software as a service (SaaS), Cloud Computing, Machine Learning and intelligent agents. The relationships of these technological concepts with SOA is worth noting. All can significantly support today's strategies in enterprise integration and information sharing.

Figure 2.4 shows an overall DT framework that models agility and stability based on EA. Services are integral to the agility of business processes. Here is a discussion of some key service types that are important in DT.

SHARED SERVICES

A series of frameworks were needed for the service provision, but Adaptiveness and Responsiveness were embedded within the project and, in turn, the service:

- **Vendor Management** – standard vendor management frameworks within the department were used, but had to be changed to support the new services. With the requirements of the service evolving during the project (from software development through Cloud hosting to application support), an iterative and staged approach with the vendor(s) was taken. A series of layered agreements for additional services were incrementally applied. The agreements had to be managed within overall government procurement guidelines including expenditure limits and spend amounts with recognized suppliers. Once negotiated, operational integration and service levels were implemented with the vendors on a staged approach, based on service commencement needs.
- **Project Management** – alignment with the overall Project Management Office was required with full auditing of outcomes and deliverables. A daily stand-up with a minimal working group approach was used.

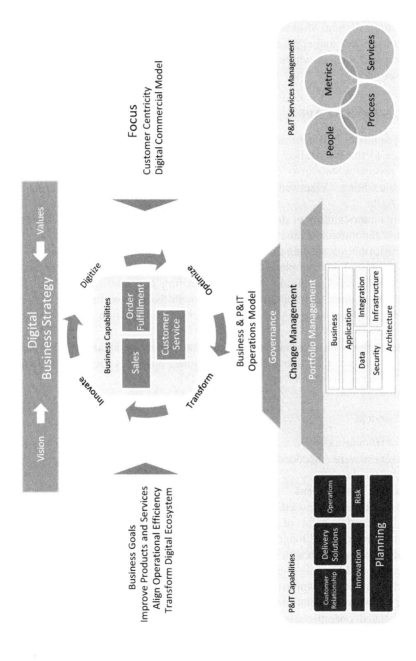

FIGURE 2.4 Digital Transformation framework based on EA and governance.

- **Financial Management** – government procurement policies had to be followed and little flexibility existed. The financial management of the services was simplified as internal cost recovery or charges for the service were not required.
- **Data Management** – aligning with departmental standards and policies, an overall series of protocols, policies, and internal standards were developed in consultation with stakeholders, including external parties.

When instituting a new service, some frameworks had to be established with a minimal approach just to commence the service, and provisions for iterative improvements and formal approval after the service commenced had to be made. This approach worked because of an absence of regulatory compliance, but an ability to audit the revisions was required.

OPERATIONAL SERVICES

The Operational Services shown are required to support software development and the establishment of a service. While much of the software development was managed using Agile methodologies, many other parts of the service and the ICT required set lead times with defined deliverables to provide the service. Iterative releases of the application, with ongoing requirement reviews and testing until the final stages, applied. Frameworks required for the service included:

- **Process (Six-Sigma)** – development and management of business processes, including IT operations and for future software development management and release coordination.
- **Requirements (BABOK)** – assists in Agile software development by enabling better elicitation of requirements.
- **Application Management** – life cycle management of an application, including data feeds and interfaces.
- **Test Management** – includes continuous testing and extended use of regression testing within Agile software development. The tools, processes, and procedures for testing were adopted from existing practices. The testing of data for assurance of service and quality, as well as ongoing performance management, was developed iteratively.
- **Request Management** – used to track requests for work, enhancements, and defects. Existing practices were modified to support the service.
- **Development (Agile)** – as discussed.
- **Infrastructure (ITIL)** – the department had a partial implementation of Incident, Problem, and Change Management, which was modified for the new service. Revisions to services with vendor(s), amendments to service desk processes, and interim processes for Release Management were developed. The prioritization was sufficient for service commencement with iterative ITIL service improvements as it matured.
- **Change Management (ADKAR)** – used in skilling and for developing the capacity and capability to undertake Agile software development, as well as in the management of the ICT service and use of the data analytics service.

CUSTOMER SERVICE

This is the final part of the data analytics service, related to customer management (of internal customers) in order to grow the service and drive the uptake of data analytics within the department. The approach was to use what existed within the department for service commencement and have the frameworks, capacities, and capabilities developed as required for:

- **Account Management** – managing the ICT relationship within the department and with vendors.
- **Market Management** – educate key internal stakeholders about the service and benefits so they could make requests for it in the budgeting cycle.
- **Product Management** – a need for product champions was identified but was dependent upon the growth of the service after commencement.
- **Customer Management** – ongoing relationship management and service provision was the starting point.

Customer servicing relied on people being adaptive and responsive to support and develop the service.

Technical architecture elements discussed thus far include data storage, services, applications, and presentations for the users. These are made up of data sourced in-house and by third parties on the Cloud. These data sources are also distributed physically on multiple nodes and servers in a Big Data environment. Big Data services and tools can be used to bring these elements together for processing. Hadoop can be used as an almost limitless database, but using that data in a meaningful way requires supporting tools and applications. Data movement and interfacing is crucial for Big Data analytics. This data manipulation and movement may not always be possible with native Hadoop tools. This is particularly true for data that needs to be integrated from structured and unstructured sources. Visual tools are most helpful in enabling back-end data manipulation that would otherwise require significant technical skills.

KNOWLEDGE WORKER SERVICES

A complex knowledge worker service[13] cannot be made using just one methodology. Consider the example of the data analytics service established for a government department in Australia.[14] There, the following frameworks (methodologies) were used for the development, management, and provision of the data analytics service (excluding shared and supporting services like HR and facilities management) required for all areas of business:

SYNCHRONIZATION OF SERVICES

Services are the basis of synchronization. Data, service, application, and user layers are based on the technology architecture. The service layer is the one that plays a major role in synchronizing these various elements.

Synchronizing technology elements adds to the challenge in the Big Data domain because the underlying distributed architecture has to also handle data that is rapidly changing. Synchronization of data needs to keep the operational (non-functional) parameters of solutions in mind. This is because a synchronization only limited to data is not going to handle the crucial performance parameters required of Big Data applications.

Synchronization has to further handle operational processes that continue to function while the data is being synchronized. This implies synchronization of not just data, but also processes and presentation. Agile processes help bring together development and operations (DevOps) to ensure that the releases of analytics and applications are in sync with existing applications.

Synchronization is also required when it comes to the presentation layer. The analytical outputs from structured and unstructured data are presented in a structured form. Analytics and presentations both need synchronization.

The synchronization of these architectural layers discussed thus far is not just a technical issue but also includes other aspects of a functioning organization, such as people and processes.

The layers shown in Table 2.1 are synchronized to ensure processes, applications and people work together. Following are some of the factors to be considered in synchronizing the elements comprising enterprise technology layers:

- Sources and availability of data – including the ownership of data across enterprise systems and the process of collecting it.
- Business processes that will be affected by the incorporation of Big Data analytics and how the change needs to be managed (e.g., training staff to start using the new processes).
- Where the data is physically stored and how compliance regulations apply to that data when it is synchronized

TABLE 2.1

EA Layers, Technologies, and Their Impact on Digital Transformation

Layers	Digital Technologies	Impact on Digital Transformation
Data	HDFS; NoSQL	Use of Tools to move, store, analyze and transform data
Service	Models for analytical algorithms (and Code Python, R)	APIs for plug in. Agile used to continuously test and promote services.
Application	CRM, SCM and in-house packages; based on HDFS, NoSQL, and associated programming	Structured and unstructured data movement, conversion, and integration for business processes. Iterative development of interfaces.
Presentation	Customers, staff, partners	Face-to-face collaboration between customers, staff, and service providers; Presentations customized to suit user needs

- How long is the data current? Synchronization efforts are required only when data synchronized in the decision-making process is current. Once the data is not current, a process to remove it needs to be initiated.
- Should the synchronized data be stored separately (to obviate the need to do the synchronization exercise again) or should it be returned to the original disparate sources after the processing is complete?

SERVICE-ORIENTATION AND BUSINESS

Using an architectural approach to roll out SOA initiatives – and specifically to build business services across the enterprise – is integral to DT. This approach is the foundation of building data-driven services now.

To establish the proposed architectural approach, begin with the simplest possible question: what does SOA really mean to the business and IT practitioners today? There are two distinguishable schools of thought on potential ways to respond to this.

One primarily relates to the business perspective and the other to the IT one. These views are often distinct and independent from each other. However, it's worth mentioning that these two schools of thought can jointly influence business and IT practitioners alike, particularly when collaboration is introduced into the mix.

At a strategic level, collaboration also addresses the synergy of innovation and execution of processes to deliver solutions for the company.

From the business perspective, SOA is always about sharing information over a network with other business users, partners, or associates. Today, the internet helps businesses leverage a global workplace. It allows professionals to create communities of practice. SOA offers consistent ways of sharing business information over a network – and they must do so by using the internet as part of that network.

Services must make an enterprise transparent to its business users, allowing them to seamlessly search, discover, identify, and connect with services relevant to their applications or use. Business users must also be able to assimilate several services to form another one (i.e., a composite service) if necessary. With the advent of the Semantic Web and software agents, practitioners can broaden the concept of discovering or identifying services further. Semantic Web and software agents can add to the capabilities of services and allow business users to search, share, and integrate information more easily beyond their corporate boundaries.

On the IT side, SOA is about providing users with visibility or transparency of business processes. To make services useful and reusable, IT practitioners must empower their business users with the ability to securely access and manipulate the services. This means employing a multitude of modern integration technologies to facilitate capabilities, such as search utilities, associated information access, and security mechanisms relevant to business users.

Enterprise Application Integration (EAI) ranges from middleware to object request broker to an enterprise information bus to an enterprise service bus (ESB) for services. These technologies primarily focus on connecting distributed, multitier, heterogeneous, and often disparate applications or systems. Through the concepts of ESBs and reference architecture-based frameworks, an SOA integrates services or their interfaces. At a strategic level, however, an SOA is still about enabling and empowering the business and improving operational efficiencies and excellence of the overall enterprise.

For many practitioners, the business goals behind creating services consist of multiple financial factors, parameters, and constraints of their organizations. No doubt, many trade magazines as well as the internet describe key difficulties in reaping business-related benefits of SOAs. However, an essential step for success is for practitioners first to identify and prioritize their prospective business service candidates in a visual model. Managers must instill this business-first approach in their teams. These services can then be transformed using a set of SOA technology, standards, and best practices. The architectural approach presented in this report can influence business and IT collaboration – the critical component of service orientation.

Currently, the standards, frameworks, and reference models supporting SOA initiatives are improving and governance processes are still maturing. As a result, practitioners can use various tools to help them assess the health of their SOA initiatives and to achieve desired objectives.

The business value of employing an SOA is in delivering enterprise agility, improved performance, and enhanced productivity. For some organizations, the benefit of an SOA may be in service reconfiguration flexibility (as the business transforms). For example, consider the changes necessary to drive ease of information access in *days* by the businesspeople of the bank rather than *weeks* by technical specialists.

SOA constructs "services" from business functions and "architecture" from IT assets. As a result, a case is created for a business-driven SOA, stressing the importance of business and IT alignment.[15] Services can also represent IT functions that support business functions. In other words, services that stem from IT functions must either support or enable business services. Many technical services are primarily used by IT (specifically application development and infrastructure) organizations internally. Typically, the system development and engineering teams of the organization manage these services locally.

BUSINESS-DRIVEN SOA

The world of SOA has evolved more rapidly than anticipated, mostly surpassing the hype and reaching the recognition of its prospective business value. Some practitioners may still argue that most early SOA adopters must have either successfully reached the valley of maturity with their initiatives or must be frustrated enough to rethink their strategies and potentially change directions. Like any other initiative, the success of an SOA project depends heavily on the effort, commitment, and the investment of resources and time that practitioners put into it.

From a business-driven perspective, the SOA must be of equal importance to both business and IT practitioners – and the responsibility of building, managing, improving, and governing services in a business-driven SOA must be *shared* equally by IT and business leaders. Once the principles and guidelines for providing and consuming services in the business are well understood, the work required to align business and IT can proceed. In the past, EA and BPM programs have helped practitioners define the ground rules for business and IT alignment. An SOA can enhance the alignment process by making services part of business solution delivery. Subsequently, practitioners can use an SOA initiative to launch a successful endeavor for information sharing across the enterprise. SOA can make companies Agile and help them adapt to transformational changes in business environments today and tomorrow.[16]

SOAs, as a business-driven concept, promise to make most business operations efficient and cost-effective. They have evolved during this decade to become one of the most effective architectural approaches for consistent information exchange or data sharing. SOA helps integrate various business components or applications as long as they are part of a network, and can be located as well as connected. Many industry leaders, analysts, and software vendors state that SOA helps them make the perfect business case for building collaborative environments that allow businesses to engineer both intra- and inter-enterprise information exchange. A significant impact on business goals follows three characteristics of business-driven services:

1. **Service Granularity and its Ability to Form Other Services** – this relates to abstracting a service so that it delivers specific business functionality and can be easily managed. The granularity of a service promotes composing other service(s).
2. **Service Coupling and its Interoperability with Other Services** – this helps detach one service from another. Many companies use an ESB to enhance interoperability of loosely coupled services.
3. **Service Reusability and its Portability to Multiple Environments** – this is perhaps the most important factor in having a direct impact on the bottom line. To support users effectively, practitioners must focus on the quality of service interfaces.

Many consider service orientation the key ingredient in building enterprise-wide innovation and collaboration strategies. Business and IT leaders should guide their teams in transitioning and deploying applications as business (web) services, leveraging a service-oriented architecture. This is based on the facts and factors related to the rapid evolution of internet technologies and the capabilities of most companies to adopt emerging web services standards.

Many organizations exert their efforts to modernize and rationalize existing business functions at tactical levels (bottom-up) while embracing new transformational business changes at strategic levels (top-down). These divergent efforts are "middle-out" initiatives.

The primary goals of these middle-out (concurrent modernization and rationalization) efforts are about finding better ways to achieve information access and sharing inside one (or across) multiple business and IT organizations by achieving enterprise goals via strategic partnerships or business relationships and delivering business results at operational levels.

As appropriate, new transformational business changes and associated challenges are dealt with at enterprise levels, where visionary leaders recommend focusing on relevant innovation and collaboration.

Innovation is essential to recognize changes needed in business functions that can be transitioned into services. Collaboration is the cornerstone of establishing SLAs or contracts between service providers and consumers. Neither innovation nor collaboration can happen in isolation; each requires concerted efforts from practitioners to share information across their organizations. Thus, an SOA can offer the most consistent architectural approach for information sharing with its ability to facilitate both innovation and collaboration in an EA. In a business-driven SOA, innovation starts early by recognizing the candidate business processes and functions that can be transformed into services. Collaboration can formalize the foundation of connecting stakeholders and the users of services. Table 2.2 highlights the key characteristics of a business-driven SOA and what its implications to business.

There is a correlation between innovation and collaboration and the adoption plan for a business-driven SOA in the case of most of the same respondents. The majority of respondents cited the following efforts in making the case for considering a business-driven SOA while promoting better information sharing across their enterprises (listed here with no specific preferences or priorities):

- Accelerated deployment of new business applications, capabilities, or service offerings.
- Simplification of most mission-critical business processes.
- Reduction in overall cost of deploying and supporting new business functions.
- Enhancement of the ROI from various existent system resources.
- Modification of business processes and their efficiencies, which ultimately improves productivity.
- Improvement in agility or flexibility of the overall enterprise.

TABLE 2.2

Business-Driven SOA: What Does it Really Mean?

Features	Description
Quality	A service in a business-driven SOA that can offer the most effective solution for the business. The quality of a service can be maintained from its abstraction to its design, and finally to its deployment. The business focus drives the level of abstraction and, in turn, the granularity and coupling of the service with other services.
Reliability	A service in the business world that comprises or supports one or more business functions that are often critical to the mission of a business. It allows information sharing across the enterprise or beyond the boundaries of it. It is crucial for a business-driven service to be available in a highly reliable manner to its consumers.
Reusability	A service that is reusable in one or more business functions across the enterprise, with the primary means of reuse being the creation of an interface(s) that can serve multiple services or business applications, as well as service-level agreements (SLAs), to bind contractually the service provider and its consumers.
Ease of Use	A service that usually transforms a business function. It is vital to improve the ease of use and interoperability of the service. For a business organization, ease of use enhances the reusability of a service. Often, ease of use also encourages practitioners to modify or improve the quality of a service and make it available to the enterprise.

AGILITY IN DIGITAL BUSINESS

"Agility" can have different meanings but, in the context of DT, is an enhancement in the ability of the organization to make more accurate faster decisions. This, in turn, leads to an increase in customer value. Accuracy and speed in decision-making are the key characteristics of business agility.[17] Typically, from a software development viewpoint, "Agile" is a method to produce a solution. Scrum and XP are examples of such Agile methods. The enterprise architect views Agility as an opportunity to provide business value through people, processes, and technologies. It is also the ability of the organization to handle change[18] – and DT brings about substantial change in the organization's people, processes, and technologies. Agile organizations are in an ongoing iterative and incremental mode – and, therefore, are in a much better position to handle DT.

The time gap between the change and the organization's response determines the "sensitivity" of an organization. The shorter the time gap in responding, the higher the sensitivity. Reducing the transactional gap and increasing sensitivity is the purpose of any initiative in an organization.

Agility is a business value resulting from DT. Agile is also a way to produce Big Data solutions and is described as both a culture and a mindset.[19,20] Thus, Agility has a lot to offer to this discussion on DT.

Agility is very important across all organizational functions. Agility in business processes is further enhanced in DT (detailed in Chapter 7). EA and its accompanying Agile techniques provide an ideal combination when implementing DT.

Software systems support decision-making in business processes based on data and its analysis. Business agility, therefore, depends on data science. Enterprises integrate their business processes with data analytics, optimize their operations and supply chains, and improve on their compliance and reporting through data science. Business agility is a strategic direction that requires commitment of resources as well as finances.

Technologies shape the future of information systems and services. Systems and services, in turn, enhance business capabilities and processes, which eventually render the business Agile.

Agility in EA enables bringing together new, incoming, high-velocity, unstructured data and existing, rigid, structured data to perform analytics.[21] Analytics in the Big Data space needs to be iterative– essentially comprising short, rapid bursts of developing analytical algorithms and database logics that are "showcased" to users, with their feedback incorporated instantaneously within the solutions development. "Trust" and "courage" – two vital Agile values are brought into play in this highly iterative Agile life cycle, wherein there is a need to rely on the inputs and efforts of a cross-functional team (trust) and the ability and freedom to throw away many different analytical prototypes (courage).

As a foundational structure, an EA provides more value than just being an aggregation of individual architectures for each technical element.[22,23] An EA is a mechanism to incorporate the long-term needs of the enterprise while keeping in mind the changing technical and business ecosystem it exists in. This enables the organization to gradually build its long term capabilities with reduced risks.

Agility of the EA itself is as important as the agility resulting *from* the EA. The Agile Manifesto, which forms the basis of software development agility, reads as follows[24]:

> We are uncovering better ways of developing software by doing it and helping others do it. Through this work we have come to value:
> - Individuals and interactions over processes and tools.
> - Working software over comprehensive documentation.
> - Customer collaboration over contract negotiation.
> - Responding to change over following a plan.
>
> That is, while there is value in the items on the right, we value the items on the left more.

The Agile Manifesto is reconceptualized to apply to EA as follows:

We are uncovering better ways of governing enterprise change by doing it and helping others do it. Through this work we have come to value:

- Sense-makers and decision-makers over processes and tools.
- Coherence in the enterprise over its comprehensive documentation.
- Promoting business and IT collaboration over contract negotiation.
- Seizing immediate opportunities over following a plan.

That is, while there is value in the items on the right, we value the items on the left more.

The Manifesto itself was backed up by twelve Agile Principles listed on the Agile Manifesto site. These principles for corresponding Agile EA can be made to read as follows:

1. Customer satisfaction by early and continuous delivery of architectural representations and diagnoses
2. Welcome changing business conditions, even in during change initiatives
3. Architecture evaluations are delivered in frequent and timely manner (days rather than weeks and months)
4. Close, daily cooperation between enterprise architects, businesspeople and developers
5. Architectures are maintained by motivated individuals, who should be practical
6. Face-to-face conversation is the best form of communication (co-location), but many forms of electronics-based communication will be embraced as needed
7. Business agility is the principal measure of progress
8. Distributed development, able to maintain a constant pace
9. Continuous attention to business and technical excellence and good design
10. Simplicity—the art of maximizing the amount of documentation not done—is essential
11. Best architectures, requirements, and designs emerge from self-organizing teams
12. Regularly, the team reflects on how to become more effective, and adjusts accordingly

The above manifesto and principles for EA form the basis for an iterative and incremental approach to technology throughout the DT process. Such an Agile-based introduction to newer technologies and the changing of business processes reduces constraints placed by a scale-up infrastructure. Iterations allow architects to think of solutions delivery in a more Agile way, as opposed to a linear or "big bang" approach to delivering solutions.

For example, consider centralization (or pooling) of data – an activity that used to happen in the past to enable the processing of that data. An iterative approach within an EA is based on the availability of a distributed structure with an exploratory version dedicated to Big Data. Such an exploratory platform facilitates Agile experimentation in developing Big Data solutions. In fact, BDFAB urges an EA to be committed to Agility. This is so because while Big Data continues to provide significant insights for business decision-making, the time available to capitalize on these opportunities is shrinking. The time available to process a data point into an actionable insight has shrunk from days to minutes. The business context in which a data point is "current" is so limited that Agile is the only way to use the EA in developing and using Big Data solutions.

EA is shifting from providing stability of technologies and systems to becoming Agile and facilitating significant technical changes that enable successful business outcomes. As argued by Cole: "Therefore, just having an Enterprise Architecture initiative isn't necessarily enough to properly leverage Big Data. EAs that are yet to focus on agility won't find as much success as those that have."[25]

Digital technologies on the Cloud promise "unlimited" data storage at low cost. There are also new opportunities for processing that data. If introduced carefully, Big Data can lead to Agility in business, characterized by lean processes, decentralized decision-making, and operating efficiency.

Using Big Data without underlying principles of Agility increases the risks of developing analytics and visuals that may not be of value to end users. For example, setting an interest rate in the banking domain requires not only the sophistication of an analytical engine but also continuous fine tuning of that engine based on feedback received from users. In the absence of Agility, such a solution may not always provide the continuous update that the bank's decision makers require.

DT focuses on data right from acquisition through to visualization. This can be machine sensor data, logs, scanners, and system-generated data. Data can also be generated by the user or crowd sourced. Data is sourced, stored, and analyzed, and the results are embedded in decision-making processes. Data also arrives from sources and different formats. Then it is stored, staged, cleansed, and transformed. Agile analytics do a lot more than sequential data-staging and processing. Agility aims at using digital technologies to collect data and conduct iterative, explorative analysis. The purpose of such Agile "prototyping" is to bring together existing structured and incoming Big Data in an experimental mode. Such prototyping provides an iterative and incremental approach to DT.

Sources of data include those generated within the organization and externally. Also, it can be unstructured data. The Big Data manipulation tools that allow data to be extracted, transformed, and loaded (ETL) for analytics imply the embedding of analytics in business processes. Decisions are continuously updated by key users who understand the relationship between analytical outputs and business outcomes.

EA provides the backbone for manipulating data in and out of technology platforms to produce effective analytics. The integration of analytics in business processes involves a lot of data movement across repositories whose handling is challenging. This integration requires the ability to not only manage data but also its context (based on metadata). The iterative and incremental aspects of Agile are most handy in integrating such data and metadata in processing.

EA reduces the friction between new technologies and existing systems and applications (typically using structured/relational data storages).[26] Agile, in its composite format, is also most helpful as a style of working – a culture – to reduce friction. The iterative and visible nature of Agile opens up opportunities for experimentation with new types of applications and analytical insights.

The scalability of technology platforms on the Cloud plays an important role in DT. For example, the challenges of capacity planning are obviated. This freed up resource can be used to enable agility in business processes in the Cloud. An EA further facilitates integration of services, resulting in the ability to create and present a unified view to the customer. For example, new analytics resulting from the integration of social media and mobile inputs can create innovative pricing models, new products, and dynamically changing business processes.

Finally, from an operational perspective, it's also important to keep DevOps in mind.[27] They enable agility in developing solutions to be operationalized rapidly and in an automated manner. Therefore, DevOps form the basis for business Agility.

CHANGE MANAGEMENT IN DIGITAL TRANSFORMATION

Business value is the desired outcome of DT. The impact of digital technology produces substantial change in the entire organization. Therefore, discussions on DT need to balance business value with risks. Business processes need to be managed as they change. Digital technologies aid business agility only when they are accompanied by change management.

Agile practices of rapid, iterative, cross-functional, and collaborative teams with just enough documentation and continuous testing are most helpful in DT efforts. Enterprise architects can also apply Agile practices in developing their architectures and synchronizing its elements.

Composite Agile Method and Strategy (CAMS)[28] utilizes Agile as a balanced practice focused on the architecture of the future and the visible delivery of the present solutions. Digital technologies can be implemented using Agile that allows for flexibility in design as well as support maintenance and upgradation of existing applications and services.

The risk of using these digital capabilities with the old mindset is real. For example, if Cloud technologies are used to provide more storage, the opportunity to develop shared and collaborative solutions may be lost.

Following are some of the factors to be considered from a change management perspective when an EA is used for DT:

- Change in the architectural mindset from developing grand designs for the future to short, sharp iterations of technical solutions.
- Ensuring the digital solutions are instantly made visible to users and that their feedback is incorporated in improving the designs.
- Ensuring that the EA is placed under formal a change management process – this will ensure that changes to the EA itself are considered in their entirety and in a holistic manner, thereby reducing the negative impact of one change on the rest of the enterprise.
- All changes to the EA are communicated to business and technical stakeholders on a daily basis (e.g., in daily standups). This is crucial to handle unforeseen impacts of changes as mentioned in the previous point. More importantly, this daily communication mechanism provides an excellent medium for "buy in" to the adoption initiatives.
- Enable the use of data from across the many different silos of the organization, as the technologies make the data available in a collaborative manner (especially on the Cloud). This collaborative use of data from a broad spectrum of organizational data creates opportunities for Lean-Agile business processes.
- Handling concerns that arise due to the decentralization of decision-making that results from EA changes, by providing an iterative and incremental change management mechanism that is based on the Agile values of "trust" and "visibility."
- Relaxing the controls in a secured manner to enable interfacing with open data provided by governments. This provides a major opportunity for analytics that will eventually change the business processes of the organization.
- Enabling integration with existing systems on a continuous basis and thereby reducing systems, applications, and process frictions.
- Enable architectural governance to control the development of organization-wide Big Data solutions that facilitate cross-functional and decentralized decision-making.

DISCUSSION TOPICS

1. Discuss, in detail, why the foundation of robust DT is the EA?
2. What is the intersection of EA, BPM, and SOA? Why is this important from a DT viewpoint?
3. What are the key elements of EA discussed in this chapter that form the basis for DT?
4. What is SOA? Why should one keep SOA in mind when undertaking DT?
5. Explore the TOGAF and Zachman frameworks. Discuss why simply following these frameworks, as they are, is not enough for DT?
6. What are the 5 layers of an EA's technology stack? Discuss them in the context of DT.

7. What is meant by "synchronization of services"? How does this help in business Agility?
8. Explore the services landscape in the context of a transforming organization.
9. How would you argue that SOA is the essential impetus for the DT journey? How would you argue against that idea?

NOTES

1 Bernard, S. A., (2005), *An Introduction to Enterprise Architecture*, 2nd edition, AuthorHouse, Bloomington, IN.
2 Tiwary, A., and Unhelkar, B., (2018), *Outcome Driven Business Architecture,* CRC Press, (Taylor & Francis Group /an Auerbach Book), Boca Raton, FL.
3 Marks, E. A., and Michael B., (2006), Service-Oriented Architecture (SOA): A Planning and Implementation Guide for Business and Technology, John Wiley & Sons, Inc., New York, NY.
4 Hazra, T. K., and Kumar, S. "Establishing the Business Architecture Practice: A Case Study." *Business & Enterprise Architecture Executive Report*, Vol. 15, No. 1, 2012, *Cutter*, Boston, USA.
5 US Government Cloud Computing Technology Roadmap, published by the US National Institute of Standards and Technology.
6 TOGAF – The Open Group Architecture Framework - http://www.togaf.org/togaf9/ accessed 27 March, 2020.
7 Zachman, J., https://www.zachman.com/about-the-zachman-framework, accessed 27 March, 2020.
8 Hofmeister, C., Nord, R., and Soni, D., (2009), *Applied Software Architecture*, Addison-Wesley Longman Publishing Co., Inc., Boston, MA.
9 Tibbetts, J., and Barbara B., (1992), *Building Cooperative Processing Applications Using SAA*, Wiley.
10 Unhelkar, B., (2009), *Mobile Enterprise Transition and Management*, Taylor & Francis (Auerbach Publications), Boca Raton, FL. 393 p, ISBN: 978-1-4200-7827-5 (Foreword by Ed Yourdon, USA).
11 Agarwal, A., and Unhelkar, B., (2016), "Influence of business context on the role of granularity in big data analytics." *Proceedings of the System Design and Process Science (SPDSnet) 2016 Conference*, Orlando, USA 4–6 December 2016.
12 Constantine L., and Lockwood, L., (1999), *Software for Use: A Practical Guide to the Essential Models and Methods of Usage-Centered Design.* Addison-Wesley, Reading, MA.
13 Sherringham, K., and Unhelkar, B., (2020), *Crafting and Shaping Knowledge Worker Services in the Information Economy.* Springer Nature (Palgrave Macmillan), Singapore. ISBN 978-981-15-1223-0.
14 Sherringham, K., and Unhelkar, B., (2016), "Service management in big data." *Proceedings of the System Design and Process Science (SDPS2016) Conference*, Orlando, FL, USA 4–6 December, 2016.
15 SOA: Understanding the Practice 2010 -- Creating Business-Driven Services By Tushar Hazra, Executive Report, Posted October 31, 2009 in Business & Enterprise Architecture.
16 Hazra, T. K. "Transitioning Business Application Components to Web Services." *Cutter Consortium Enterprise Architecture Executive Report*, Vol. 5, No. 12, 2002.
17 Unhelkar, B., (2018), *Big Data Strategies for Agile Business,* CRC Press, (Taylor & Francis Group/an Auerbach Book), Boca Raton, FL. ISBN: 978-1-498-72438-8 (Hardback).

18 Unhelkar, B., (2013), *Art of Agile Practice: A Composite Approach for Projects and Organizations*, (CRC Press/Taylor & Francis Group/an Auerbach Book), Boca Raton, FL. Authored ISBN 9781439851180.

19 Ibid.

20 Unhelkar, B., *Agile in Practice: A Composite Approach,* (16,000 words), Cutter Executive Report, January 2010, USA. Vol. 11, No. 1, *Agile Product and Project Management Practice.*

21 Hazra, T., and Unhelkar, B. "Leveraging EA to Incorporate Emerging Technology Trends for Digital Transformation." *Cutter IT Journal, Theme - Disruption and Emergence: What Do They Mean for Enterprise Architecture?* Vol. 29, No. 2, pp. 10–16, 2016, February.

22 Unhelkar, B., (2008), *Mobile Enterprise Transition & Management*, Taylor and Francis (Auerbach Publications), Boca Raton, FL.

23 Unhelkar, B., (2008, April), *Mobile Enterprise Architecture*, Cutter Executive Report. Vol. 11, No. 3, *Enterprise Architecture Practice*, Boston, MA.

24 http://www.agilemanifesto.org/history.html.

25 Cole, Z., "Big Data, Agility, and Enterprise Architecture" available on https://www.corso3. com/blog/big-data-agility-and-enterprise-architecture; accessed 10 November, 2016.

26 Tiwary, A., and Unhelkar, B., (2018), *Outcome Driven Business Architecture,* CRC Press, (Taylor & Francis Group /an Auerbach Book), Boca Raton, FL.

27 http://www.disciplinedagiledelivery.com/devops-data-management/ accessed 1st December 2016.

28 Unhelkar, B., (2013), *The Art of Agile Practice: A Composite Approach for Projects and Organizations,* CRC Press, (Taylor & Francis Group /an Auerbach Book), Boca Raton, FL. ISBN 9781439851180.

3 Strategic Planning for Digital Business

SUMMARY

This chapter discusses the importance and relevance of planning in Digital Transformation (DT). Strategic planning is important because DT needs to be holistic to benefit the entire organization. Successful DT is not possible if only one part of the organization and its associated processes is digitized. However, holistic change while the organization is still in operation is a very complex endeavor. Enterprise Architecture (EA) is integral to DT because it provides the backbone for evaluating the impact of digitizing one business function or process over another. Delivering increased value to the customer is one of the most important strategic goals of DT. Engaging key business and technology stakeholders early in the transformation is vital to strategic planning. This chapter reviews the main activities involved in the planning stage, as well as how to leverage and capitalize on existing and new IT investments. How to recognize organizational challenges that may arise due to DT and incorporate them into business strategies is also covered. This chapter considers how to prepare and perform cost-benefits analyses and investment planning for digital business sponsors.

PLANNING FOR A DATA-DRIVEN DIGITAL BUSINESS

Digital business is based on the value of data as a strategic asset. Strategic planning for digital business revolves around data and how it can be used to provide customer value. The validation of data and the creation of new and relevant business models that drive customer value are a part of the strategy. Digital business strategies include embedding data-driven analytics in every decision, including those around developing innovative products and process optimization.

A Digital Transformation (DT) strategy is a multi-disciplinary function, as it integrates data with processes and people. Such data-driven strategy gives due consideration to governance, security, storage, and usage, while basing itself on the Enterprise Architecture (EA). DT strategies also factor in reengineering business processes to be more collaborative.

Strategic planning for digital business is creating a plan for the company to achieve its vision and goals. Such plans also focus on the alignment of business functions with all service and support functions, including – especially – IT. An EA provides the necessary impetus to align and synchronize functions and capabilities. The strategic plans, goals, objectives, and expectations of a digital business are periodically synchronized with the capabilities and project initiatives of the organization. An EA leads, orchestrates, contributes, and facilitates the synchronization of capabilities for digital business. Strategic planning identifies goals, builds a road map, and develops a blueprint for implementing change. It results in modifications and upgrades to IT capabilities that aid in transitioning to a digital business.

Strategic planning, aligning, and synchronizing IT with the business functions of an enterprise help reduce the risks of DT. A checklist of tasks and activities as well as effective practices for developing a strategic plan is helpful for any business enterprise embarking on DT.

Strategic planning is also associated with qualitative and quantitative measures. Metrics and measurements enable buy-in from the business for DT. The business must be engaged as early as possible in the EA life cycle and key stakeholders must be actively involved throughout the delivery of EA values. The interactive, innovative, and collaborative coalition of IT and business has significant influence on delivering the right business results.

"Agile" as a business characteristic carries immense value. The agility goals of DT are included in the strategic planning effort. The balance between customer focus and operational continuity can be achieved only with business agility. In turn, this strategy depends on an Agile approach to knowledge management and project management. Since EA is the backbone for DT, the strategic planning for a digital business needs to be based on an Agile, Innovative, Digital Enterprise Architecture (AIDEA). AIDEA requires digitized data to be integrated throughout the business, all the way to the edges and even beyond. The hallmark of AIDEA is the ability to make informed business decisions, at a strategic level and also in real-time customer interactions and transactions, informed by the following analytical matrix:

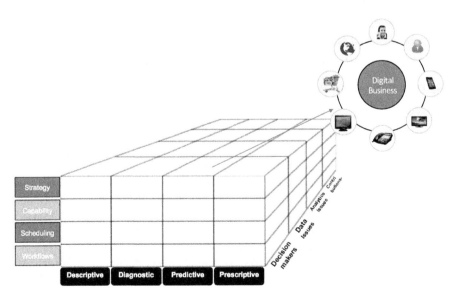

FIGURE 3.1   The strategy planning matrix.

The strategy planning matrix in Figure 3.1 includes:

- On the x-axis, the four main categories of decisions that benefit from analytics:
  - **Strategy** – decisions to pursue business-defining goals
  - **Capability** – decisions to invest in specific capabilities
  - **Scheduling** – decisions about how and when to deploy capabilities
  - **Workflow** – minute-to-minute decisions made in real time while performing the work of the enterprise
- On the y-axis:
  - **Descriptive** – what happened?
  - **Diagnostics** – why did it happen?
  - **Predictive** – what will happen next?
  - **Prescriptive** – what should be done?
- On the z-axis, the key concerns of analytic support for the functional areas of the business
  - Who (what roles) are involved in decision-making for this business area?
  - What issues may exist in the underlying data?
  - What issues may exist in the algorithms and implementation of analytics?
  - What contributions does this business area make to the data used by other business areas for *their* decision-making?

This analytics matrix provides an essential structure for how to consider digital business strategy planning based on EA. It provides guidance and governance for any company that hopes to successfully pursue the DT journey.

DIGITAL BUSINESS STRATEGIES

Digital business strategy starts with the vision and definition of the goals of DT. The key goal of DT revolves around providing customer value. Digital business strategy comprises a set of decisions that enable changes in organizational structure and the behavior that affects the long-term competitive position of the organization. Metrics to monitor strategy execution (e.g., satisfaction, loyalty, and costs) help control it and ensure continuous alignment with projects. The strategy execution plan keeps the customer, infrastructure, and resources in continuous alignment. Strategies are continuously aligning capabilities to achieve business outcomes.[1]

Digital business strategy needs to keep the context of a particular market or industry in mind. Consider, for example, the retail grocery industry. The strategy to digitize such an organization would include decisions related to store location, store refurbishment, advertising, promotions, and investments in staff development. The social, legal, and political climate and its patterns would be inputs in long-term decision-making. These decisions impact the organization's ability develop digital capabilities. The vision and aspirations of the organization are tied to the products and services it delivers to customers. Digital business strategy would also ensure that its products and services do not end up competing with each other.

DT involves an organization's technologies culture, business process, systems, and data, and it directly impacts the customer. The digital business strategy includes the digitization of various organizational functions. Furthermore, it provides direction to optimize operational areas of business.

Strategies specifically include:

- Identifying opportunities and associated risks in undertaking DT.
- Analyzing key investments in providing and increasing customer value.
- Digitizing the marketing and sales functions.
- Optimizing business processes (operational) through analytics and Artificial Intelligence (AI).
- Ensuring governance, risk, and compliance of all business functions and their digital reporting.
- Innovating in products and services, including improvement of existing ones, through utilizing digital technologies.
- Applying the principles and practices of cybersecurity holistically.

These strategies require enterprise to extend the use, understanding, and trust of its data across every business function.

INPUTS TO STRATEGIC PLANNING FOR DIGITAL BUSINESS

Figure 3.2 shows the inputs that need to be considered in strategic planning for digital business:

- **Current Decision-Making Process** – this is important to understand, as it will likely have gaps in delivering value to the customer. Any changes to the overall decision-making process need to be based on the current process. Also, the risks associated with changing it based on data-driven decisions need to be evaluated.

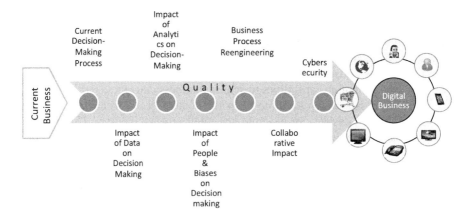

FIGURE 3.2   Inputs for strategic planning for digital business.

- **Impact of Data on Decision-Making** – including the sources, storage, and manipulation of data. Data sourced from collaborative business partners, third-parties, and government sources, as well as data generated in-house and stored on the Cloud, are all going to impact decision-making in the new digital organization, so they need to be included in the strategic planning process.
- **Impact of Analytics on Decision-Making** – especially as this impact will change (improve) the accuracy and time taken for making decisions.
- **Impact of People & Biases on Decision-Making** – strategies need to factor in the effect that digital business has on people and the way they make decisions. Changes associated with human bias and sensitivity require careful strategic planning as these are perhaps the most important and difficult parts to change during DT.
- **Business Process Reengineering** – DT undertaken while the organization is still in operation requires substantial and holistic strategic planning. This is so because the impact of digitizing one process on another and functions of the organization can be substantial.
- **Collaborative Impact** – especially because DT will render the business much more collaborative on electronic platforms than ever before. Strategic planning needs to give due consideration to the services offered and consumed from collaborative business partners, the policies governing those services, and the impact on the value being delivered to the customer.
- **Cybersecurity** – is a vital strategic consideration in DT as changes to the electronic platform open up the organization to the possibility of cybercrime and other related risks. Data, analytics, and digital business assets need additional protection and those need to be factored into strategic planning.

STRATEGY FOR DIGITAL TRANSFORMATION – FOCUS ON CUSTOMER EXPERIENCE

The Figure 3.3 presents a comprehensive and holistic approach to developing a consistent and succinct road map for the DT journey. As also shown in that figure, the DT journey primarily focuses on providing improved customer experience. In general, this means engaging customers, offering desired business services, and providing better and timelier responses to customer needs.

A business starting its DT journey must recognize the challenges, issues, and risks associated with meeting the customer requirements. The digital journey begins with considering changes in the following three areas:

Business Capabilities – a set of business capabilities that addresses the key business requirements of target customers. Often, business capabilities and gaps therein are directly connected to the values, objectives, and goals of the business.

Business Processes – these present a conduit for various business capabilities to deliver desired outcomes to target customers. In most cases, a business considers modernizing its processes to improve or enhance its ability to realize the values of its business capabilities. A modernization effort includes automation, consolidation, and integration of disparate or siloed business processes.

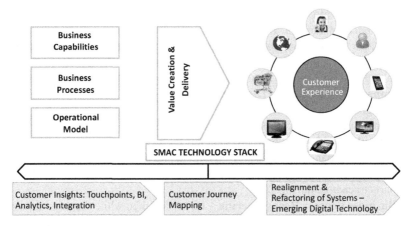

FIGURE 3.3   Strategy for Digital Transformation – the focus is on customer experience.

Operational Model – DT often requires a significant change in the way a business operates. The operational model is transformed from an "inside out" one to an "outside in" one. This means that the organization changes its business processes to make sure that the operational model aligns itself to meeting customer needs – rather than creating or offering business values in such a way that target customers have to change their requirements to receive what the business offers.

OBJECTIVITY IN DEVELOPING DIGITAL STRATEGIES

The digital business strategy of an organization is created and maintained in a formal manner. Senior decision-makers identify and define organizational goals. These are then are dispersed across the organizational structure, depending on its size. Risks associated with individual personalities and their biases may come into play in strategy development. Decision makers may influence strategies based on their own beliefs and understanding.

A truly consultative and objective approach to developing digital business strategies is required. Visibility, collaboration, discussions, and an understanding of the objective reality of the environment the business operates in is beneficial to developing a digital business strategy. Cross-functional teams at the business, corporate and departmental levels iteratively define and manage these strategies on an ongoing basis. Each strategy outcome is mapped to business capabilities and desired business outcomes.

ELEMENTS OF DIGITAL BUSINESS STRATEGIES

A digital business strategy has the following elements:

- Vision and aspirations
- Goals that define outcomes

- An implementation plan
- Measurements and metrics
- Feedback loop

The vision and goals of the organization provide the basis for digital outcomes. Outcomes are defined, measured, and implemented as part of DT. Organizations define an enterprise vision, but the actions necessary to achieve this vision are assigned to business divisions. Strategies are broken down into projects with corresponding implementation plans. Each division further plans how to achieve KPIs and related measures of success.

Implementation deals with the actions needed to achieve goals and a method to manage these actions. Strategic risk associated with the implementation is managed. Implementation results in numerous projects. An important criterion of success for projects is how closely they are aligned to outcomes.

STRATEGIES RELATE PROJECTS TO CAPABILITIES TO GOALS

Figure 3.4 shows how digital business strategy encompasses visions, goals, capabilities, and projects. The strategy implementation plan of an organization focuses on projects related to capabilities. Multiple departmental implementation strategies are accompanied by actions through projects. While strategies deal with aspirations and goals of the organization, actions and projects enable goal implementation.

The success of a project is equal to the success of a DT. The time lag between defining strategies and the commencement of corresponding implementation projects causes friction. This is mainly because of the rapidly changing business context. Strategies need to be continuously aligned to this context to reduce friction and for the business to succeed.

BUSINESS CAPABILITIES

A business capability is a combination of skills, tools, processes, and resources[2] (see Figure 3.4). "Business capability" is a generic term that groups management practices, resourcing, intelligence, and processes that coordinate and allocate tasks. Business capabilities can also be thought of as a collection or container of people,

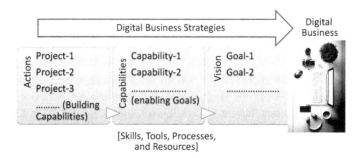

FIGURE 3.4 Strategies relate projects to capabilities to goals.

process, and technology gathered for a specific purpose. A business capability brings together multiple dimensions of an organization to enable quality response to the company's core functions.

The specific definition of business capability varies for different organizations. Following are some key aspects of business capabilities to be considered in DT:

- Business capability is a combination of multiple attributes. These attributes, or dimensions, are customized based on the organization but the definition of the capability is same across the organization. Each attribute has multiple perspectives depending on the context.
- Business capabilities provide an excellent way to understand the organization's technical priorities. Assessing current performance levels (including gaps, risks, inefficiencies, and opportunities) against required performance provides an understanding of where technical investment is required.
- Capability management is applied by organizations in order to align strategic intents and outcomes with capability-building initiatives.
- Capability management provides resource allocation to meet various competitive dimensions.[3]
- Projects enhance or develop new business capabilities. The key requirement is to have capability-based governance of organizational resource allocation and an enterprise-wide prioritization of the resource allocation.
- Business capabilities are able to help the organization achieve its objectives in a pragmatic and timely manner. The mindset of the organization changes from being a technical, solutions-oriented one to a business outcome-driven one.
- Capabilities help the organization move away from disparate and disjointed recommendations from external stakeholders. Furthermore, independent projects across different divisions and departments are stopped and a "big picture" approach is instituted in building business capabilities.

One of the most challenging aspects of this exercise is to define the capabilities uniquely. The effort to define them requires a great commitment of time and resources. When embarking on a DT journey, existing processes and policy frameworks are helpful in defining business capabilities. The more capabilities and processes are understood within the organization, the easier the transition. In some cases, a maturity assessment is in place as well, making adding the capabilities to it a step up.

Digital business value results from models that blend the physical, electronic, mobile, and collaborative domains. Data transforms everything, including capabilities and processes. Data as a strategic asset in itself opens up opportunities for new revenue streams.

Developing capabilities that provide insights for decision-making at the point of action is a crucial goal of strategic planning.

DT expands the use of data beyond IT and makes it visible to the rest of the organization. Unless data can improve business performance decision-making, it does not provide value. Also, decisions that handle operational optimization are based on data-driven analytics. Digital strategy needs additional effort to secure business data to ensure regulatory compliance.

Mergers through acquisition lead to technology silos. Digital strategic planning has to handle the crucial challenge of data integration.

Integrated data leads to proper analytics and accurate insights. EA engenders complete and accurate data used in analytics.

Digital business strategies are based on singular customer views, enhanced quality and governance, and greater collaboration between technical and business stakeholders. As a result, silos are broken down and a unified approach for DT is developed.

Structured and unstructured data are part of Big Data. They can be stored locally on the premises or in the Cloud. Data sources and usage require model-driven tracking. Services, applications, and processes utilize the data and its analytics.

DT strategies are all data-driven strategies. Strategies for collaboration and sharing of data result in a singular customer view. Integration with other applications and processes is based on collaborative business strategies. The following capabilities are strategically developed during DT:

- Creating a unified view of data.
- Aligning people, processes, and technologies with new capabilities.
- Developing models for data assets.
- Managing and governing change.
- Implementing policies and rules electronically.
- Cybersecurity.

BUSINESS STRATEGIES AND ENTERPRISE ARCHITECTURE

EA plays a vital role in digital business transformation. The impact of EA on digital business ranges from IT alignment, Big Data analysis, the Internet of Things (IoT), and Cloud to governance, risk, and control.

EA makes a direct and positive contribution to digital business as follows:

- Identifies capabilities to meet strategic goals.
- Plans and executes business transformation.
- Provides enterprise-wide technical insights.
- Supports multiple projects to develop organizational capabilities,
- Develops actionable insights.
- Automates IoT sensors for business data collection.
- Integrates data and processes with decision-making.
- Combines IT devices (the IoT) with existing systems.
- Optimizes for the Cloud.

DT depends on data and the ability to integrate data-driven decision-making to achieve goals.

Figure 3.5 is an example of how a digital strategy (based on Big Data in this case) is mapped to an EA. The figure is a variation on the Zachman framework for EA.

BDFAB	What (Data/ Artefact)	Why (Purpose)	When (Time from Start)	Where (Location)	How (Process)	Who (People)
Business Context	Budget; Competition	ROI; Risk Mgmt; Value	1-3 months	Local – within business	SWOT; Decentraliza tion	Investor Owner, CxO, Data Scientist
Concept Explorati on	Feasibility; Optimum Granularity Levels	Establish KPIs – Opportuniti es; Value	2-4 months	Global (location- independent)	Proof of Concept; Update EA	Data Scientist, Architect
Process Model Analytics	BPM; Des– Predictive NPS	Embedding Analytics; Decision- Making; Set Granularity	3-6 months	Depending on Partners	BPMN; Statistical Modeling	Process Modeler; Data Analyst
Technol ogy	HDFS; NoSQL; SMAC	Distribution; Handling 3V	3-12 months	Cloud- location	Prototyping (Iterative); Agile	Data Architect; Developer
Impleme ntation (Agile)	Big Data Solutions (Code, Data)	Quality in Code, Data	6-8 months	Co-location	CAMS Practices (Iterative)	Coach, Quality Analyst, Developer

FIGURE 3.5 Mapping digital strategy to Enterprise Architecture (initial, high-level iteration in the context of Big Data).

The rows are not an exact replication of those representing a functioning enterprise as described in Zachman. Instead, the scope, business model, system model, technology model, its implementation details, and organizational sections are all replaced by appropriate equivalent rows based on a Big Data Framework for Agile Business (BDFAB)[4]. These rows are:

- **Business Context** – business objectives, strategy, and service requirements from Big Data and their alignment with existing business strategy are discussed here. This is the focus of outcome-driven strategies. Big Data is viewed from outside facing in. A timeframe of 1–3 months is suggested. The people involved are primarily the investor, the CEO, the data scientist, and their equivalents.
- **Conceptual Exploration** – the research and analysis required to establish Big Data products and services; e.g., establishing the technical and business feasibility of linking real time data to Customer Relationship Management (CRM). This exploration is well supported by composite Agile as it is undertaken iteratively and in close collaboration with all stakeholders. The KPIs for success are specified here and a proof-of-concept is created.
- **Process Models and Analytics** – undertaking an analysis of business rules, processes, and processing rules. This analysis is then modeled using Business Process Management (BPM). These models are based on conceptual exploration outputs but, in turn, also aid deeper exploration of business and technical concepts. This layer is given a 3–6 month time period. The process modeler and data analyst are the key drivers.

- **Technology (Hadoop, NoSQL)** – the distributed data architectures of Hadoop and the large data stores that can handle lack of structure and schema through "Not only Structured Query Language" (NoSQL) databases, along with Big Data, form this layer of the EA. This layer has to consider interfacing and integrating with existing (and mostly) structured data. The Cloud forms the primary location for data. This layer of the EA can work to separate how data is stored and how it is used. This can reduce the impact of changing the adoption of Big Data technologies. Data architects and developers are the primary roles here.
- **Implementation (Using Agile)** – the use of Agile to develop a solution creating a minimum amount of viable product releases is part of this layer. The technical integration of previous layers is further implemented here.

ARCHITECTURES AND DIGITAL STRATEGIES

Enterprise Architecture

EA defines the structure and operation of an organization with the purpose of determining how it can achieve its current and future objectives most effectively. It translates those goals into a blueprint of IT capabilities. Its advantages are improved decision-making, the ability to adapt to changing demands or market conditions, eliminating inefficient or redundant processes, and optimizing the use of assets.

Data Architecture

Data architecture involves models, policies, rules, or standards that govern what data is collected and how it is stored, arranged, integrated, and used within an organization and its various systems. It starts with data modeling – the creation of a unified view of any data (structured or unstructured) from anywhere (within your walls or in the Cloud). Such an integrated, visual representation of enterprise data enables stakeholders to see critical business information, regardless of its source, and relate to it from their unique perspectives.

Business Process Architecture

Business process architecture represents the elements of a business and how they interact, with the aim of aligning people, processes, data, technologies, and applications to meet organizational objectives. It provides a real-world picture of how an organization functions, including opportunities to create, improve, harmonize, or eliminate processes in order to improve overall performance and profitability.

The EA team sees business requirements and can make technology decisions based on real business scenarios.

- The business architecture team supports the EA team by providing goals and constraints of the business.
- The data architecture team sees how data is used in the context of the customer journey and how it fits into the technology roadmap.

- The process team sees available data sources and their quality, and can refine processes accordingly.
- The cybersecurity team ensures that every deliverable from the DT effort is secured on an ongoing basis

SOURCES AND DIGITAL STRATEGIES

KNOWLEDGE CUSTOMER

The customer today is as knowledgeable as the business. The "knowledge customer" links with the business electronically in order to customize his/her needs. By one estimate, 1.7 megabytes of new data are created every second by every human.[5] This is a knowledge customer – one who produces and demands data. The knowledge customer uses the IoT to collect, analyze, and share information that he/she may not even be aware of. The knowledge customer uses this data to make buying decisions, demand improved and personalized service, and connect with the rest of the world. The knowledge customer also collaborates with other customers to check, evaluate, and demand improved and personalized services.

KNOWLEDGE WORKER SERVICES

Knowledge worker services are a type of electronic support (e-support) that allows customers and employees to access information and perform routine tasks over the internet without any direct interaction with a representative of an enterprise. These knowledge worker services are electronic "plug and play" components that are customized by the knowledge worker to suit his/her needs when providing personalized services to the customer.

BIG DATA

Big Data is high-volume, high-velocity, and high-variety information assets. These Big Data require innovative forms of information processing that are also cost-effective. Big Data analytics provide enhanced insights that result in process automation and improved decision-making. Big Data is thus integral to all business decisions. Data-driven businesses thrive on Big Data and, obviously the more the data, the greater the impact on business decision-making.

SENSORS (IoT)

Sensors are IoT devices that are interconnected through the internet to sense, record, analyze, and share data and information. The IoT is significant because an object that can represent itself digitally becomes something greater than the object by itself.[6]

ANALYTICS

Data analysis is conducted to identify historical patterns and trends. Analytics also help narrow down the effects of decisions and evaluate business performance. Thus, it improves decision-making at all levels of business.

MACHINE LEARNING

The complexity and enormity of Big Data is such that computing is required not only to provide answers but also to find the right questions to ask. This is where Machine Learning (ML) comes into play in a digital business. ML algorithms are put to use to find hidden patterns in Big Data that can be found only by machines.

SOCIAL MEDIA

Performance and popularity of the business on social medial is an important criteria in DT. Various digital, audio, and video channels provide opportunities for businesses to discover where they stand through analyzing traffic and chats amongst visitors to social media sites.

MOBILE APPLICATION

Mobile apps provide one of the easiest means for customers to connect with the business independent of time and location.

MAKING DIGITAL STRATEGY WORK

Figure 3.6 shows at a high level how a digital strategy works. It starts by creating a value map – the vision and the goals of DT derived from it. The strategy provides input for the EA. The EA and project management offices enable understanding existing business capabilities and projects, actively involving the business and ensuring the DT is treated like a business initiative. Setting the right expectations with the business is the responsibility of the EA. But if the business is involved right from

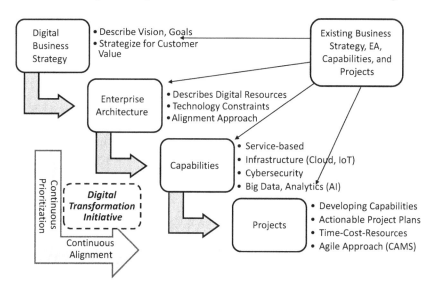

FIGURE 3.6   Making digital strategy work.

the beginning, then the expectations are set in collaboration and projects are based on an actionable plan to deliver capabilities. A DT initiative continuously prioritizes capabilities and continuously aligns with projects.

DIGITAL BUSINESS STRATEGY AND PLANNING

Integrating the vision, goals, objectives, and requirements specific to digital business with each other is a part of the strategy and planning. The goals need to be relevant and appropriate for the application, data, and infrastructure layers of the architecture. While emerging technologies bring up a myriad of challenges, issues, and concerns for the EA, the most disrupting factor can be the incorporation of security. Therefore, it is important to first prioritize security requirements in terms of risks, issues, and concerns across the Cloud, Big Data, and IoT implementations. Evaluating and assessing the existing business strategy helps develop a new digital strategy. Digital is an integral part of the entire enterprise. Digital business strategy must consider an optimal approach that can work across the enterprise — with the caveat that it may or even will change during the course of the transformation — as well as a plan to counter disruption.

ENTERPRISE ARCHITECTURE RESOURCES AND CONSTRAINTS

The EA identifies the right set of standards, tools, technology, and architectural best practices that can be leveraged across the life cycle of Cloud, Big Data, and IoT adoptions and implementations. These standards, technology, and best practices are all evolving rapidly. Leveraging open-source is cost-effective at times, although that decision also depends on the situation. Often, companies have successfully managed the learning curve with less initial investment and have created an effective ramp for their DT. In many cases, the transition plan from using open-source to industry-standard technology and proven processes, along with a few subject matter experts, has streamlined disruption and kept it to a minimum.

CAPABILITIES AND SERVICES

As mentioned earlier, a capability is a combination of skills, tools, processes, and resources. Capabilities form the backbone of EA of an organization. Capabilities are delivered by organizations through services. Capabilities bring together people, processes, and technology in order to deliver a specific service. Ability to offer services – primarily electronic – forms the backbone of most modern-day digital businesses. These services not only provide value to the end-users but they also support the knowledge workers.[7]

When the organization is embarking on a DT journey, it is prudent to look for existing definitions, understandings, and implementable options for capabilities and corresponding services. The EA contains a rich repository of such definitions and options that help define business capabilities in a consistent manner. Therefore, existing EAs and policy frameworks are valuable assets in an organization's journey of digital transformation.

PROJECT IMPLEMENTATION

Projects deal with the implementation of technologies to create capabilities. Projects use "what if" scenarios to explore various solution options before rolling out the actual implementation. Carefully implemented projects uplift capabilities and provide cost benefits as well as operational excellence. Project leaders prepare, describe, compare, and select ideal options to develop capabilities, keeping the business context in mind. Data is the most important element when it comes to implementation of Cloud, Big Data, or the IoT. Implementation needs to keep existing technology, the business, and devices in mind. Organizations taking a hard look at their current technology and capabilities can define their expected outcomes better and can achieve the desired project success.

Identifying and analyzing new ideas across the organization is the first step in the strategic planning process of successful organizations.

While portfolio management and the project management office (PMO) evaluate the initial concept, the EA team evaluates top priority ideas and compiles a business case for pursuing (or not pursuing) each of them.

The team examines whether the new idea contradicts or extends existing projects. It examines risk, time schedules, effects on corporate goals, and how the changes would be constrained by the principles and controls of the organization.

It develops transition plans and suggests solution alternatives that describe the impact of the change, including estimates on cost, risk, resources, etc.

The business case is shared across the PMO, IT, portfolio management, and the business teams to help them make an informed decision about whether to pursue the idea for implementation.

A review board can regularly evaluate returned business cases and prioritize them based on a range of objective and subjective factors such as cost, financial return, strategic relevance, opinions of stakeholders, and potential risk.

The EA team compiles and analyzes structured information on:

- The internal capabilities of the organization, the goals and long term strategies they support, and the resources that support the goals and strategies.
- High priority initiatives and the capabilities and resources they affect. Initial analysis can be made on the impact of new initiatives on existing projects and whether they are in line with current strategy.
- Building a target state architecture that provides details for each capability.

DISCUSSION TOPICS

1. What are the key elements to consider in developing strategies for Digital Business? Provide examples.
2. How can an EA help and how should it be mapped in developing digital strategies?
3. What is the difference between vision, goals, capabilities, and projects?
4. What are the sources of digital strategies and how do they help in strategic planning for DT?

5. How does an EA map to digital business strategy (Figure 3.5)?
6. How do you address your diagnostic of business capabilities for DT?

NOTES

1 Tiwary, A., and Unhelkar, B., (2018), *Outcome Driven Business Architecture,* CRC Press, (Taylor & Francis Group /an Auerbach Book), Boca Raton, FL.
2 Ibid.
3 Hammer and Champy *Op Cit.*
4 Unhelkar, B., (2018), *Big Data Strategies for Agile Business,* CRC Press, (Taylor & Francis Group/an Auerbach Book), Boca Raton, FL. ISBN: 978-1-498-72438-8.
5 Bernard Marr in "Big Data: 20 Mind-Boggling Facts Everyone Must Read" (Forbes, 2015, No. 2).
6 https://www.techopedia.com/definition/28247/internet-of-things-iot accessed 3 April, 2020.
7 Sherringham, K., and Unhelkar, B., (2020), *Crafting and Shaping Knowledge Worker Services in the Information Economy,* Springer Nature (Palgrave Macmillan), Singapore, 2019. ISBN 978-981-15-1223-0.

4 Collaborative Digital Business

SUMMARY

Digital business collaborates electronically with customers, partners, staff, and regulators. This chapter recognizes, establishes, and develops the concept of collaborative digital business based on electronic interactions amongst businesses. Collaborative Enterprise Architecture ("Collaborative EA") is the mainstay of this chapter. Discussed here are the evolution of architectures in the context of collaboration, further details of collaborative elements, active matrix modelling in action, and practical steps for deployment of a Collaborative EA together with its road map. Emerging trends in technologies provide the foundation for the electronic collaboration of multiple organizations. These include Cloud Computing, Social Computing, Mobile Computing, Machine Learning, and Big Data analytics. They are discussed in this chapter in terms of how they impact a collaborative digital business enterprise. The opportunities created by digital collaboration for the business are also outlined.

A DIGITAL BUSINESS IS A COLLABORATIVE BUSINESS

Collaboration is not a new concept. Organizations, large or small, interact with each other through various operational units (business, engineering, or technical) in order to deliver services. Physical collaboration, based on paper contracts, is not the way a digital business collaborates. Digital technologies – in particular "services" – enable businesses to automatically connect, exchange data and information, execute contracts, and increase overall value to their customers. The tools and technologies of electronic collaboration also support globally dispersed workforces within the same organization. The focus of collaboration is on integrating and extending corporate operations or service delivery options beyond the boundary of a single enterprise.

Digital business uses electronic mediums to collaborate with customers, partners, staff, and regulators. Therefore, every digital business is essentially a collaborative one. Collaborative technologies enable a digital business to explore many opportunities in order to provide additional customer value. Enterprise Architecture (EA) plays a crucial role in enabling and executing electronic collaborations. A collaborative digital business becomes a complex and challenging entity because its boundaries are fuzzy and are continuously changing. A Collaborative EA enables handling the complexity and dynamicity of collaborative digital business.[1] In addition to business-to-business collaboration, even knowledge customers and knowledge workers associate electronically. A Collaborative EA also offers major benefits in enabling safe collaboration amongst customers and workers.

There are three typical ways in which organizations collaborate: physical, electronic, and mobile.

PHYSICAL COLLABORATION

This is the traditional way in which businesses relate to each other. This is the people-to-people, face-to-face, manual process of collaborating. Physical collaboration is understood as working together. Such collaborations can be long-drawn and bureaucratic, limiting the opportunities for agility. This is so because in physical collaborations there is a need to establish partnering organizations, setup an alliance, and undertake formal agreements. Legal contracts and their execution become a bottleneck in collaboration. Physical collaboration can be slow and time consuming, leading to lost market opportunities. Whenever physical collaborations are formed, it is imperative that stakeholders and players in these partnering organizations quickly understand and establish working relationships. Socio-cultural issues in physical collaborations are most crucial. Agility is limited in such collaborations as each organization is required to maintain full and independent operability. Yet, understanding the structure and dynamics of physical organizations provides the basis for their collaborations through electronic and mobile communications technologies.

ELECTRONIC COLLABORATION

An electronic collaboration uses internet-based technologies to enable automated and continuous exchanges of information between suppliers, customers, and intermediaries. This is supported by tools that facilitate communication and the information sharing needs of collaborators, either as individuals or in groups. Electronic collaborations, although tool based, still face challenges of mapping trust between partner organizations during the collaborative work establishment and life cycle. Web service-based solution architectures provide opportunities for organizations to collaborate through their portals. The enhanced ability of information systems to connect and communicate with each other leads to a collaborative opportunity for Agile enterprises. Electronic collaborations also open up Agile opportunities as they enable organizations to reuse IT infrastructure and databases.

MOBILE COLLABORATION

This is an extension of electronic collaboration, with the additional characteristic of being independent of location and time. This is based on the features of mobility that enable multiple parties to connect and collaborate with each other using mobile/wireless devices and networks. Mobility leads to dynamicity in collaborations, enabling real-time sharing of information and knowledge between different parties that take part in the collaborative work. This results in flexibility and support as well as ad hoc relationships between multiple parties that unite to work together for short-term customer-focused goals. Agility is most enhanced in mobile collaborations as the infrastructure associated with physical and electronic organizations is further reduced due to both location and time independence.

COMPLEXITIES OF COLLABORATIVE DIGITAL BUSINESS

Enterprises are consumer-oriented, widely dispersed, and serve many (millions) of users in diverse industries such as healthcare, financial services, and energy. The processes of producing goods and providing services are heavily intertwined with myriad underlying technologies, applications, and data warehouses.

Various complexities emerge in applying EA to a collaborative business. Studying these complexities are essential for the success of a collaborative digital enterprise. The complexity arises not only due to multiplicities of applications, but also due to the fact that they are serving dynamically changing business processes. Multiple collaborating applications that are widely dispersed over physical servers (or in the Cloud); many different input/output points over fixed and mobile devices; and dynamically changing data comprising text, audio, video, and graphics – all result in a melee of services that is daunting to decipher for sensible decision-making. Following are the factors that add to the complexities of collaborations amongst businesses:

BUSINESS PROCESSES

As they traverse the boundaries of multiple organizations in order to collaborate, business processes become complex. Assessment and evaluation of collaborative business processes or workflows, modification to business interactions, information-exchange components, and understanding the dependencies between associated business applications is required and is part of a Collaborative EA. Process management also includes collecting such metrics as user access logs and user fulfillment surveys, and tracking the volume of collaborative activities.[2]

ENTERPRISE IT GOVERNANCE

Enterprise IT governance promotes the use of standardized technology and techniques and helps incorporate best practices while deploying, maintaining, or supporting a collaborative enterprise. This becomes complex because of cross-functional knowledge customer demands and the empowerment of knowledge workers in the decision-making process.

COLLABORATIVE TECHNOLOGIES

The multitude of technology available presents yet another significant challenge in deploying a Collaborative EA. With the evolution and maturity of web services, collaboration techniques become complex too. Ranging from simple instant messaging and chat sessions to real-time audio and video conferencing, from video streaming to e-learning and online communities of practice – the complexity is enormous. The availability in the marketplace of best-of-breed and integrated technology tools reflects continued progress in the area of collaboration and, subsequently, makes it easier to deploy a Collaborative EA.

COMMUNICATION NETWORKS

Broadband technologies overcome network bandwidth limitations and, as a result, most organizations are well equipped to handle enterprise-level collaboration. A Collaborative EA has to provide the framework and processes for integration of these communications networks. Applying a set of best practices, open standards, and process improvement models helps alleviate this complexity.

In order to make sense of these IT assets, enterprises put together their application inventories, database inventories, heat-maps, and solutions' impact under the EA umbrella. Digital Transformation (DT) strategies make provisions for Collaborative EA – including an understanding of technologies and a road map to empowering collaborative enterprises with web services.[3,4] Such EA provides the basis for making informed decisions when incorporating emerging technologies into business on an ongoing basis. The EA feeds into multiple systems and multiple functional groups within an enterprise, ensuring their alignment with business.[5,6] A Collaborative EA takes this understanding of multiple systems and groups beyond the organization, in order to help it utilize its technical capabilities to reach out to a group of businesses that have shared and common goals of enhancing customer value. For example, the Internet of Things (IoT), social engineering, Cloud analytics, Big Data informatics/Machine Learning (ML), and mobile applications can all be used by a group of organizations in the collaborative digital business processes enabled by a Collaborative EA.

The EA's mechanism to measure,[7] compare, and contrast technology investments helps highlight the risks of DT. This mechanism also helps align myriad business and technology elements with the business' strategic objectives and vision.[8] Thus, an EA offers a technical foundation that provides long-term and strategic input into the business decision-making of a digital enterprise.

DT is a business endeavor that requires a well-orchestrated, innovative, and collaborative approach from the EA perspective. It is also an ongoing and, perhaps, an unending activity. Disruption of operations has been identified as a major risk factor for many organizations that are traversing the path of DT. Continuous technological changes result in continuous transformation. Thus, in a way, DT is "Agile" in an organizational sense. And since such business agility is a customer-centric effort, enterprises consider collaborating with other enterprises in their space to enhance the user experience.

EVOLVING TECHNOLOGY TRENDS AND EA

EA facilitates the alignment of business visions and processes with operational capabilities.[9] The impact of an EA as shown in Figure 4.1 – each paradigm and its shift has disruption associated with it. Small and mid-sized organizations were either acquired and/or merged with other organizations to avoid potential disruption. Large and complex organizations, on the other hand, tackled disruption by simplifying and federating their architectures, while integrating or consolidating the majority of their distributed or dispersed "silo" systems.

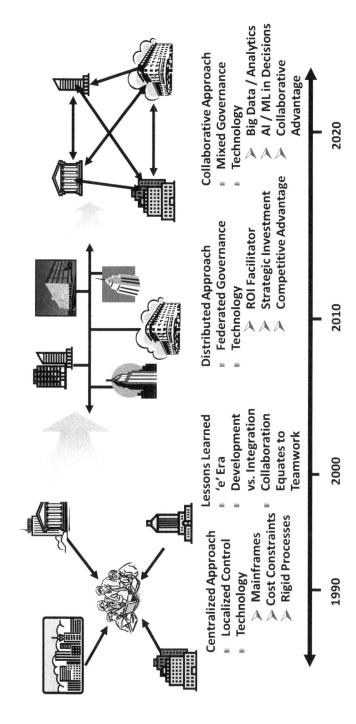

Centralized Approach
- Localized Control
- Technology
  - ∧ Mainframes
  - ∧ Cost Constraints
  - ∧ Rigid Processes

Lessons Learned
- 'e' Era
- Development vs. Integration
- Collaboration Equates to Teamwork

Distributed Approach
- Federated Governance
- Technology
  - ∧ ROI Facilitator
  - ∧ Strategic Investment
  - ∧ Competitive Advantage

Collaborative Approach
- Mixed Governance
- Technology
  - ∧ Big Data / Analytics
  - ∧ AI / ML in Decisions
  - ∧ Collaborative Advantage

1990   2000   2010   2020

FIGURE 4.1 Evolving enterprise approaches: from centralized to distributed to collaborative.

Portals, web services and apps are transition vehicles that help transition business application components to web services[10] and the use of web services technologies to deploy Collaborative EAs.[11] As a result, the performance or quality of existing business services can be improved, and the skills or expertise of available resources can be enhanced.

Collaborative EAs benefit from portals, web services, and apps through orthogonal values. While an organization can use an enterprise portal to integrate internal and external business applications, it can also employ web services to extend its ability to make business services accessible over communication networks for its entire user community. Enterprise portals integrate a set of distributed, network-centric, federated, and locally controlled portals and/or business applications to deliver specific functions for collaborative enterprises. This eliminates the issues presented by centralized data-centric solutions as illustrated in Figure 4.1.

On the other hand, web services use the service-orientation approach to extend the enterprise's information exchange capabilities over the internet. Business applications create a collaborative enterprise (acting either as a requester or provider in a service-oriented paradigm) as long as they are seamlessly integrated over the network and can locate (using a broker) and connect to one another during their operations. Organizations can significantly reduce the risks associated with deploying a Collaborative EA initiative by harnessing the benefits of portals and web services. But this requires special attention given to strategies that integrate specific key elements of the Collaborative EA and, more importantly, to the interdependencies and interpretabilities of these components.

Strategies for a Collaborative EA incorporate frameworks, patterns, and government and industry regulations, as well as best practices, corporate policies, and previously adopted standards. These strategic choices make collaborative enterprises agile and flexible enough to adapt to and manage changes in the corporate IT environment. Furthermore, strategies must consider the ease of integration and the portability of key elements in existing heterogeneous or disparate operating platforms and environments. Utilizing portals and web services can provide an added advantage through the reuse of expert resources. This is particularly true when the ability to reuse existing skill sets is a decision-making factor in building strategies when deploying Collaborative EAs.

Teamwork as a part of collaboration is necessary to successfully integrate enterprises. Hence, evolving business requirements and corporate strategies together make a strong business case for developing Collaborative EAs.

Effective business collaboration also requires effective IT collaboration. The involvement of business decision makers is imperative. Such involvement is critical in empowering IT and securing the active participation of business units in a strategic DT. Business unit sponsors play a crucial role in determining the level at which IT must participate or offer their support when delivering collaborative business solutions.

The corporate governance model is more business-centric and allows business units to become independently responsive to changing requirements. This is largely because most business units are globally (in both a physical and a logical sense) dispersed today and organizations now use global resources to take advantage of the current economy. They establish federated environments to unite socioeconomic and technology cultures with the way that each sector delivers business goals.

The governance of distributed enterprises focuses on establishing federated environments that facilitate the incorporation of best practices, open industry standards, and a cultural mix of existing technologies and globally located expert resources. Federated environments facilitate collaboration while leveraging autonomous management of individual components of the federation – a true conglomeration of operational business units.

Outsourcing development and production are other focal points in the industry. Operational outsourcing models reflect the true distributed nature of most enterprises today.[12] Outsourcing entails complexities and challenges that practitioners experience when solving problems for their entire organization, including connecting various facilities or locations that contain people (employees, partners, consultants, or associates), processes, and – more importantly – the applications used to perform transactions or make business decisions. Outsourcing initiatives reinforce the need for collaboration in a delicate way, as many solution providers are not typically physically co-located with the enterprise. And, in the case of offshore developments, they may be culturally divided as well.

The benefits of collaboration rest primarily on integrating all organizational units across all corporate entities. In many cases, an organization's divisions and departments operate in silos, creating a heterogeneous environment without sufficient interaction. Systems are disparate and require significant business-process automation or reengineering. Ideally, business drivers and technology imperatives must be thoroughly reviewed as one evaluates corporate strategies to build and empower a Collaborative EA.

Widely accepted EA frameworks and integration processes provide a road map for deploying Collaborative EAs. These frameworks are based on the following:

- A set of organizational or corporate business reference models.
- Standards, policies, procedures, and regulations influenced by industry standardization bodies or regulators.
- Best practices and a culture inculcated by practitioners throughout the industry.

For example, an organization may utilize the TOGAF,[13] comply with the regulations of the Sarbanes–Oxley Act (SOX), and incorporate its own culture when building a collaborative enterprise that allows it to interact with partners, employees, and customers. On the other hand, an organization working primarily with US federal government agencies may view its Collaborative EA as part of a large program or mission and may rely on frameworks such as the Federal Enterprise Architecture (FEA) framework, SOX regulations, and Federal Information Processing Standards (FIPS) to collaborate with its partners and customers. Either way, most organizations will develop a collaborative enterprise primarily for digital business goals.

The impetus for deploying a collaborative enterprise is manifold.

First, it reestablishes a basis on which to do business with partners and customers in a distributed world, enforcing a set of ground rules such as service-level agreements (SLAs) or trading-partner agreements (TPAs).

Second, it gives the EA and infrastructure the flexibility to handle growing business needs and to connect globally with prospective partners, customers, or vendors.

Third, a collaborative enterprise also lays the foundation for establishing communities of practice and promotes reusing an available knowledge base without reinventing the wheel.

Collaboration as an inherent, ubiquitous aspect of business processes and operational activities in an enterprise is also discussed by Hazra.[14]

To collaborate means to participate in a mutually beneficial joint venture. It means connecting, communicating, coordinating, and making commitments between the two or more parties involved in a single or multiple initiatives. Depending on established roles and responsibilities, an organization or a business unit of a company assumes the leading role in a collaborative effort. This entity institutionalizes various agreements such as SLAs, TPAs, subcontracting, and sourcing agreements with other involved parties. From a technical perspective, a collaborative approach involves sharing appropriate information, technology, and techniques, and using a common medium for the exchange of information such as application data, decision-making data, or transaction processing-related data.

A collaborative environment establishes an operational conduit for two or more entities to collaborate, whether they are located within a single organization or in different ones separated by geographical distance. In general, a collaborative environment is a logical concept that provides various common services, a set of information exchanges, or a delivery mechanism. This environment offers connectivity or interfaces to various components of the environment – collaboration, knowledge management, content management, user experience and relationship management, and security. A corporate portal is an example of a collaborative environment.

A collaborative business enterprise involves people interacting with one another using processes, policies, best practices, and a collaborative environment. It also includes a set of technologies and techniques accepted by practitioners across the business. The human component of a collaborative enterprise emphasizes the complexity of interactions, given the cultural (i.e., socioeconomic and organizational) diversity of participants. In a typical collaborative engagement, interactions may include human-to-system, system-to-system, or system-to-human forms. The system component of a collaborative enterprise includes the integration of business applications, business processes, frameworks, and reference models inside or beyond the boundaries of a specific enterprise, to provide appropriate access to participants.

COLLABORATIVE EA

A Collaborative EA combines a set of principles, architectural patterns, frameworks, and best practices for setting up a collaborative enterprise. Like any other EA, it represents the strategic objectives and goals of an enterprise. A collaborative EA supports a common environment and connects various business application components with a set of common architectural services. It is usually connected to front- and back-end or external systems using integrators, connectors, adapters, and brokers. From a technical perspective, Collaborative EAs differ from other EAs in their agility and flexibility to utilize portals and web services for deployment. Portals can be distributed or federated in a way that preserves autonomous control, and web services can be considered the basis for service orientation in a collaborative enterprise. From a business perspective, Collaborative EAs involve the integration of business processes that empower the business community in its decision-making. They differ from other EAs in that business users and sponsors are more actively involved in the process, right from defining architectural strategies to the integration, deployment, and use of the practices that typify collaborative enterprises.

From an enterprise architect's viewpoint, defining a Collaborative EA may sound similar to conceptually defining and refining any other EA. Building Collaborative EAs require meticulously integrating business application components with the following:

- Service-oriented infrastructure support.
- Business processes and workflows with a technology foundation.
- A set of standard frameworks, reference models, and best practices.

From a business perspective, a Collaborative EA demands much more direct involvement from business units. In fact, business units or partner organizations must play a pivotal role in defining and employing the Collaborative EA. Unlike when building traditional EAs, in this case IT teams must involve business units in technology selection and implementation decisions throughout the initiative.

Internal business units have also been the chief catalyst in deploying Collaborative EAs. Thus, successfully empowering business units is a key factor for successful deployment. In most of these organizations, business units assumed prime responsibility for gathering business requirements that were architecturally significant to their collaborative enterprise. In many cases, gathering requirements involved understanding current business processes and workflows, so as to define how the Collaborative EA should work and how it could support ongoing activities for users inside and outside corporate firewalls.

Various organizational best practices, policies, and procedures have been collected as part of business requirements. SLAs and TPAs form the basis of interaction among external associates, partners, and vendors when collaborating or interfacing with external business applications.

Defining a Collaborative EA means addressing such questions as:

Who are the users of the collaborative enterprise? Which applications must be integrated to support current and future business operations?

As Figure 4.2 shows, different users may have specific needs, and collaboration may serve these users' purposes differently. Collaboration also may involve granting various levels of access control to certain business applications for different users. Furthermore, managing various business applications or the users accessing these applications involves determining the associated requirements for knowledge management, content management, user experience and relationship management, and security.

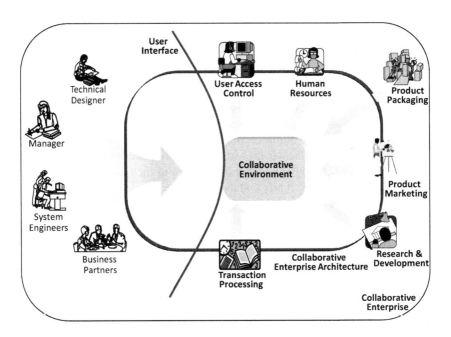

FIGURE 4.2   Users and applications in a collaborative enterprise.

Key Elements of a Collaborative EA

Figure 4.3 illustrates collaboration between applications and users. This, knowledge management, content management, user experience and relationship management, and security compose the five key elements of a Collaborative EA. These core components along with environment management and the repository constitute the collaborative environment. Environment management offers basic services to support the operations of the environment. The repository, on the other hand, stores and maintains relevant information (including metadata) during the operations of the environment.

In addition to these components, the Collaborative EA includes two other significant sets of elements:

1. Enterprise application integrators, adapters, brokers, and connectors.
2. Business intelligence, operational reference models, and integration platforms.

These elements connect the collaborative environment with the business infrastructure to build a collaborative enterprise. Two activities must be performed while consolidating the key elements of a Collaborative EA:

1. Formalizing architectural principles to adopt widely accepted frameworks and patterns and to comply with government and industry regulations
2. Incorporating best practices, policies, and standards as established across the existing enterprise

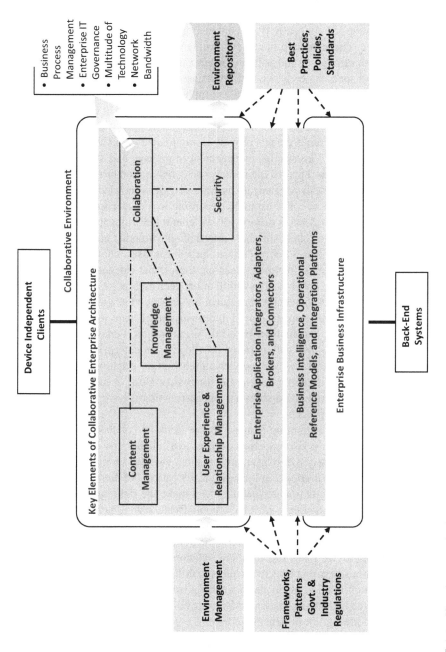

FIGURE 4.3 Key elements of a Collaborative Enterprise Architecture.

As previously mentioned, and as Figure 4.3 demonstrates, collaboration is one of the five core components of a collaborative enterprise. From a simple communications standpoint, collaboration addresses network connectivity and essential interactions among various users and applications. The complexity of collaboration, however, increases as the scope of connectivity and interaction broadens to encompass a community of practice. The need for a secure environment arises to protect data integrity, ensure application efficiency, and validate or authenticate user accessibility. Based on the enterprise's specific needs to comply with associated government or industry regulations, security may become a critical component of the Collaborative EA.

Similarly, depending on the complexity of information exchange or data sharing, managing knowledge capital can become another inevitable part of business requirements. In practice, these requirements provide a way to size up a Collaborative EA. Most organizations utilize knowledge management to manage and share knowledge (i.e., data or information as a part of their enterprise collaboration process during normal business operations). Many organizations, however, view knowledge management as a decision-making practice. For example, according to a reader survey conducted by *Government Computer News*, a majority of US federal government agencies utilize knowledge management to collect and share information with other national and international government agencies.[15] For medium-to-large businesses, knowledge management offers an effective set of features to search, locate, and categorize information that users can share while collaborating within or between enterprises.

Over the past few years, content management has expanded its usage from simply being a means of manipulating structured and unstructured data to one of categorizing and personalizing information based on users' needs. Personalization adds another practical dimension to collaboration by allowing an enterprise to share with individual users a consistent, customized view of relevant information. Furthermore, content management addresses the requirements of assimilating or merging information developed by federated and distributed enterprises that is to be used or viewed during the collaboration process.

User experience and relationship management present the collaborative enterprise with considerable versatility. User experience relates to a collaborative enterprise's flexibility in providing users access to relevant information, with the device (e.g., handheld, mobile, or browser) of their choice, at their physical location. No doubt, providing the right information at the right time so that users can make the right business decisions provides a positive user experience in collaboration. Relationship management, on the other hand, pertains to formal agreements, such as SLAs and TPAs, and to compliance with these agreements, as well as adherence to the policies and procedures established as corporate standards. In many organizations, relationship management is dealt with at the portfolio or business-unit level, with multiple initiatives considered a portfolio. In light of collaboration, relationship management helps institutionalize best practices, patterns, standards, and industry regulations to facilitate building a collaborative enterprise.

Security has added a new dimension to human-computer interactions and affects collaboration significantly. It plays a definitive role in protecting information and associated applications and in ascertaining information delivery and user identity management. A critical component of a Collaborative EA, security also supports other components apart from collaboration.

STRATEGIES FOR COLLABORATIVE EA

Business users and project sponsors are empowered to help formulate EA strategies as well as similar movements toward establishing Collaborative EAs. In strategic planning for Collaborative EAs, practitioners usually consider the benefits of collaboration in addition to the advantages of traditional EAs (Figure 4.4).

The three different perspectives of EA that are integral to Collaborative EAs are driven by (1) technology, (2) business processes, and (3) enterprise information systems.[16]

The premise of technology-driven EAs is technological advancement. It offers practitioners a viable path of transition from traditional to Collaborative EAs. Business process-driven EAs focus on identifying the value proposition of operational workflows from a business perspective. But as the IT industry continues to evolve, the marriage of technology- and business process-driven approaches has become inevitable.

Even in the case of the US federal government agencies, the FEA enables Business Process Management (BPM) in integrating federal information systems with multiple EAs that originate from different federal programs and their technology choices. Overall, a Collaborative EA emphasizes the people, process, and technology aspects of an enterprise and incorporates all three perspectives.

The human aspect involves user experience, organizational culture, and relationship management, as well as human interactions with the available technologies. The process aspect identifies and subsequently prioritizes the architecturally significant business process flows in order to define the scope of collaboration. Finally, the technology aspect reveals the gap between existing and future investments in technologies and the cost-effectiveness of initiatives, including delivery, support, and maintenance activities.

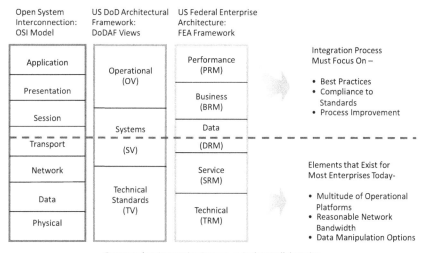

FIGURE 4.4   Collaboration from an industry-wide architectural frameworks perspective.

There are three key parts of a corporate strategy to develop a Collaborative EA:

1. Aligning IT strategy with existing or new business goals.
2. Preparing a blueprint that can ready the enterprise for change.
3. Instituting a new enterprise IT governance structure that is flexible enough to implement and influence the deployment of a Collaborative EA.

These activities often depend on one another. Therefore, there is a need to evaluate interdependencies to determine how and to what extent these tasks must be conducted. Further, the complexity of these tasks intensifies more rapidly for large organizations than for small and medium ones. For many enterprises, these complexities depend primarily on how strategic business goals and drivers of the organization are tied to corporate technology investments and resource skills. IT imperatives and constraints serving strategic business drivers may change over time.

In an attempt to create a decision model that can facilitate identification of critical areas in building Collaborative EAs, an active matrix model (depicted in Figure 4.5) is most helpful. As the figure shows, the model allows for "what if" scenarios in the event of changes in IT risk factors or business driver priorities. Using active matrix models, business and IT teams can prioritize activities that must be performed by weighing risks and the availability of resources for the collaborative initiatives at any time. In the case of the hypothetical organization represented in Figure 4.5, for example, the risk associated with innovative techniques is low. Meanwhile, the

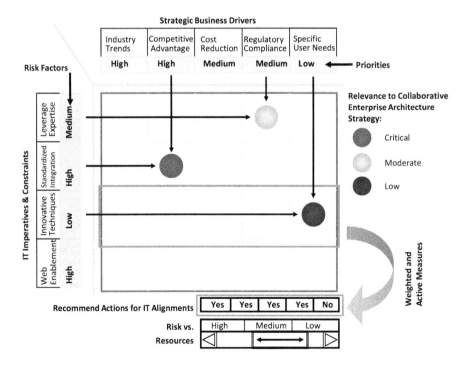

FIGURE 4.5 Active matrix modeling to track business-IT dependencies.

priorities of business drivers such as keeping pace with industry trends, achieving competitive advantage, reducing costs, complying with regulations, and meeting specific user needs is high, high, medium, medium, and low, respectively, at the time of assessment. With adequately available resources, recommended actions for IT alignments to move forward with a Collaborative EA initiative are yes, yes, and no, respectively, for fulfilling the listed business drivers. As the priorities and risk factors are weighed and measured periodically, the recommendations may change, given personnel availability and associated risks.

Aligning IT strategy with existing or new business goals begins with making the business case for developing a Collaborative EA. Ideally, the appropriate business and IT executives (i.e., stakeholders), along with financial sponsors, should have already established the corporate strategy, identified critical success factors, and analyzed common business values to be delivered via a Collaborative EA, before preparing a business case. Additionally, a business case must contain the following:

- An estimate of how a Collaborative EA can affect current systems and/or business processes.
- A cost-benefit analysis of the deployment of a Collaborative EA.
- A set of well-defined risk management strategies to generate stakeholder support and secure commitment in mitigating probable risks.

In practice, aligning IT strategies with business goals when deploying a Collaborative EA can be iterative and incremental. This approach allows practitioners a more feasible transition from the existing to the new technology base, lower initial investment in technology and techniques, and greater flexibility in allocating resources that fit the skills needed to deploy a Collaborative EA. It also helps IT executives establish realistic expectations for business sponsors. In addition, IT can demonstrate ROI to its business counterparts. This strengthens the confidence level and the business case concerning IT's capabilities by evaluating user experience and measuring performance during each phase of funding. Such alignment opens the door to building consensus-driven teams, starting with the enterprise IT governance board or steering committee (which typically consists of business sponsors and senior IT leaders). The governance board or committee has the responsibility to approve or reject any activity that is conducted to achieve alignment, with the decision based primarily on the activity's conformity with the collaborative blueprint or with a set of enterprise-adopted best practices.

Many recognized thought leaders such as John Zachman,[17] Steven Spewak,[18] and Bernard Boar[19] have addressed practical concepts for developing blueprints for corporate IT organizations.

By engaging individuals or teams in delivering business solutions to customers in an active –rather than a reactive – mode, collaboration provides effectiveness and efficiency, even when customers' business requirements change rapidly.

Blueprinting provides a systematic approach for the entire collaborative enterprise to:

1. capture business processes using standard notations and visual models or diagrams,

2. transform business processes into technology choices, and
3. implement business solutions.

A well-conceived blueprint directly affects strategic business goals and identifies competitive advantages.

Furthermore, blueprinting keeps business users actively engaged by developing a big picture that uses standard notations and models. It also helps by making gradual refinements that relate to the different phases, business contexts, and needs of multiple users or stakeholders. And the blueprint allows all involved parties to interact and access each other's business applications as needed, to promote mutually beneficial cooperation. Blueprints with multiple views allow different users to visualize how their requirements are captured and their impact on the Collaborative EA.

Preparing a blueprint for deployment of a Collaborative EA is very much a part of ongoing initiatives to build Agile EAs. In blueprinting a Collaborative EA, the focus is directed towards:

1. defining appropriate levels of abstraction for interfaces and
2. presenting complex interactions or information exchange among various users and/or business applications.

Additionally, understanding the levels of abstraction (or granularity) and exploring relationships between overall enterprise systems (in the case of currently existing traditional EAs) are equally important. It is imperative to emphasize that a great deal of effort is necessary to prepare a blueprint for a Collaborative EA, primarily because of the complexity of these three factors:

1. Understanding the essence of collaboration as a means to ensure competitive advantage.
2. Ascertaining the ongoing active involvement of internal, client, and partner business units or organizations.
3. Establishing an appropriate work environment for clients, partners, and associates alike as the key value proposition for a Collaborative EA.

Blueprints offer various fundamental benefits throughout the life cycle of building a Collaborative EA, the most important of which is establishing a road map for the transition from the existing architecture to the collaborative one. The road map outlines a process for IT teams to meet business needs and allows the enterprise to monitor the progress of activities during the transition.

Another step in establishing the strategy for deploying a Collaborative EA is to define and employ an enterprise IT governance model that focuses on how much value it can deliver for the company, financially or otherwise. Most organizations embarking on instituting Collaborative EAs also confront the challenge of building and managing consensus-driven partnerships between business and IT. Many organizations have revitalized IT governance by focusing on business-IT relationships and by formally integrating all the enterprise's best practices.

In building a Collaborative EA, the governance team makes the greatest contribution in two major areas:

1. Risk management for a consensus-driven approach in terms of roles, responsibilities, and accountabilities, while also ensuring the adaptation of IT to changes in its culture
2. A strategic direction to measure the progress of deployment via user experience metrics and fulfillment measures. Typically, the larger the organization, the greater the risks associated with establishing business-IT partnerships.

In many cases, the governance team mediates the negotiation of a formal contractual agreement (also known as a "chargeback") between the business and IT functions. Usually, the road map provides input on the rules of engagement, which become the formal contractual agreement. The agreement further spells out necessary activities, milestones, and deliverables, as well as the level of involvement of each of the teams.

An important part of the strategy is to reorganize IT operations, because the business-IT partnership mostly affects that function. This means evaluating how IT activities can support critical business services and operations requirements while also ensuring that the change supports the enterprise's goals and objectives. The evaluation process requires dialogue between IT and business organizations, building on the collaborative approach to prioritizing business requirements. The level of effort needed to support ongoing business operations determines the level of collaboration and the involvement of business teams during the initiative life cycle of a Collaborative EA deployment. A clear understanding of the big picture provides a holistic approach to balancing complexities and constraints with the objectives of the entire enterprise. And establishing the big picture determines the level of effort needed to deliver those objectives. For many organizations, this approach means:

- A thorough evaluation of ongoing projects or initiatives.
- A comprehensive inventory of currently used technology, tools, techniques, and standards across the enterprise.
- A meticulous assessment of business domain knowledge and subject matter expertise.

By investing in ongoing projects or initiatives, business application components or services that – from the collaboration perspective – are enterprise-critical can be considered architecturally significant for a Collaborative EA (at a very high level, of course). This helps identify already functional application services that may not be in the critical path for Collaborative EA initiative life cycles but need to be supported during the transition. An inventory of the current technology base offers a broad view of the enterprise's heterogeneity as well as its disparities and level of compliance with industry standards. This offers a means to determine the ROI of the existing technology. Existing knowledge capital in business domains directly linked to collaboration requirements can provide insight into the capabilities of an IT organization in supporting ongoing business and in continuing their own operations. In short, this prioritization exercise determines both resource needs and how well current operations can be supported in light of Collaborative EA development.

Establishing strategies that can help enterprises transition their portal and web services initiatives to build Collaborative EA is discussed next.

CHALLENGES AND ISSUES WITH COLLABORATIVE EA

Collaborative EAs have associated challenges, issues, and risks. This is so because most of the common issues they encounter are related primarily to enterprise-wide application integration techniques. Some of these organizations have used a multitude of technologies such as adapters, brokers, connectors, and middleware-oriented integrators, along with web integration (including J2EE and. NET) techniques.

Challenges, issues, and risks of deploying Collaborative EAs fall into the following categories:

- Organizational culture.
- Architectural foundation and principles.
- Key elements that build collaborative environments.
- Practical concepts of collaboration.
- Recognizing the existing business processes.
- Prioritizing the business processes to be managed as services.
- Providing continued IT support to ongoing business operations.

Obviously, these categories may overlap. Hopefully, they will still reflect the specific challenges of practitioners as they assume different roles and responsibilities.

From the organizational culture perspective, the foremost challenge is to assign the roles and responsibilities of all parties involved in deploying Collaborative EAs, from building strategies to making the collaborative enterprise operational. Hence, the assignment begins with defining effective IT governance so that appropriate decision rights, responsibilities, and accountabilities can be attributed to the appropriate team of executives and managers. Governance sets the tone for strengthening the business-IT relationship while institutionalizing a set of best practices, standards, and principles, and prioritizing IT investments based on ROI. Major issues concerning organizational cultures are the following:

- How can the IT organization best align business priorities with IT investments?
- What kind of SLAs or contractual agreements should be in place in order for the business and IT to comply with the best practices, standards, and principles that have been set forth by IT governance?
- Who should monitor the execution of business-IT contractual agreements, and what is the minimum level at which the line items in these contracts must be executed to prevent warning or punitive action from the governance board for noncompliance?

- How should the business and IT teams jointly evaluate new technologies? Should senior management be involved to ensure the business value of such technologies?
- Who should obtain approval from the governing structure and senior management for funding the adoption of newly evaluated technologies (primarily based on the existence of portfolio or project management offices in most organizations today and their roles and responsibilities)? When should they obtain approval?
- Who is charged with readying the enterprise and choosing and prioritizing business applications that are considered architecturally significant enough to integrate with the Collaborative EA?
- Once strategies for deploying the Collaborative EA are in place, who measures the improvements needed or achieved in enterprise productivity?

Furthermore, organizational challenges include transitioning away from the existing technology base and retiring legacy technology-based applications in order to exploit the benefits of advanced technologies. This may include improving the skills of available personnel, adapting to a new set of best practices, and incorporating new guiding principles for Collaborative EAs.

Common challenges in architectural foundation and principles extend from the business-modeling context and the selection of processes and tools for integrating business applications to the deployment of Collaborative EAs (see Figure 4.6). In following the informal flow of activities shown in Figure 4.6, practitioners confront multiple challenges. The diagram captures only a small number of these challenges.

As presented in the figure, challenges posed during various stages of the architecture development activity flow are usually linked to business processes, technical transformations, application integration, deployment, and collaboration. In the business process context, primary challenges center around gathering requirements that can define the scope of Collaborative EA initiatives. Current business processes provide a point of reference for defining potential collaborative enterprises if associated users and their business applications are brought on board during the early stages of initiatives. In a technical transformation context, major issues center around studying current technology and data exchange mechanisms as part of a gap analysis and defining architectural blueprints and best practices for the initiative. Application integration challenges lie in identifying the right candidate applications or services to transition as part of the Collaborative EA. For deployment, the main challenges are likely to be the capture of appropriate business operation continuity requirements and the choice of the right tools and implementation languages. Finally, from a collaboration perspective, gathering specific requirements in establishing SLAs and TPAs presents basic challenges.

Table 4.1 summarizes the most common challenges and issues related to the five elements of Collaborative EAs. Table 4.2 shows an additional list of challenges and issues associated with collaboration. These are linked to the four integral parts of collaboration: connection, communication, coordination, and commitment.[20] The complexity of the challenge usually varies according to the size, heterogeneity, and disparity of the enterprise's systems.

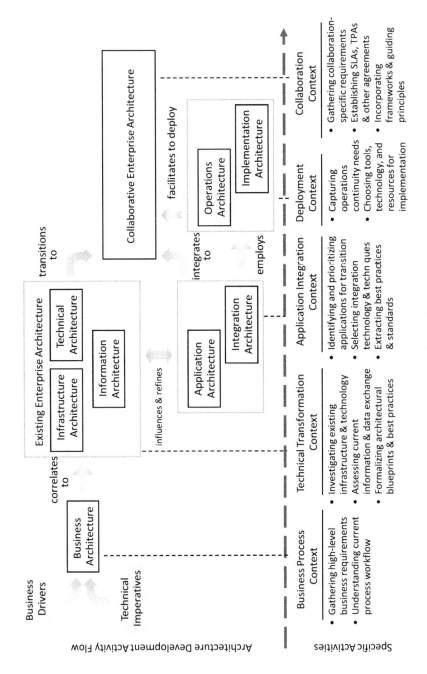

FIGURE 4.6 Challenges and principles in the context of architectural foundation.

TABLE 4.1

Challenges and Issues in Collaborative EA Initiatives

Key Elements	Challenges and Issues
Collaboration	Data sharing and information exchange across an integrated and extended enterprise

1. Event notification/messaging

   Delivering alerts, messages, updates, or notifications for occurrence of specific events as appropriate

   Allowing synchronous and asynchronous message passing among users over the network

2. Communities of practice

   Establishing messaging (via e-mail, instant messaging, or text messaging over cell phone or PDA), discussion (chat sessions or whiteboarding), and videoconferencing facilities

   Allowing sharing or exchanging information across multiple users with common goals or interests (partners, vendors, clients, or associates)

3. Decision-making or sharing responsibilities and accountabilities

   Coordination or monitoring of various activities and decision-making as appropriate; commitment to delivering the right information at the right time (maintaining accountabilities and responsibilities)

4. Establishing and managing enterprise-wide IT governance

   Facilitating the practicality of Collaborative EAs by involving business and IT users as appropriate

   Defining a charter of governance to successfully achieve business goals, allowing appropriate level of access to ease the decision-making process

Knowledge management	Information organization and management to support seamless collaboration

1. Categorization

   Organizing, cataloging, and indexing business application processing information based on user access patterns while improving user productivity

2. Repositories and data stores

   Collecting structured data, unstructured data, and metadata for current, interim, or future collaborative enterprise initiatives utilizing advanced technologies and techniques

3. Reporting

   Generating personalized reports for users with specific needs and presentation styles; creating on-the-fly or ad hoc reports of user metrics (security logging, for example) to facilitate the decision-making processes of managers and executives to improve the quality of collaboration

4. Logging information usage

   Creating and maintaining a log of information accessed by users pertaining to critical business applications in accordance with established service-level agreements or trading-partner agreements

Content management	Preparing and managing data, policy and document contents for collaboration in distributed and federated environments

1. Generating and assimilating contents

   Incorporating static or dynamic contents generated by different users (internal or external resources) or portals for sharing in collaborative environments

   Merging contents developed and published by different sources as appropriate to other users in collaborative enterprises

(Continued)

TABLE 4.1 (*Continued*)
Challenges and Issues in Collaborative EA Initiatives

Key Elements	Challenges and Issues
Content management	2. Personalizing and customizing the views Enabling users to view information based on specific needs, choice, or level of interest Offering flexibility to modify view of the information 3. Delivering the information with a consistent look and feel Distributing data in multiple client devices while maintaining consistent presentation
User experience and relationship management	Offering succinct experience and fulfillment to all users of collaborative enterprises 1. Ease of access and navigation for data and business application components and services Facilitating the process to access and navigate relevant information (using remote or on-site collaboration facilities for information exchange) from different user access devices (PDA, wireless, or browsers) and comfort levels (from home or on the road) 2. Supporting a multitude of user interfaces Allowing users to utilize available or existing technologies to establish collaboration while transitioning to collaborative enterprises using advanced technologies 3. Evaluating collaborative needs to improve quality of service of collaborative enterprises Offering online (or otherwise) help, updates, or critical warnings, as well as technical support to facilitate collaboration (including creation of new user accounts and maintaining accessibility) Offering continuous improvement of services for collaborative activities
Security	Secure collaboration to maintain entitlement, privacy, and confidentiality 1. Single sign-on capability Formalizing access to appropriate business applications or services based on policies, procedures, agreements, or profiles 2. Identity management Verifying the identity of users by matching or validating encrypted passwords, digital certificates, and public or private keys for participation in collaborative enterprise initiatives 3. Access authorization and validation Defining special privileges for users to access specific information to perform certain activities (with or without updating any information) or to control specific tasks 4. Logging user metrics Maintaining a log of user access (usage, time, and number of business applications or services accessed) to determine access violation, denial, and breach of policies or for audit trails 5. User account management Creating, managing, and supporting user accounts and access privileges; supporting activities such as forming user groups or communities of practice

TABLE 4.2

Common Collaboration Challenges and Issues

Key Areas	Challenges and Issues
Connection	Managing disparity and heterogeneity of collaborative enterprise systems 1. Business Process Management (BPM) Effectively automating relevant business processes involved in collaboration and establishing and maintaining their connectivity to Collaborative EAs, promoting ROI of current investment in existing technologies and resources 2. Transformation Assessing the viability of transforming the identified and prioritized components as services (web or otherwise) to reduce the cost of change or total cost of ownership
Communication	Data-driven versus process-level integration of business application components and services 1. Technology or service vendor selection Choosing vendors for technologies and techniques that can support API to reduce complexity and to increase flexibility of integration 2. Data exchange mechanism Establishing a consistent and integrated information delivery process 3. Network access management Streamlining the changes in network access of business processes using standard protocols such as HTTP over TCP/IP
Coordination	Reliability of information sharing 1. Information assurance Providing guaranteed and reliable delivery of messages between business application components or services over secure collaborative environments 2. BPM Formalizing BPM activities (reengineering or automation), internal or external, to improve quality of service of collaborative enterprises
Commitment	Improvements in level of interaction 1. Best practices and standards Enforcing use of standards-based integration and connectivity to promote flexibility and dynamic relationships with business partners or internal allies Managing enterprise-wide adoption and adaptation of best practices, patterns, standards, and regulations as well as architectural guidelines 2. Organizational culture Eliminating barriers of cultural changes to extend the capability of a collaborative enterprise and strengthening business-IT relationships by unifying "big picture" visualization models

DEPLOYING A COLLABORATIVE EA

Before proceeding with deployment efforts, practitioners must have an understanding of the principles of Collaborative EAs (which, as might be expected, many organizations already follow). The most widely accepted principles are the following:

- **Service and Component Orientation** – the orientation promotes reusing existing business components and services in the transition to web services- and portals-based Collaborative EAs.
- **Loose Coupling** – in a collaborative initiative, loose coupling between the business application components and services allows the enterprise to formulate roles and responsibilities for business users who need to collaborate and to define rules of engagement.
- **Rules of Engagement** – established rules (including SLAs and TPAs) among various users (internal or external) identify the business protocols as well as the technology imperatives that have significant impact on a Collaborative EA.
- **Technology and Tools Selection** – the enterprise often defers its choices of technology (including platforms, operating environments, or programming languages) to a later stage of the deployment life cycle so that it can focus on defining business processes and establishing business-IT relationships.
- **Open Standards, Best Practices, and Corporate IT Culture** – these standards are incorporated to improve the productivity of initiative teams and to make an enterprise Agile enough to accommodate advances in technology as well as to meet future business requirements.

To fully gain the benefits of these principles, business units must be involved from the requirements-gathering phase through to the incremental stages of deployment. At an enterprise level, business teams must be actively involved in situations such as choosing technology partners, evaluating best-of-breed products, or simply custom building business applications. This involvement strengthens the relationship between business and IT, allowing practitioners to establish a single, standardized measure of progress that tracks the responsibility and accountability of all parties, along with the dependencies and interfaces of various projects leading up to the Collaborative EA.

Figure 4.7 presents a snapshot of the approach many organizations use today to build their Collaborative EAs, while following the previously mentioned five principles. The Model-Driven Architecture (MDA) approach supports service and component orientation, and – together with service-oriented and component-based approaches – spans the life cycle of a Collaborative EA. Open standards, best practices, and existing IT culture form the organizational foundation that supports the architecture deployment life cycle, while frameworks and reference models – as well as *a priori* selection of tools, technologies, techniques, and infrastructure-support capabilities – lay the foundation.

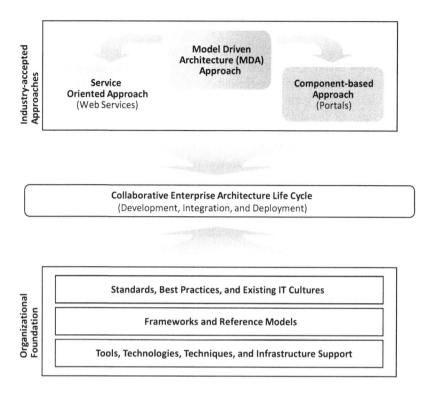

FIGURE 4.7 A high level snapshot of the most commonly used approach in deploying a Collaborative EA.

Deploying a Collaborative EA – in contrast to the traditional approach of building an EA – is a momentous step forward. Its significance lies in three vital points that empower Collaborative EAs:

1. Leveraging the service orientation of web services technology and enterprise integration capabilities of ongoing portal initiatives
2. Reaping the benefits of the maturity and the prospects delivered by the application of the component-based approach throughout the enterprise
3. Establishing mutually beneficial relationships between business and IT, starting with the early involvement of business sponsors and users in identifying their enterprise's collaborative needs

J2EE and .NET frameworks are used to substantiate the relevance of service-oriented architecture in a pay-per-use digital business.

Web services empower collaborative enterprises mostly through two basic principles:

1. A business-centric focus (i.e., making internal and external business users central to the decision-making process throughout the life cycle of web services)
2. An emphasis on service-based collaboration among enterprise systems and business partners, customers, and vendors (i.e., using SLAs and TPAs as contractual agreements to offer or receive pay-per-use services).

Portals and Collaborative EA

Portals (for employees, customers, or enterprises), portal technologies, tools, and platforms are part of Enterprise Application Integration (EAI). Software vendors and system integration leaders provide integrated portal suites. Other organizations provide niche expertise in assimilating legacy business applications, services, and federations of heterogeneous or disparate portals to deliver business solutions at large.

The use of portals has evolved from focusing on a specific set of users, such as customer portals that interact with customers and employee portals that deal with HR-related issues, to enterprise portals that provide a consistent view of corporate assets, including internal business applications and services. They also provide employees, customers, vendors, and partners a gateway to access and manipulate appropriate transaction process applications or services.

The synergy of portal initiatives with Collaborative EAs originates from the significance of their five key elements: collaboration, knowledge management, content management, user experience and relationship management, and security (see Figure 4.3). From the architectural perspective, critical dependencies as well as interfaces of collaboration with the other four elements make enterprise portals integral to Collaborative EA deployments. Many consider the following portal features benefits when merging existing portal initiatives to Collaborative EA ones:

- Security to protect and control access of crucial information and data exchange across the enterprise to maintain secure collaboration.
- Reliability to ensure failover, crash, or disaster recovery of mission-critical business processes or services, ensuring fulfillment of user expectations.
- Continuous ability to support 24/7 user access or interactions that establish and cultivate progressive user experience and relationship management.
- Scalability to accommodate ever-changing business goals or clients' and partners' objectives that require interactive information exchange and processing.
- Performance to responsively deliver users demands that enhance the enterprise's overall productivity and efficiency.
- Search capability that allows users to navigate the organized and/or relevant information collected as a part of knowledge management repositories.
- Personalization and customization to present relevant information to an individual or community of users, facilitating their ability to make decisions or take action.
- Collaboration to form a community of practice that shares, communicates, and exchanges specific information and interacts with other involved parties.

Tools help assimilate portal applications and create integration solutions or services. Standardized tools are used to incorporate web services with solutions. Enterprise portals and Web services can jointly help build Collaborative EAs by:

1. Providing a consistent view of the distributed and fragmented (politically or geographically) enterprise systems with federated portals, and

2. Connecting business applications and services (internal or external to organizations' firewalls) with enterprise-wide service integration buses. Federated portals focus on connecting multiple organizations and their existing portals to facilitate collaboration with consistent views of the enterprise, while service integration buses provide the functionality to execute transaction processing for content routing or information exchange.

Components can represent both software and system (business application) units and business services. Visual modeling tools support the notion of components with today's modeling notations and views. In general, the component-based approach enforces loose coupling by allowing different parts of systems to be built or to evolve independently on an incremental and iterative basis. It also provides support to "plug and play" modularity, change manageability, built-in technology independence, and the reusability of components as services. As the component-based approach has matured over the past decade, the IT community has widely accepted it as a mainstream method to build, integrate, and deploy enterprise systems. Hence, it has a definite impact on building Collaborative EAs.

PRACTICAL STEPS AND MODELS FOR COLLABORATIVE EAS WITH MDA

Decisions to buy, build, or lease specific components or services in order to integrate Collaborative EAs are important (Figure 4.8). From a business perspective, an MDA establishes a common ground for business modeling and information sharing among business and IT teams. It also encourages customer-focused and customer-driven arrangements that promote collaboration among those teams. From a technical perspective, an MDA ensures ROI for technology and promises the extensibility to adopting and adapting to emerging technologies. Above all, the MDA and the component-based approach together can enable practitioners to build Collaborative EAs based on open standards, modular, and "plug and play" business components and services.

Once Collaborative EA components and associated interfaces are designed, initiative teams work to find and integrate the pieces of the architecture. During this deployment stage, the following activities may be performed: (1) deciding between build-versus-buy versus pay-per-use components and services; (2) generating transition modules and plans for their removal; and/or (3) integrating existing components and services with new ones.

These three stages also offer an organized way of allocating roles and responsibilities to enterprise-wide teams and of answering such questions as "Who owns which responsibility for a collaborative enterprise and to what extent?" As the building of the Collaborative EA proceeds, the responsibilities and accountabilities between business and IT teams usually swap in the following manner:

- During business modeling, business users are owners (accountable) and participants (responsible) in providing their requirements and helping IT teams visualize business models.

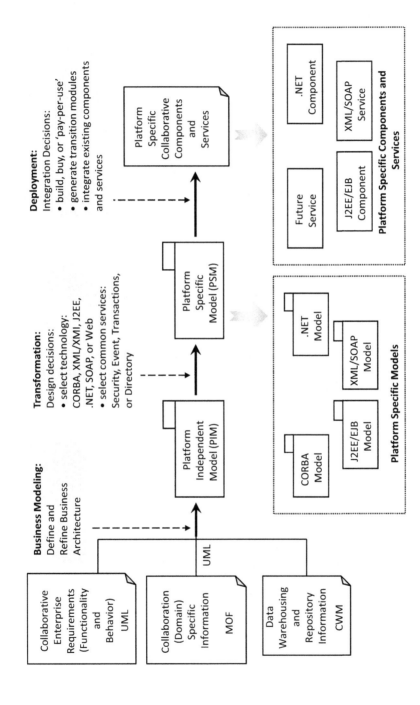

FIGURE 4.8 Practical steps and models for Collaborative Enterprise Architectures with MDA.

- During transformation, IT teams take charge of transferring business requirements to technical specifications; they solicit the participation of business users in critical decision-making processes.
- Finally, in the deployment stage, business users and IT teams coordinate the integration of the collaborative enterprise, then the business teams take over the final delivery while IT offers ongoing support.

In general, the linking of the component-based approach, service orientation, and the transitional integration of business application components and services paves the way for establishing consensus-driven collaborations between business and IT teams. In well-disciplined organizations, business and IT teams share a set of corporate goals and a vision. Agreements between business and IT as well as a flexible road map and performance-measuring metrics provide significant impetus to Collaborative EAs. In order to measure the progress of the collaboration, performance metrics are usually presented in a scorecard and include three major focus areas: business objective measures, technology management measures, and resource planning measures. Conducting periodic progress reviews to track, validate, and update such performance metrics can expose many issues, risks, and concerns that business or IT managers and leaders experience. In some organizations, senior executives and governance committee members often offer their expertise and experience in dealing with similar situations to help navigate a consensus between IT and business units. In general, a consensus-driven collaboration promotes stronger communication, firmer commitment, and more responsive accountability. Overall, it facilitates the deployment of Collaborative EAs.

CHARTING A ROAD MAP FOR COLLABORATIVE EA DEPLOYMENT

To successfully deploy Collaborative EAs, business-unit and IT leaders, senior executives, and DT sponsors chart a road map that makes the best use of existing portals and web services. A pragmatic road map evolves from focusing on many well-known system development or integration life cycle processes into looking at refining architectures and improving process frameworks to alleviate financial constraints that affect the majority of business and IT industries. This road map encapsulates most industry-standard software integration processes and frameworks in order to deliver collaborative enterprise solutions incrementally and over multiple stages. Therefore, a basic advantage of using this road map lies in its ability to secure the transitional changes of existing business application components and services into a Collaborative EA.

The primary business success factors of this road map include:

- **A Focus on Current Business Processes** – this emphasis enables initiative teams to identify, analyze, and prioritize the business components and services that are ready, mission-critical, and architecturally significant to be transitioned into Collaborative EAs.

- **An Enterprise-Wide Ease of Integration** – this approach allows teams to build "plug and play" modular components or services, enabling transition over multiple phases.
- **Leveraging Existing Technology and Expert Knowledge** – taking advantage of existing resources helps visualize the ROI of various technologies, reduces cost of ownership, and assesses overall impacts of the collaborative enterprise on corporate goals and objectives.
- **Agility of the Enterprise** – this characteristic preserves scalability, availability, performance improvement, productivity, quality of service, and operational support and maintenance features.
- In the context of clients' utilization of web services technologies in deploying Collaborative EAs.

Before proceeding with a detailed discussion of these activities or steps, it's important to provide a summarized view of the road map for reference purposes. As shown in Figure 4.9, the proposed road map consists of four essential phases of a component- and service-based integration approach: discovery, gap analysis, mediation plan, and solution integration. It can also be partitioned into three stages of system engineering based on the concepts of the MDA approach: business modeling, transformation, and deployment.[21] Figure 4.9 also shows appropriate levels of effort (LOEs) for each phase and stage during normalized life cycles of the road map.

These steps are consistent with commonly available system integration processes in applying a unified approach based on component-based and model-driven disciplines. During the discovery phase, the initiative team prepares a business case for deploying a Collaborative EA and establishes the customer focus by recognizing customers, vendors, partners, and associates. The business application components and services to be transitioned as portal components or web services are also defined during this phase.

In a gap analysis, teams evaluate the identified business requirements and prioritize them based on how critical they are. They also weigh them against IT imperatives and constraints using active matrix modeling (as shown in Figure 4.5). This phase also includes building an inventory of existing technology investments in an effort to size and scope out the initiative.

The mediation plan focuses primarily on managing and resolving challenges, issues, risks, and concerns associated with the Collaborative EA initiative. In most cases, business risks are assessed periodically to adjust the resource allocation plan and to mitigate technology-based design constraints. Prototyping efforts are directed toward minimizing prioritized business risks.

Finally, the solution integration phase involves designing, developing, and/or buying portal components and web services elements prior to integrating them with the Collaborative EA. In this final phase, the goals of the teams are directed toward delivering business values.

Using the road map, transitional Collaborative EAs can be rolled out over multiple repetitive stages. Appropriate feedback can help initiative teams refine or modify previously completed deliverables while using the road map. Continuous life cycle management (inspection, walkthroughs, reviews, and approval processes),

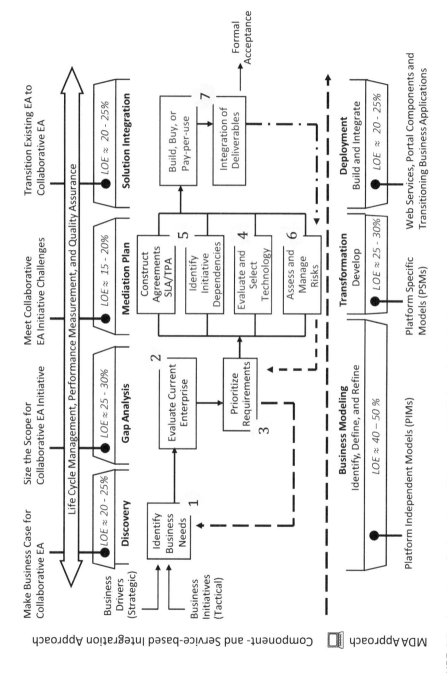

FIGURE 4.9   A road map for iterative and incremental Collaborative EA deployment.

performance measurements (user metrics), and QA program activities proceed concurrently with the other steps in the road map. There are seven major steps in road map[22] most commonly used to help an enterprise transition to a Collaborative EA:

- **Step 1** – identify business requirements for Collaborative EAs and validate their impact on the enterprise. This allows IT teams to initiate partnerships with business users and sponsors and prepare a business case for obtaining financial sponsorships.
- **Step 2** – evaluate the current enterprise for existing tools, technologies, techniques, standards, best practices, and organizational culture. This step prepares a matrix of IT organizational capabilities and skills inventory, and builds the foundation of a gap analysis.
- **Step 3** – prioritize business requirements identified in Step 1 using the concepts of active modeling (see Figure 4.5) and weigh their priorities with technical imperatives and constraints to highlight their significance in the transition to and integration with the Collaborative EA.
- **Step 4** – evaluate and select appropriate technologies and, if necessary, perform prototyping with relevant business requirements. This step usually requires due diligence to establish the case for portals- or web services-based Collaborative EAs.
- **Step 5** – revitalize business-IT relationships and embrace active business involvements to identify how the initiative depends on other tactical projects. This ongoing step strengthens the relationship among all parties involved. During this step, lessons-learned sessions are usually conducted to explore the pitfalls and benefits of portal and web services power.
- **Step 6** – assess, manage, and resolve business challenges, issues, and risks. This step offers an opportunity to revisit and reassess business users' needs and allows teams to evaluate how to make best use of portals and web services, while resolving any associated risks they may impose on the enterprise.
- **Step 7** – Deploy the Collaborative EA by integrating portal components and web services as a part of build, buy, or pay-per-use solutions. This step entails detailing captured requirements for the extended enterprise and charting agreements with the partners involved in the final deployment of a Collaborative EA.

Several leading software industry vendors offer integrated portal suites while supporting XML and web services technologies.[23] Most of these offer drag-and-drop tools to help build interfaces and test functional capabilities, and they can be used in deploying Collaborative EAs. Transitioning to a Collaborative EA with portals and web services needs to leverage existing technologies, business application components, and the culture of the enterprise. It is important to carry out an in-depth investigation of commercial tools and/or technologies, as well as their vendors, to determine the feasibility of future support and growth plans to accommodate changes in business requirements.

OBSERVATIONS FROM THE TRENCHES

The most pressing questions concerning evaluating technologies and vendors have been:

- What are the criteria in evaluating technologies, or how is a set of evaluation criteria created?
- What should be expected from vendors? How are they examined?
- How is a sourcing model to interact with multiple vendors and partners created?
- How are SLAs with selected solution providers and vendors created?
- How do selected technologies relate to internal enterprise-wide resources and the integration process?
- How does project or portfolio management incorporate standards and best practices with selected technologies?

A simplified technology evaluation model is shown in Figure 4.10. The steps focus on external IT vendors when preparing for tools and technology selection. For a large organization, the evaluation process may be more elaborate and complex and may take up to a year to complete. For medium and small businesses, it may vary from three weeks to three months. The number of iterations matches the complexity of evaluation criteria and the time taken for evaluation is proportional to the combination of the number of resources involved, the number of vendors qualified to be evaluated, and the complexity of the evaluation criteria. As Figure 4.10 shows, for a majority of organizations, technology evaluation consists of four of the previously mentioned seven steps:

- **Step 2** – evaluate current enterprise to define the scope of technology evaluation (step 3 facilitates this by providing the prioritized requirements and applicable updates).
- **Step 4** – evaluate and select a set of technologies so that a smaller number of vendors can be identified based on their relevant technology capability and support strengths.
- **Step 5** – construct agreements to initiate technology-based alliances or partnerships with previously selected vendors.
- **Step 6** – assess and manage risks by establishing appropriate risk mitigation strategies and negotiating various risk factors that may affect the progress of enterprise-wide initiatives.

The start and end of evaluations are presented under Steps 1 and 7. These present a simplified technology evaluation model and in some respects are very similar to the evaluation models many practitioners use today. The two most intriguing parts of this model are (1) engaging business sponsors early in the evaluation and (2) its iterative and repetitive nature in defining and refining the evaluation criteria. By engaging business sponsors and users early, evaluation criteria can be closely connected to business needs for collaboration, and therefore vendor strengths and weaknesses can be exposed early for timely consideration by business sponsors.

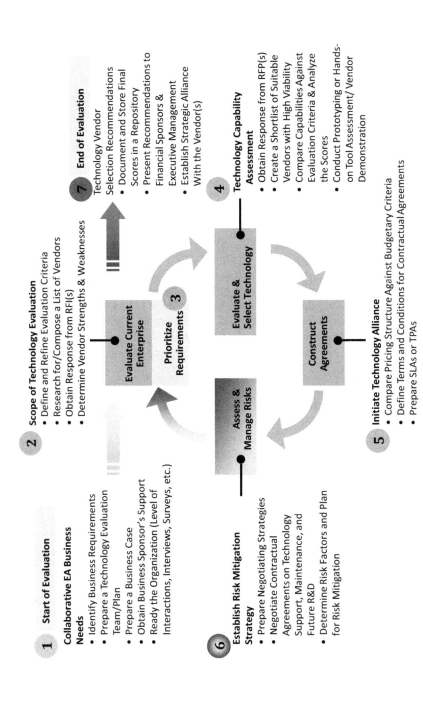

1　Start of Evaluation

Collaborative EA Business Needs

- Identify Business Requirements
- Prepare a Technology Evaluation Team/Plan
- Prepare a Business Case
- Obtain Business Sponsor's Support
- Ready the Organization (Level of Interactions, Interviews, Surveys, etc.)

2　Scope of Technology Evaluation

- Define and Refine Evaluation Criteria
- Research for/Compose a List of Vendors
- Obtain Response from RFI(s)
- Determine Vendor Strengths & Weaknesses

7　End of Evaluation

Technology Vendor Selection Recommendations

- Document and Store Final Scores in a Repository
- Present Recommendations to Financial Sponsors & Executive Management
- Establish Strategic Alliance With the Vendor(s)

4　Technology Capability Assessment

- Obtain Response from RFP(s)
- Create a Shortlist of Suitable Vendors with High Viability
- Compare Capabilities Against Evaluation Criteria & Analyze the Scores
- Conduct Prototyping or Hands-on Tool Assessment/Vendor Demonstration

3　Prioritize Requirements

Evaluate Current Enterprise

Evaluate & Select Technology

Construct Agreements

Assess & Manage Risks

5　Initiate Technology Alliance

- Compare Pricing Structure Against Budgetary Criteria
- Define Terms and Conditions for Contractual Agreements
- Prepare SLAs or TPAs

6　Establish Risk Mitigation Strategy

- Prepare Negotiating Strategies
- Negotiate Contractual Agreements on Technology Support, Maintenance, and Future R&D
- Determine Risk Factors and Plan for Risk Mitigation

FIGURE 4.10　A simplified technology evaluation model.

This approach also promotes awareness of the Collaborative EA within the enterprise as a whole and cultivates business-IT relationships, both internally and externally.

The evaluation criteria is business-focused, and the steps addressed in their evaluation model include business challenges as part of due diligence to provide technical solutions. Some evaluation criteria include general information such as vendors' past performance, current customer base, pricing structure, financial viability, allocated R&D budget, technology upgrade schedule, and their position in the field of collaboration. Some of the tool-specific criteria include ease of integration with other products, interoperability, and the ease of use for developers and end users (as appropriate). There is no straightforward approach to defining technology evaluation criteria. While transitioning portals and web services to a Collaborative EA, the only caveat is that collaboration has already been considered a significant part of existing portals. Similarly, SLAs and TPAs have been recognized as part of doing business together while incorporating service-oriented architectures. Since many organizations consider web services helpful in improving enterprise agility, productivity, and competitiveness, sourcing them internally or externally must be factored in at a strategic level. In this respect, sourcing can be looked at as a vehicle for the build-versus-buy versus pay-per-use decision-making process. In today's business environment, sourcing models as defined by many organizations are performance based and measure vendors' ability to comply with open industry standards and support relevant regulations. As a result, SLAs and TPAs are just two parts of the sourcing life cycle and must be constantly evaluated and looked after to guarantee successful delivery of a Collaborative EA. Most organizations inadvertently follow these seven steps in their sourcing approach:

1. Focus on current business processes that help directly achieve enterprise-level business goals.
2. Conduct gap analyses to prepare current technology and skills inventories.
3. Perform industry research to recognize market trends in involving technology partners and vendors in Collaborative EA initiatives.
4. Evaluate and select technologies, processes, and solution partners that meet the business' needs.
5. Prepare SLAs that commit sourcing partners to follow specific rules of engagements.
6. Identify and manage associated risks early in the sourcing process and, if necessary, locate alternate solutions or services to eliminate critical risks and the concerns of business sponsors.
7. Establish a flexible and appropriately involved governance model to disseminate corporate vision, principles, and best practices-driven guidelines across the board.

In practice, these steps can be considered essential elements of technology evaluation and selecting sourcing options. However, it may be necessary to consider tradeoffs in establishing the most suitable sourcing strategy for a particular enterprise.

Two common issues experienced are related to (1) linking existing technologies and integration processes with sourcing options and (2) incorporating selected technologies with already established IT cultures, best practices, and standards. The transition road map addresses the first issue. The best-of-breed or integrated solution options while retiring legacy systems and technologies over time is part of this approach. Addressing the second issue requires participation by the senior leadership and enterprise governance. Once leaders establish and approve policies, the portfolio management office executes and controls the progress of inculcating the standards, best practices, and compliance.

MANAGING USER EXPECTATIONS

The successful deployment of a Collaborative EA depends primarily on human factors such as trust, reliability, confidence, dependability, and commitment. For two organizations doing business together to collaborate optimally, they must build a trusting relationship. The concept of trust is not new to practitioners; however, building of trust takes time and patience. The best principle of trust building is to share or exchange information incrementally. Building trust does not necessarily translate into a written contract. In most cases, it's purely based on verbal understanding. For internal purposes, a consensus-driven partnership can be built between the business units and IT to examine the trust. The terms of the partnership agreement can be formally accepted as an official contract and followed up with a flexible road map, as well as periodic performance measurement with a set of interactive performance evaluation metrics or scorecards. For internal peers, trading partners, or vendors (service providers or solution providers), trust is equated with many activities, including the following:

- Verbal promises followed by commitment
- Ability to deliver on time and within budget
- Earning the confidence of customers when things go wrong
- Preserving the confidentiality of protected corporate data

There are no processes that allow an organization to measure trust. Therefore, it's best to rely heavily on measuring user experience to create performance metrics to examine the success rate in building trusting partnerships between two or more organizations involved in deploying Collaborative EAs.

Steps of building confidence or trust between organizations include:

1. launching a collaborative initiative on a small scale;
2. considering a win-win situation for all parties; and
3. establishing trust between peers inside the enterprise.

In order to strengthen these qualitative measures, two additional associated and practical measures are:

1. employing SLAs and TPAs in the Collaborative EA deployment; and
2. using quantitative measures in creating performance metrics.

The business community already knows the typical use of technology that enforces SLAs in providing web services. Some vendors already offer management of SLAs in their product or tool suites.[24] The concept of SLA management can be extended to include various levels of support for connecting, communicating, coordinating, and committing in collaborative enterprises. Similarly, portals offer web-based access to SLA management-related information to appropriate users.

It is possible to collect data related to user experience and expectations using various web-enabled tools. These tools provide a mechanism to build performance metrics for evaluating and establishing the level of collaboration, abstraction, and interaction. Scorecards (similar to what IT and business call "balanced scorecards") that measure performance and access, as well as the volume or extent of usage of a Collaborative EA, can provide valuable user experience data. Once the data is collected, it must be analyzed to determine the changes necessary to successfully deploy the Collaborative EA. At this point, content management, knowledge management, and security also become key factors in providing the best solutions for Collaborative EAs. In general, managing the user experience depends on measuring the people, process, and technology pieces of Collaborative EAs.

There are three major factors that can significantly affect the next generation of Collaborative EAs:

FORMULATING EFFECTIVE USE OF FEDERATED PORTALS

The effective use of federated portals will drive the establishment of a network-centric approach to collect and store enterprise data. It will empower Collaborative EAs to attain the advantages of distributed computing environments. From a business perspective, it will allow local business units to maintain and manage their own portals and handle budgetary constraints at their own organizational levels. Executives and business sponsors will be able to visualize and eliminate bottlenecks in transitioning the applications of their areas of interest to Collaborative EAs as a basis for distributing traditionally centralized authorities, accountabilities, and responsibilities in EA initiatives. Federated portals enable organizations to transition their existing EAs to collaborative ones via incremental investments over a period of time, with ample opportunities to assess ROI. It facilitates utilizing lessons learned from previous efforts. It also will allow for the instilling of a corporate culture based on best practices, standards, and consensus-driven partnerships.

ACHIEVING CONSENSUS ON WEB SERVICES STANDARDS

The standardization of various web services are currently underway as a part of W3C, OASIS, WS-I, and other initiatives. The benefit is that these processes will unify standards floating around across vertical (commercial and government) markets. However, the long process of establishing standards makes the position of adopting web services technologies difficult for many organizations. As this progresses over the next few years, utilizing web services more effectively will become a surmountable task. At this point, core web services standards such as XML, SOAP, WSDL, and UDDI play a major role in establishing Collaborative EAs.

Incorporating Value Propositions from Grid Computing Concepts

Many practitioners see grid computing as a means to facilitate the allocation, selection, and aggregation of a variety of geographically dispersed computational resources. Adding to the principles of federated portals, Grid Computing can divide and farm out business applications in network-distributed, clustered environments to take advantage of the computationally intensive processing power of multiple systems. Collaborative EAs will benefit from using the parallel and distributed processing powers of Grid Computing as it becomes more popular among practitioners in the field.

Visionary business leaders guide their organizations to utilize the benefits of portals and web services. Additionally, an approach to establish consensus-driven business-IT partnerships via effective use of a pragmatic road map and the OMG's MDA will continue to facilitate progress in building Collaborative EAs.

DISCUSSION TOPICS

1. Why and how is the digital business enterprise landscape changing? Discuss in the context of collaborations.
2. What are the key elements of a Collaborative EA and how can they help cope with changes in the organization as it undertakes DT?
3. How would you apply strategies for business collaboration based on EA?
4. Discuss the practical steps and models for s Collaborative EA from the points of view of their practical advantages and risks.
5. What are the potential challenges your organization could face without a road map for Collaborative EA deployment?
6. How do portals and services enable collaboration?
7. What is the role of metrics in facilitating Collaborative EA?

NOTES

1 Hazra, T., and Unhelkar, B. "Leveraging EA to Incorporate Emerging Technology Trends for Digital Transformation." *Cutter IT Journal*, (theme - Disruption and Emergence: What Do They Mean for Enterprise Architecture?), Vol. 29, No. 2, pp. 10–16, 2016.
2 Hazra, T. K. "EA Metrics Deliver Business Value: Going Beyond the Boundaries of the EA Program." *Cutter IT Journal*, Vol. 22, No. 11, November 2009.
3 Ibid.
4 Hazra, T. K. "Aligning Business and IT Architectures: A Seven-Step Approach." *Cutter IT Journal*, Vol 21, No. 12, December 2008. pp. 22–27.
5 Unhelkar, B. "Relating Business Analysis to Enterprise Architecture, Enterprise Architecture Service." *Cutter Executive Update* Vol. 13, No. 4, May 2010.
6 Ibid.
7 See Note 2.
8 Based on McGovern, J., Ambler, S., Stevens, M., and Sharan, V., (2004), *A Practical Guide to Enterprise Architecture*, Prentice Hall PTR, Upper Saddle River, NJ.
9 Tiwary, A., and Unhelkar, B., (2018), *Outcome Driven Business Architecture,* CRC Press, (Taylor & Francis Group /an Auerbach Book), Boca Raton, FL. Co-Authored.

10 See Note 4.

11 See Note 8.

12 Unhelkar, B., (2014), *Agile Outsourcing: Cross-Cultural, Cross-Regional Perspectives*, Cutter (Cutter Executive Report, Agile Product & Project Management Practice) Boston, MA, Vol. 15, No. 5.

13 TOGAF — The Open Group Architecture Framework.

14 See Note 2. (Special issue on "Employing Web Services Technologies to Deploy Collaborative Enterprise Architectures").

15 US Government Cloud Computing Technology Roadmap," published by the US National Institute of Standards and Technology.

16 Hazra, T., and Unhelkar, B., (2015), "Cloud-Analytics for Digital Business: A Practical EA Perspective in the Age of Big Data," *SDPSnet Conference* (1–5 November, 2015. Dallas, TX). Proceedings to be published in the USA by 2015 Society for Design and Process Science. (www.sdpsnet.org).

17 Zachman, (1984), *A Framework for Enterprise Architecture*, https://www.zachman.com/ea-articles-reference/54-the-zachman-framework-evolution, accessed 27th June, 2020.

18 Spewak, S. H., & Hill, S. C., (1993), *Enterprise Architecture Planning – Developing a Blueprint for Data, Applications, and Technology*, QED Publishing Group, Boston, MA.

19 Boar, B. H., *Constructing Blueprints for Enterprise IT Architectures*, John Wiley & Sons, New York, NY.

20 See Note 2.

21 See Note 8.

22 See Note 4.

23 Rosen, M., Krichevsky, T., and Sharma, H., (2010), "Strategies for a sustainable enterprise." in *Handbook of Research in Green ICT*, (Ed. B. Unhelkar), Hershey, PA: IGI Global.

24 Taft, D. K. "IBM Tests Web Services SLA Technology." *e-Week*, 30 June 2003.

Part B

The Digital Enterprise
Architecture Life Cycle

5 Cloud Capabilities in Digital Transformation

SUMMARY

This chapter focuses on the use of Cloud capabilities in Digital Transformation (DT). The role of analytics and how the Cloud enables the offering of analytics as a service are also discussed. This chapter positions the Cloud in the overall Enterprise Architecture (EA). An EA-based approach to incorporating Cloud analytics in digital business processes is important. This is so because, with the advent of Big Data, Cloud analytics plays a pivotal role in sharing analytical insights in decision-making. This sharing of analytics goes way beyond sharing of infrastructure, services, and platforms. Sharing of data and analytics in the Cloud opens up the doors to virtual digital organizations – as there are no in-house installations and maintenance of digital assets. Without the backdrop of the EA, Cloud analytics has risks such as degenerating into a stand-alone activity, siloed insights, and contradictory intelligence in decision-making. Therefore, Cloud analytics is discussed in terms of the overall EA, including the challenges and risks associated with it.

CLOUD AND THE ENTERPRISE ARCHITECTURE

EA enables the incorporation of Cloud-based services in business processes.[1] The Cloud is commonly understood as a pool of computing resources accessed and shared via the internet. Before the increase in ease of internet connectivity, data was managed within organizational boundaries and stored on a local data server. With the ease of communications, however, the local data server moved away to a remote location and started offering "shared services". This was the start of Cloud Computing (Cloud), which shifts computing activity to a centralized, shared server away from the device that is used to access data and display (visualize) results.

Cloud Computing describes a system where users can connect to a vast network of computing resources, data, and servers that reside somewhere else, usually on the internet, rather than on a local machine, a LAN or in a data center.[2] Furthermore, IoT devices generate high-volume, high-velocity sensor-data that can be directly placed in the Cloud. The Cloud provides the storage and services aspect of Big Data. The ease of electronic connectivity and the use of Cloud create digital business opportunities other than simply resource sharing.[3] The Cloud renders a variety of resources as utilities or service. Digital businesses can draw upon these, depending on how their business grows and also their ability to handle the costs. After extracting the key elements and characteristics of more than 20 Cloud Computing definitions, Vaquero et al (2009) define Cloud as:

> "Clouds [are] a large pool of easily usable and accessible virtualized resources (such as hardware, development platforms and/or services). These resources can be dynamically reconfigured to adjust to a variable load (scale), allowing also for an optimum resource utilization. This pool of resources is typically exploited by a pay-per-use model in which guarantees are offered by the Infrastructure Provider by means of customized SLAs [service-level agreements]"[4]

The actual execution of applications and analytics also occurs on the Cloud. The Cloud obviates the need to install software and analytical applications locally. Instead, results from the analytics carried out on the Cloud are visualized on the user's devices. Thus, analytics become a utility or a service sourced by a digital business. Analytical applications are made available on demand on the Cloud. The distributed nature of this approach to computing without the need to know the physical location of the computing resource is a crucial element of Enterprise Architecture (EA) and Digital Transformation (DT).

The Social Media and Mobile (SoMo) elements of SMAC-Stack are responsible for input and output of user data. SoMo is based around interactions with the user. SMAC technologies are imbued with versatility and visibility; they also comprise high volumes of data of different types (e.g., structured, audio, video, graphics) derived from varied sources.[5] When SoMo data and information are analyzed in a Cloud-based infrastructure, SMAC technologies come to fruition by generating diverse insights and knowledge immensely useful in rapid decision-making. Based on such insights, a digital business can change directions, new product lines can be introduced (or withdrawn), and new services marketed. DT is facilitated by a strategy based on collaboration that welcomes change and facilitates dynamic decision-making – in short, "Agile."[6] SMAC, by nature, is thus very close to Agile. Digital business transcends the storage aspect of the Cloud and strategizes to use it for analytics-as-a-service.

The memory and power of SoMo devices (e.g., a smartphone) are primarily used to enhance the presentation of outputs (using visualizations and sensors) rather than to undertake detailed analytics. The Cloud also shifts the responsibility of storing data away from local machines and devices. This serves to consolidate data storage, backup, and recovery options.

Web-based applications when hosted in a Cloud environment leads to thin-client architecture. To others, the Cloud architecture also creates utility computing, which behaves like a grid that enables charging metered rates for processing time. The Cloud also represents distributed or parallel computing, designed to scale complex processes for improved efficiency.

Cloud architecture shares conceptual closeness with Mainframe Computing. Although far from being a centralized server (mainframe-like computers), the Cloud stores, processes, and shares data from a "common platform" that is akin to how a mainframe computer stores data. The ways in which data is stored and resources scaled up and down is quite different, though. The sophistication of tools and technologies accompanying the Cloud influences its implementation.

The back end of Cloud storage is extremely "elastic". This means the capacity and services offered on the Cloud grow and shrink rapidly depending on the demands of users. The Cloud opens up a vast amount of cheap storage with multiple redundancies.

The Cloud domain has incrementally evolved from offering data storage, sharing software applications, and enabling computing platforms to eventually offering infrastructure as a service. Sharing of data in the Cloud also opens up doors to sharing analytics that can be used without the usual technical overheads. The Cloud frees businesses from the limitations of their local technical environments and devices. Data, analytics, applications, and processing can all be used on a shareable basis with other collaborative businesses.

Connectivity is the key to using the Cloud in digital business as it opens up many opportunities.[7] For example, treating computing resources as utilities creates opportunities to offer them as services, depending on the needs and ability of an organization to pay. Shareability of data creates an opportunity to collaborate with varied data providers – resulting in new types of data analytics.

The shift in the computing paradigm due to the evolution of the Cloud covers technologies, architectures, data, and business models. This paradigm change also includes user viewpoints and attitudes that change as they use a thin client or a smartphone to access data, applications, and process. The Cloud also changes the notion of security since data is stored in a shared, centralized, remote, secure data center (the Cloud). The remote storage of data has the potential to reduce risks due to local environment failure or the loss of a device.

CLOUD CHARACTERISTICS FOR DIGITAL BUSINESS

The Cloud is the basis for virtualization of resources, their configurability, shareability, and scalability. Thus, the Cloud is the basis for a data-driven digital business. Early adopters of the Cloud are now ideally positioned to expand into the use of Big Data analytics on the Cloud. The Cloud can be considered an effective conduit to deal with the ever-expanding deluge of data – especially in the Big Data age.

The key characteristics of Cloud (as discussed by many, including Murugesan, 2009[8]) can be understood in the context digital business is as follows:

1. Cloud Computing allows access to capabilities and services over the internet. Digital business offering services can strategize to present pluggable service API to clients.
2. Enterprises that do not have the capacity to own an installation will be able to use the analytics.
3. Computers and storage are housed in one or more huge, off-site data centers. This takes away the pressure to host Massive Parallel Processing (MPP) capabilities over a large cluster of computers – and to secure them.
4. Clients and users don't need to own the hardware for analytics. This allows the provider of the analytical service (vendor) to keep their installation

updated with the latest hardware, as well as operating and analytical applications.

5. Users pay for what they use, similar to how utilities such as electricity, water, or telephone service work. Big Data analytics can thus be made scalable (for use in large enterprises on demand, as also for small and medium enterprises – SMEs – for their analytical insights)

6. Services over the Cloud are much safer with increasing cybersecurity sophistication.

7. Improves compliance due to transparent available data and audit trails to authorized personnel.

Cloud-based architecture shifts the focal point of data management away from an enterprise. The routines of data management are moved to third parties who are specialist vendors in Cloud Computing. Thus, capacity planning recedes into the background and enterprises can continue to focus on growth (or handle shrinkage) without undue concern from a data management perspective. This is not to say that large enterprises need not be concerned about where the data is stored and how it is accessed. The shift of emphasis to the Cloud, however, opens up many opportunities for enterprises in the Big Data age. This is not only because of the size and unpredictability of both structured and unstructured Big Data, but also the core need of Big Data analytics to correlate seemingly unrelated suites of data and information.

These information stores are available on the Cloud and, thus, the EAs of modern digital business need to interweave the Cloud in their solutions. This is also the way to handle the exponential growth of demand (for analytics and related business intelligence) from various types of users. Often, different users view the data differently – and look for different patterns or different behavior the data presents. This element of visualization is much easier to handle by professionals with specific expertise in that area of data analytics and informatics. These professionals (aka data scientists) are able to make use of tools that support the use of data analytics in Cloud environments. Thus, where data storage and accompanying analytics were once considered two separate entities, in the age of the Cloud, they are closely intertwined.

With increasing sophistication in connectivity and storage, it is now becoming feasible to undertake Big Data analytics in the Cloud itself. This phenomenon changes the way in which digital businesses are organized and operated. Table 5.1 lists key Cloud characteristics, what they mean, and their relevance to Big Data analytics and digital business. The successful implementation of analytics on the Cloud requires careful consideration of the EA and the way in which the Cloud is positioned within it.

These aforementioned characteristics are opportunities in the digital space to provide dynamic visualization, data virtualization, data consolidation, and enhanced decision-making. For many decision makers, cost reduction or containment are the key business drivers for leveraging Cloud Computing. Cloud is, not meant to replace the IT workforce or associated assets.

TABLE 5.1

Cloud Characteristics and Digital Business

Cloud Element	PA	PB	
Cloud characteristics	What it means	Relevance in Big Data analytics	Relevance to digital business
User centric	Single point of contact for user	Can provide analytical insights in user's time and space	Enables mass-personalization of services
Task centric	Driven by the needs of the user rather than offering of the application	Analytical needs vary vastly, requiring highly flexible application suite	Provides ability to focus on specific user needs
Greater computability	Large number of interconnected computers	Highly relevant for Big Data clusters for Massive Parallel Processing	Harnesses power for digitization
Ubiquitous access	Over multiple devices and in many different formats	Enable provisioning of decision-making intelligence in multiple formats and on many devices	Enables ability to spread digital services over devices, reports
Scalable	Can size up or down depending on needs of the user (enterprise)	Enables performance of analytics for small and large data	Frees up the enterprise from the non-core job capacity planning
Economical	Utility-based model allowing users to procure only that which they want	Highly relevant for users that may be interested in Pay-per-Analytics	Enables digitization of small business
Collaborative	Enables sharing of data	Vital for Big Data analytics based on widely varying data suites	Provides collaborative opportunities over regions
Self-Healing	Able to reconfigure its installation with multiple points of failure	Eases the opportunity for Commodity Computing (key precept of Hadoop)	Provides stability for digital business

Challenges in Cloud Computing initiatives are discussed by Blitstein.[9] There are different ways of establishing and managing Cloud-related issues, risks, and challenges. Strategies for the Cloud and its architecture are part of the overall EA. This facilitates Cloud implementations that also benefit business intelligence and analytics initiatives.

There is a real need to define a Cloud architecture that can facilitate leveraging the business strategy and harnessing the due diligence of EA to prepare the blueprints or road maps for Cloud implementation. It is important to understand and explain the challenges associated with Big Data analytics and then show how these are better handled with a good EA.

FOUR PHASES OF CLOUD ADOPTION THROUGH ENABLEMENT AND THEIR CORRESPONDING BUSINESS VALUE

Figure 5.1 shows the four specific phases of adopting the Cloud for digital business. They are: Cloud assessment, Cloud transition, Cloud deployment, and Cloud enablement.

CLOUD ASSESSMENT

In this first phase, enterprises undertake self-assessment in terms of their Cloud-readiness and their Big Data strategies. Essentially, adoption is driven by strategic business requirements. During this step, the known business drivers to define the value proposition of Cloud-analytics is undertaken. Additionally, there is a need to rely on best practices for adopting Cloud Computing as recognized in the industry. This step helps concentrate on the enterprise strategy as a whole and resolve situations where business users may have a preconceived idea about the Cloud as a replacement for internal IT organization. It is important to work closely with business units in making the business case to leverage the Cloud effectively based on their requirements while conforming to federal "Cloud first" policy. During this step, it is essential to keep an open mind while analyzing the value of Cloud Computing to support the goals and objectives of the business strategy. Here, there are two basic characteristics: business strategy guides the IT strategy that provides opportunities for Cloud analytics, and business and IT strategies must be continuously aligned to support ongoing operations.

CLOUD TRANSITION

Once all stakeholders have agreed to the requirements of Cloud adoption, the enterprise can initiate the transition process to the Cloud. It is possible that there are some analytical applications that the enterprise uses without the benefit of the Cloud. In this step, there is a strategy for transitioning all data and applications (including existing analytics, if any) to the Cloud. Attention is directed toward extending the views, models, and frameworks of business and IT architecture to incorporate the value proposition

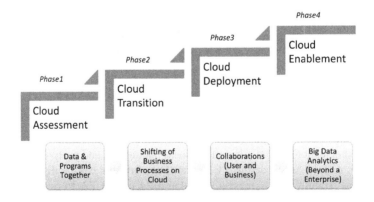

FIGURE 5.1   Four phases of Cloud Assessment through enablement and corresponding business value.

of Cloud Computing. The scope, benefits, and limitations of Cloud Computing architecture components such as Software as a service (SaaS), Platform as a service (PaaS), and Infrastructure as a service (IaaS) in formulating Cloud strategy are considered, in addition to espousing the reference models and specifications from the Federal Enterprise Architecture (FEA) and the Federal Segment Architecture Methodology (FSAM). This step includes identifying risks, issues, and challenges with each of these architecture components as part of efforts to formulate the Cloud strategy. As part of EA organization, critical business applications and associated business processes are identified. Subsequently, a set of Cloud transformation blueprints is developed (during the next step). It is necessary to analyze lessons learned from applying these blueprints to review and modify (if appropriate) the Cloud strategy periodically.

CLOUD DEPLOYMENT

In this phase, the work is done with business portfolio, program management, transition and operations support organizations, and associated teams. The primary intention in this step is to continue helping business and IT teams identify, evaluate, and select the right Cloud solution or service providers; prepare and establish SLAs; and get the right set of IT assets and resources allocated for the transition to the Cloud-based enterprise and the subsequent operational support. As a result, it is possible to deploy all enterprise IT assets on the Cloud.

CLOUD ENABLEMENT

In this phase, the focus is on helping various business organizations and IT teams in their initiatives to undertake Cloud analytics based on the previous phase. Strategic principles are utilized, as well as Cloud transformation blueprints, to enable an enterprise undertaking insightful decision-making based on the Cloud. The Cloud Computing strategy actively supports information-, application-, and technology-focused solution architecture development efforts to offer transparency across architecture domains. It also suggests the utilization of insights to avoid potential pitfalls in Cloud implementations.

THREE SYNERGISTIC AREAS OF EA AND CLOUD

There are three areas of understanding between EA and the Cloud. They are the EA governance, EA measurement and maturity, and EA implementation associated with the Cloud.

EA GOVERNANCE AND THE CLOUD

The role of EA governance principles, guidelines, frameworks, and models to establish and cultivate Cloud governance is created. Business and IT teams are engaged to collaborate in this effort. Adopting a "Cloud first" policy has helped set expectations for stakeholders from the beginning. This is particularly important in the Big Data analytics space where, without strong EA governance, analytics can get easily out of hand.

EA MEASUREMENT AND MATURITY FOR THE CLOUD

Metrics and measurement programs are started early in the DT initiative. A set of metrics is defined, starting from business drivers, business and IT strategies, as well as identified business objectives and goals, while creating the business case for incorporating Cloud Computing and its adoption in DT. These metrics and associated parameters are established throughout the life cycle of the Cloud architecture. This exercise enables business sponsors to make informed decisions and to progressively mature the Cloud architecture, its processes, principles, and frameworks.

FROM STRATEGY FORMULATION TO SOLUTION DEPLOYMENT

This is the stage of deliberating whether the adoption of Cloud Computing has become a paradigm shift for the client organization. There is a clear shift in focus during the execution of the four steps in Cloud architecture practice. In the first two steps, the focus was directed at identifying business needs for the Cloud. The next two steps concentrate on identifying the changes or transformation required to implement Cloud-based solutions and deploy the right Cloud solutions.

Deployment of the Cloud within EA was discussed in Chapter 2 (Figure 2.2). The adoption and migration of the Cloud is integral to DT. Cloud adoption is made up of four strategic activities aligned with the activities and tasks of the EA. These activities are:

1. Create a Cloud value proposition
2. Formulate a Cloud strategy
3. Facilitate Cloud planning
4. Support Cloud deployment

These activities in the areas of strategic planning and solution delivery during DT are described in greater detail:

1. **Create Cloud Value Proposition** – this activity analyzes the value of Cloud Computing from the perspective of their requirements. During this step, known business drivers are used to define the value proposition of Cloud Computing. Additionally, industry best practices for adopting Cloud Computing are employed. This step helps concentrate on the enterprise digital strategy as a whole and resolve situations where business users may have a preconceived idea that Cloud Computing can completely eliminate an organization's dependency on the internal IT organization. Business units leverage the Cloud effectively based on their requirements while conforming to federal "Cloud first" policy. During this step, it is essential to keep an open mind while analyzing the value of Cloud Computing in supporting the goals and objectives of the digital business strategy. Business strategy guides the IT strategy, both of which continue to be aligned.
2. **Formulate Cloud Strategy** – the result of the analysis conducted during the first step is used to formulate Cloud strategy. The primary attention during this step is directed toward extending the views, models, and

frameworks of the business and IT architectures, to incorporate the value proposition of Cloud Computing. In addition to espousing reference models and specifications – e.g., the FEA and the FSAM – the scope, benefits, and limitations of Cloud Computing architecture components such as SaaS, PaaS, and IaaS are included in formulating the Cloud strategy. The identification of risks, issues, and challenges with each of these architecture components is part of efforts to formulate the Cloud strategy. The overarching EA identifies critical business applications and associated business processes – and subsequently develops a set of Cloud transformation blueprints (during the next step). The lessons learned from applying these blueprints are used to review and modify (if appropriate) the Cloud strategy periodically.

3. **Facilitate Cloud Planning** – this step focuses on helping various business organizations and IT teams in their initiatives to prepare for Cloud Computing. Strategic principles, as well as Cloud transformation blueprints, are used to develop a road map for the enterprise to follow in its Cloud migration. The plan is revised and refined based on experience and lessons learned during the next step. A decision framework similar to the one presented in Federal Cloud Computing Strategy is created. As was shown in Figure 2.2, information-, application-, and technology-focused solution architecture development efforts are supported.

4. **Support Cloud Deployment** – the business portfolio, program management, and transition and operations support teams work closely to aid the deployment of the Cloud within the overall EA deployment. The primary intention of this step is to continue to help business and IT teams identify, evaluate, and select the right Cloud solution or service providers, prepare and establish the SLAs, and get the right set of IT assets and resources allocated for the transition to the Cloud-based enterprise and the subsequent operational support for it.

EMBEDDING ANALYTICS IN CLOUD-BASED DIGITAL PROCESSES

Undertaking analytics in the Cloud and embedding the results in business processes is one of the key activities of DT. A Cloud-oriented EA determines the value proposition of Cloud-based digital processes. The experiences and lessons learned are shared. In establishing Cloud deployment activities as a practice, an ideal approach is outlined by Rosen (2011).[10]

To get started with Cloud architecture, the focus is on understanding the business strategy, goals, and objectives coming out of the EA. The primary intention is to capture the vision as well as business policies that may impact the implementation of Cloud Computing, in addition to the risks and issues associated with adopting Cloud Computing concepts. The following business drivers as part of the overall DT strategy are also applicable for Cloud deployment:

• Lowering cost of deployment and operations – in particular, analytical software and applications.

- Increasing efficiency and productivity of business users by providing them with timely intelligence that enables rapid decision-making.
- Improving the quality of service delivery by providing greater information about a client, a situation, or a competitor.
- Managing IT assets, with the appropriate level of security and threat management.
- Enhancing the response time for the users, with better customer satisfaction.

An active matrix (one that helps decision makers evaluate risks against the benefits, as discussed in Figure 4.5 in the previous chapter) is used here. This matrix is based on the original Cloud Decision Matrix presented by Rosen[11] and further developed by Hazra.[12] In addition, there is an emphasis on factors such as enterprise efficiency, its overall agility or flexibility, and the potential of applying innovation and improving collaboration across the enterprise. Recognition goes to server utilization, server virtualization, and the performance of existing data centers – and subsequently to reverse engineer the requirements appropriate for meeting business needs of users across the enterprise.

A set of shared resources and IT assets that can be considered a part of the EA and dedicated to establishing Cloud architecture are identified. Also important are existing business processes, components, and applications as part of business architecture (again, a subset of EA), as well as revisited business strategies to ascertain business and IT alignment.

The next task is to create a set of blueprints that represent the IT strategies identified in the previous task. To be considered are security requirements, government agency policies and regulations, known constraints to design and develop solution architectures, and evaluate the potential of Cloud use from the solution architecture perspective. This task determines the value of Cloud implementation; evaluates the potential of using private, public, or hybrid Clouds; and analyzes the cost and benefits for business sponsors.

At this point, the principles and guidelines are established, and architecturally significant components for the enterprise are defined. Cloud architecture elements can be mapped directly into three layers: the service layer, the resource abstraction and control layer, and the physical resource layer. These are depicted in the reference models presented in the "US Government Cloud Computing Technology Roadmap," published by the US National Institute of Standards and Technology.[13] In addition, these levels establish a governance framework that can be leveraged in enforcing Cloud architecture principles and in vetting any major investments to be made in Cloud implementations.

LESSONS LEARNED IN PRACTICE

Lessons learned are categorized into three major areas: strategy, architectural blueprints, and Cloud implementation.

- At the strategy level, the most important lesson learned has been about integrating security goals, objectives, and requirements as relevant and appropriate to the business, application, data, and infrastructure layers of the architecture from the beginning. It is also important to prioritize security requirements in terms of risks, issues, and concerns, as well as the critical success factors they pose to Cloud implementation.

- At the architectural blueprints level, the primary challenge has been in identifying the right set of standards, tools, technology, and best practices that can be leveraged across the life cycle of Cloud adoption and implementation. It is important to keep an open mind, as these are all evolving rapidly.
- At the Cloud implementation level, the lessons learned are quite remarkable. Using a number of "what if" scenarios, there are various solution options before rolling out the Cloud implementation. These solution options, and in many cases, achieved cost benefits as well as operational excellence. Business leaders need to make informed decisions and avoid making substantial initial investment for private Clouds. Cultivating the Cloud architecture practice and documenting lessons learned from this initiative continues.

Leveraging the benefits of Cloud computing for Big Data analytics and avoiding corresponding pitfalls are not possible without recognizing the big picture and understanding the limitations of existing resources. Additional considerations include how the Cloud might improve or impede the productivity and performance of the business.

In order to leverage the benefits of Cloud Computing effectively, a simple charter that aligns business vision and mission to support a "Federal Cloud Computing Strategy" is established. This a "Cloud first" policy. To avoid pitfalls or limitations of Cloud Computing implementations, incorporate the principles and guidelines of the "US Government Cloud Computing Technology Roadmap" discussed previously into the foundational principles of the Cloud architecture practice charter.

CHALLENGES IN USING CLOUD-BASED ARCHITECTURE

Hayes (2008)[14] and Murugesan (2009)[15] have discussed challenges for Cloud Computing. Hazra (2012b)[16] has also documented several important challenges. Most of these are encountered while establishing a Cloud architecture practice for an enterprise. These are the challenges in the context of undertaking Cloud analytics:

SCALABILITY

In deploying software to run in the Cloud (for Cloud applications), scalability is a major issue. Resources need to be managed in such a way that the operations continue to run smoothly even as the number of users grows – servers must respond to hundreds or thousands of requests per second, and the system must also coordinate information coming from multiple sources. For example, a typical Hadoop cluster can run on commodity computing, ranging from a handful to a few thousand computers. This adds to the challenge of scalability from the Cloud vendor's perspective. Besides, it is important to note that in Cloud analytics, not all the computing resources would be under the control of the same organization.

User Interfaces

A web browser-based user interface presents challenges of another kind. Over the decades, the familiar window-and-menu layer of the operating system has been fine-tuned to meet user needs and expectations. Duplicating this functionality inside a web browser is a challenge, and has to be done in a comparatively primitive Web Computing development environment, compared to creating a desktop application for Windows, assembled from a broad array of prebuilt components.

Shifting Enterprise Computing to the Cloud

In Big Data analytics, the need to integrate enterprise applications with other data suites from multiple vendors is very high. Cloud analytics is of most value when enterprise applications are also on the Cloud platform. Moving applications to the Cloud may need skills in multiple languages and operating environments.

Open Source Development

Cloud Computing represents a competitive challenge to vendors of shrink-wrap software. The open source movement could also have a tough time adapting to the new computing model and creating web services to compete with those offered by major corporate players (e.g., Google).

Control and Ownership

Allowing a third party to take custody of personal documents raises tough questions about control and ownership of data. Furthermore, moving from one Cloud service provider to another can also be a challenge.

Privacy and Confidentiality

Ensuring privacy and confidentiality of data are key concerns for Cloud users. For instance, if a government agency presents a subpoena to the third party that has possession of your data asking them to surrender your information, the third party is less likely to contest the order. If you had retained physical custody of the data, at least you would be able to decide for yourself whether to contest the order or not. In worst case scenarios, you might not even be informed that your documents have been released. Despite this situation, it seems likely that much of our digital information will be living in the clouds long before such questions are resolved.

DISCUSSION TOPICS

1. What are the key characteristics of the Cloud that make it important in DT?
2. Why should the Cloud be considered integral to EA in the context of DT?
3. What are the key phases of Cloud adoption by a digital business?
4. Discuss the approach to embedding analytics in Cloud-based business processes

5. What strategies would you develop in order to overcome the challenges of using Cloud-based architecture in your digital business?
6. What is the importance of governance in Cloud deployment?
7. How is the Cloud able to open up opportunities for collaborations for digital business?

NOTES

1 Hazra, T., and Unhelkar, B., (2015), "Cloud-analytics for digital business: A practical EA perspective in the age of Big Data." *SDPSnet Conference* (1–5 November, 2015. Dallas, TX). 2015 Society for Design and Process Science. (www.sdpsnet.org).

2 Kay, R., "QuickStudy: Cloud Computing." *Computerworld*, 4 August 2008 (www.computerworld.com/action/article.do? command=viewArticleBasic&articleId=321699).

3 Hazra, T. K., and Kumar S. "Establishing the Business Architecture Practice: A Case Study." *Business & Enterprise Architecture Executive Report*, Vol. 15, No. 1, 2012.

4 Vaquero, L. M., et al. "A Break in the Clouds: Towards a Cloud Definition." *ACM SIGCOMM Computer Communication Review*, Vol. 39, No. 1, January 2009. 50–55.

5 Unhelkar, B., *SMAC with Agile,* Agile Product & Project Management Practice, (Cutter Executive Update, 2014, 4 of 5), Boston, MA, Vol. 15, No. 9.

6 Unhelkar, B., (2013), *The Art of Agile Practice: A Composite Approach for Projects and Organizations,* CRC Press, (Taylor & Francis Group /an Auerbach Book), Boca Raton, FL. ISBN 9781439851180.

7 Hazra, T. K., (2012), *Cloud Architecture: Leveraging Strategies, Blueprints, and Road maps – What's Different Today?* Cutter (Cutter Advisor), Boston, MA.

8 Murugesan, S., (2009), *Cloud Computing: A New Paradigm in IT,* Data Insight and Social BI Resource Center (Cutter Executive Report), Boston, MA.

9 Ron B., (2011), *Cloud Computing –A CIO's Perspective*, Cutter IT Journal, Cutter (July 2011, Guest Editorial), Boston, MA.

10 Rosen, M., (2011), *Enterprise Architecture for the Cloud*, Cutter IT Journal, Cutter (EA Practice Director), Boston, MA, Vol. 24, No. 7.

11 Rosen, M. "Understanding and Evaluating Modeling and MDA Tools", *Enterprise Architecture Advisory Service Executive Report, Cutter Consortium*, Vol. 6, No. 5, May 2003.

12 See Note 7.

13 "US Government Cloud Computing Technology Road map," published by the US National Institute of Standards and Technology.

14 Hayes, B. "Cloud Computing." *Communications of the ACM*, Vol. 51, No. 7, pp. 9–11, July 2008.

15 Murugesan, S., (2009), *Cloud Computing: A New Paradigm in IT,* Data Insight and Social BI Resource Center (Cutter Executive Report), Boston, MA.

16 See Note 7.

6 Business Process Digitization and Customer Value

SUMMARY

This chapter discusses the importance of digitizing business processes as a part of Digital Transformation (DT). The chapter starts with a description of various types of activities within the business process discipline. The common steps used in the digitization of business processes is discussed next. Since business processes are interdependent, the need for a holistic approach – as a part of the overall strategy for digitization – is outlined. How to monitor the progress in process transformation, develop business capabilities, and handle governance and management are discussed next. Finally, a road map for transforming business processes is discussed.

BUSINESS PROCESSES AND DIGITAL TRANSFORMATION

Business processes form the backbone for the delivery of value to the end-user. Therefore, Digital Transformation (DT) requires a reengineering of all business processes in order to improve customer satisfaction, productivity levels, and, most importantly, end results.[1] Business processes are the workflows that provide output and help achieve outcomes for the key end-user. Modeling and optimization of business processes is a crucial part of DT. Business process transformation (BPX) is an initiative within the overall DT of the business. Business process automation, reengineering, integration, and optimization are some of the popular ways in which business processes benefits from digitization.

Business analysts, data analysts, developers, and security specialists are involved in all aspects of BPX initiatives. Both business and IT must be equally responsible or accountable for managing the change. BPX requires tools, technology, and an expertise of the business and the workflow. In order to undertake DT, business analysts must articulate their BPX needs. Depending on the associated risks and critical success factors (CSFs) identified for BPX, internal IT organizations or external technical partners are engaged in DT.

Following are some of the topics to keep in mind when digitizing business processes:

1. delivery of business value at the end of the process,
2. the scope of the change,
3. opportunity to optimize the process,
4. the time assigned for change, and
5. availability of resource levels and funding

BPX occurs in a number of iterative and incremental phases. Agility in DT provides an opportunity to try out-of-the-box or packaged solutions and test drive niche outsourcing organizations for their services. Iterations and increments within the transformation allow control and monitoring over the rate of progress, governance of enterprise-level DT, and vendor relationship management. Once business processes are formally prioritized, they are transformed with data analytics embedded in them.

Ideally, improvements in business value occurs via BPX. The "X" stands for transformation, which represents the integration, automation, management, outsourcing, and reengineering of business processes. BPX with digital technologies and data-driven analytics achieves enterprise-level business efficiencies.

Leadership and an understanding of industry trends help define the impact of changes on business processes. A road map and due diligence provide clarity and a line of action for delivering BPX to enterprises. Effective use of the road map helps deliver the desired expectations, typically through business process outsourcing (BPO) or business process management (BPM). Digitization of business processes involve significant functional change to the core of a business.

BPX starts with an understanding of the impact of the transformation on the end user. Will BPX increase the value being delivered to the end user? That is the key question.

Additionally, digitizing business processes keeps the following in mind:

• Current business processes are not efficient or don't deliver solutions, end results, or business functionality as fast or as accurately as end users anticipate. The performance of business processes is directly correlated with the level of experience, expectation, or satisfaction achieved by customers while interacting with the system or business function.
• Business processes are siloed, which means that they are brittle or don't connect relevant business applications with one another.
• Business processes are manual and don't have the interfaces or interaction points to connect with other business processes in the organization.
• Existing business processes are time-consuming or don't address changing business requirements or needs of customers well.
• In the early stages of a system development life cycle, efficient business modeling may rectify the flexibility or agility of such business processes significantly, but it is important to revisit these business processes later in the life cycle to identify areas that address qualities such as scalability and extensibility to meet changing business requirements.

- Many organizations suffer from redundant business processes as a result of mergers and acquisitions. As a result, too many processes do the same thing; staff in each business segment are used to working with their own systems and continue to do so even after the merger. Technologies, applications, platforms, and operating systems of the merging entities are different from one another and may not be easily consolidated. Another major challenge is to consolidate multiple organizational cultures and remove any resulting barriers. These are important considerations in transition of business processes.
- Existing business processes can be costly in terms of integration and subsequent cost of ownership. Such processes add to the complexity involved in mergers and acquisitions and reduce overall efficiency.

Digitizing business processes is not only for improving efficiency and effectiveness of the business processes. Digital business processes help better interaction with sourcing and collaborating partners and, as a result, help manage these relationships to deliver enhanced productivity.[2]

The following conditions are the most common root causes of business process inefficiencies[3] and failures during DT:

- **Disparate, heterogeneous, disconnected, or manual systems** – such systems are built with little or no vision of the future. They are also the reason for silos and stovepipes. In other cases, they are the outcome of band-aid practices in which organizations try to fix inefficiencies by repairing only a localized part of a business process pertaining to a larger complex system.
- **Mergers and acquisitions** – organizations may intend to gain competitive advantage or technical excellence, but nonetheless end up with a multitude of identical business processes during mergers and acquisitions. Such redundancy adds to the complexity of existing organizational cultures and to political battles about how to streamline business processes for efficiency.
- **Complexity and inflexibility of corporate policies; standards; and government laws, rules, or industry-specific regulations** – in these situations, business processes are affected by compliance issues, and imposed restrictions may be too rigid to avoid the inherent complexities of existing business processes.
- **Lack of a well-thought-out transition plan** – while most organizations formalize a consistent, successful strategy and a pragmatic road map for legacy modernization, many fail to recognize the significance of a transition plan that reflects the impact of BPX on an enterprise. Ultimately, for many organizations, the transition plan delivers less-than-anticipated results.

At this point, several questions about BPX arise:

- What are most organizations doing about BPX?
- Subsequently, what should be done to successfully transform business processes and to benefit from the resulting efficiency and gained productivity?
- How can an enterprise prepare to deal with BPX?
- What are the different avenues for improving business process efficiencies?

Answering these questions are part of the overall DT experience.

BPX is made up of many activities, terminologies and acronyms. These are described next.

Business Process Reengineering (BPR)

Business process reengineering (BPR) is a set of principles adopted and employed by organizations to rethink, realign, and redesign existing business processes across the enterprise to achieve significant performance, efficiency, and overall measurable customer satisfaction via effective delivery. BPR includes "rethink," "realign," and "redesign" to emphasize the need for the right people (for rethinking), the right process (for realigning), and the right technology (for redesigning). BPR has previously been known as the concept of Total Quality Management (TQM). BPR is an ongoing phenomenon that must empower practitioners to recognize continuous process improvements and associated cultural changes.

Business Process Automation (BPA)

Business process automation (BPA) is a mechanism to automate disparate and manual business processes. Existing business processes may be disconnected from their mainstream business processes or disjointed due to mergers and acquisitions. Many functional business processes may have been managed by domain experts and maintained by their knowledge of the systems. BPA activities are interpreted in terms of people, process, and technology: that is, the resource pool, the means by which BPX is performed and managed, and the specific standards, platforms, and so forth that are required. People-related issues involve transferring the knowledge base to analyze and design consistent and hopefully repeatable business processes; process involves aligning the IT solutions to business needs or requirements; and technology involves enabling and establishing the environment for automation of critical business processes.

Business Process Analysis (BPAn)

Business process analysis (BPAn) is a way to understand existing business processes or functionality by delving into the details of a business application or focus area that represents a relevant business context under consideration for transformation. It also allows practitioners to make a business case when there is a need to transform a specific business process and its impact on the overall business goals of an enterprise. Furthermore, BPAn allows practitioners to determine the initiative's specific needs as well as the costs and benefits (if any) associated with transforming a business process in multiple iterative and incremental stages.

Business Process Integration (BPI)

Business process integration (BPI) is a step in the BPX life cycle wherein multiple business processes are connected or consolidated (automated, reengineered, or outsourced). BPI relates to retooling, redesigning, or re-orchestrating existing business processes, which directly impacts their strategy for managing future business processes. For organizations involved in outsourcing specific business functionalities, BPI provides a vehicle for transitioning business components to the outsourcing organization. BPI can be interpreted in terms of people, process, and technology: people to unite the diversity of organizational cultures, process to reduce or eliminate reinventing the wheel, and technology to connect the disparate and disjointed functional components.

Business Process Improvement (BPIm)

Business process improvement (BPIm) is a set of well-thought-out steps that results in a measurable outcome and quantifies the change in business value delivery. BPIm can be illustrated in light of people, process, and technology concepts. In order to perform activities pertinent to BPIm, organizations require the right people with the right skills and domain knowledge, the right process to identify the gaps between the existing and future business functionality, and the right technology in the form of tools and products to engineer and deploy improvements. The concept of BPIm must take place in multiple iterative and incremental stages as a part of a continuous improvement program.

Business Performance Management (BPrM)

Business performance management (BPrM) is an approach to identify, measure, monitor, and maintain the performance levels or parameters of specific business functionality as it relates to the objectives of an enterprise. In order to establish the right measures for BPrM, it is essential to prioritize the business processes that are most important. A lack of BPrM undermines business goals, particularly in cases where changes in requirements and needs are common. Many organizations strive to maintain a desired business performance level while simultaneously complying with corporate policies and procedures, government regulations, and legal mandates. As a result, BPrM is closely connected with business process management, outsourcing, or transformation. From a people, process, and technology perspective, BPrM facilitates prioritizing business processes based on their significance or criticality for the organization, setting appropriate measuring standards or metrics, making recommendations for BPIm or change, and establishing costs and benefits to justify business cases for further funding.

Business Process Management (BPM)

Business process management (BPM) is a commonly used industry term. It is often misrepresented as a suite of tools that can be employed in managing or reengineering existing business processes associated with the essential business functionality of an organization. While BPM may involve tools and technology, it is also about incorporating organizational cultures (people), aligning IT with business objectives (process), and achieving a level of capability or process maturity. BPM is an ongoing initiative, and the transformation is a step forward in this effort. In other words, BPM may involve multiple consistent transformation stages to deliver desired business value.

BUSINESS PROCESS OUTSOURCING (BPO)

Business process outsourcing (BPO) is another commonly used industry term. It primarily involves utilizing the global workforce or expertise to reduce the cost of development or integration of specific business functionality without sacrificing quality, efficiency, or performance. BPO is often used interchangeably with "offshore outsourcing." BPO is aimed at gaining cost advantage, competitive edge, and better customer focus, as much as it means employing offshore outsourcing. In practice, however, BPO can be considered outsourcing a number of business functions to be implemented as packaged solutions (or customized) separately by third-party solution or service vendors and then integrated with rest of the enterprise. BPO provides an important opportunity of BPX.

BUSINESS PROCESS OPTIMIZATION (BPOp)

Business process optimization (BPOp) allows practitioners to identify, prioritize, measure, and modify business processes that can deliver improved performance, enhanced productivity, and increased customer satisfaction. In general, BPOp provides a means to improve business efficiency by introducing necessary changes to the way in which business processes perform and by actively monitoring the outcomes or metrics produced by measuring the results. From a people, process, and technology perspective, BPOp involves incorporating changes in organizational cultures (people), redesigning or refining certain business functions (process), and employing a new set of tools (technology). In practice, business process analysis, automation, management, reengineering, and/or outsourcing-related activities are precursors that lead to BPOp. Overall, BPOp enables business and IT executives recognize the role of each organization and helps manage realistic expectations.

BPIm SCENARIOS

Depending on the tasks or activities involved in a BPX initiative, there may be many ways of transforming business processes (see Figure 6.1). Most of the tasks presented in Figure 6.1 can also be considered a single unit of BPX initiative in their own right. However, practitioners usually consider a combination of these activities in transforming their organizational or enterprise-level business processes.

BUSINESS PROCESS DIGITIZATION

Prior to embarking on a BPX initiative (whether for internal enterprise partners or external customers or partners), it is essential for practitioners, business units, and IT alike to explore the benefits of BPX. Most organizations evaluate the benefits of BPX strategically in terms of ROI and total cost of ownership (TCO). Many senior executives have also discovered that the long-term cost savings, financial benefits, and opportunity cost must be factored into the analysis. But from a tactical standpoint, organizations still make decisions about transformation of business processes on a case-by-case basis.

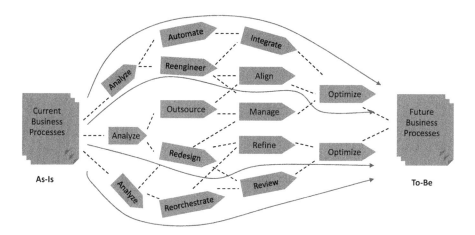

FIGURE 6.1   Many ways of transforming business processes.

The business case for pursuing BPX initiatives is part of the strategic planning for DT (see Chapter 1). The level of detail varies based on the significance of the respective business process to the enterprise.

Prioritization is based on the significance of the potential practical impact of BPX on the entire enterprise. Depending on the anticipated impact, appropriate approval from the business sponsors is obtained.

A business case for BPX is a complex and time-consuming. Depending on whether the initiative is designed for internal or external customers, the level of effort in collecting relevant information to make or recommend business decisions may vary.

In order to capitalize on the factors that make a BPX feasible, most organizations focus on two questions: "how does the proposed BPX initiative improve the operational excellence of existing business processes?" and "how will the organization deliver the practical benefits of BPX initiatives?" Answers to these questions must address the challenges of customer satisfaction, competitive advantage, and changes in organizational culture. In both cases, the level of due diligence in serving internal and external customers is related to the time and effort directed in performing the following seven steps (also presented in Figure 6.2):

1. **Identifying the Need for Change**

   A preliminary assessment of business scenarios exposes how current business functions operate, and subsequently allows practitioners to identify the real reasons for the proposed change. For many organizations, involves incubating ideas for change and conceptualizing the change. For others, this step may involve only a vision or mission statement. Whatever the case, this step explores the basic reasons for change and documents the expectations of business users in pursuing the change. This step also helps initiate a collaborative engagement between business and IT and formalizes these units' intention of working together as partners.

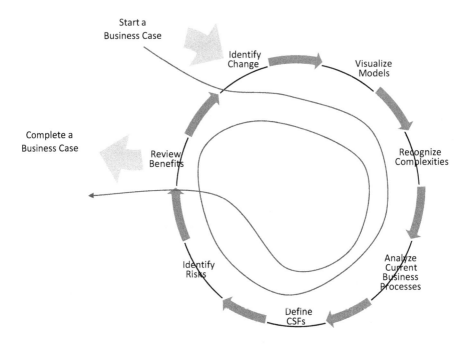

FIGURE 6.2   Common steps in making a business case for BPX.

2. **Visualizing Models of Current Business Functionality and their Usage**
      Substantiating the case for change can be aided by preparing visual mod-
   els of relevant business processes. Many organizations begin with simple
   diagrams that depict existing or anticipated process flows and how a typical
   business function operates. While in the past practitioners used data flow
   diagrams or business context diagrams, today most create business use case
   diagrams to represent the usage(s) of a business function. A visual model
   allows business and IT decision makers to determine the impact of change
   on current business operations. From a business perspective, a visual model
   presents the opportunity to capitalize on business domain knowledge associated with a business process. From a technical perspective, business process modeling may leverage the concepts of Model Driven Architecture
   (MDA) and encapsulate platform-independent models (PIMs).
3. **Recognizing Challenges**
      While performing the previous two steps, challenges are inevitable in
   transforming business processes. The business case must acknowledge
   these issues. This step reveals the opportunity for automation, reengineering, or outsourcing business processes. It also allows practitioners to estimate the level of effort required to successfully deploy a BPX initiative.
   Furthermore, this step provides a high-level view of the people-, process-,
   and technology-related needs that are necessary for transformation and that
   are further explored in the next step.

4. **Analyzing Current Business Processes and Business Contexts**

It is imperative to understand current business processes and the context they create for specific functional areas or operations. A clear understanding of existing processes can help practitioners determine which cost-benefit business process changes may result. While this step is intended for initial due diligence, in enterprise-level initiatives, it also identifies the components or business services associated with business processes and explores their interfaces and dependencies with the other business processes or focus area-related initiatives. Many organizations consider preparing both a conceptual business domain model as well as use case models when adopting a use case-driven approach.

5. **Defining critical success factors**

It is essential for the initiative teams as well as financial sponsors to recognize the factors that affect the successful implementation of a BPX initiative. This step also manages senior executives' expectations during a BPX initiative. Stakeholders are interviewed and observed, and their understanding of what will make or break the initiative is documented. A list of prioritized success factors is compiled and then monitored throughout the life cycle of the initiative. This step also enables recommending the change or modification of priorities for an initiative based on associated CSFs. Financial sponsors usually consider these and identified risks to determine their comfort level in pursuing the appropriate BPX initiative. CSFs and risks directly impact the outcome of business case development.

6. **Identifying Risks and Preparing Risk Management Plans**

As mentioned, CSFs are identified from a sponsor's point of view. Identifying risks and associated mitigation plans provides practitioners with an understanding of what a BPX initiative entails. Embarking on a BPX initiative can pose threats to the operational excellence (i.e., improved productivity and performance) of current business functions. Threats may concern an organization's available resources, domain knowledge, or simply their technical know-how to perform the tasks involved in the BPX initiative. As a result, it is important to identify and document potential risks as well as how the initiative team plans to mitigate them in a business case.

7. **Reviewing Viable Benefits and Limitations**

This step is a vital element of preparing a business case for any BPX initiative. Reviewing significant benefits and terms of financial-, productivity-, and performance-related gains that a BPX initiative can deliver are documented. This step usually answers the questions that arise for various stakeholders. For a COO, this step may reveal how many current business processes can be outsourced, which can result in significant benefits. For a CFO in the same situation, this step can indicate the savings that the outsourcing initiative delivers. Similarly, for a CEO, this step indicates whether it is worthwhile to make a long-term commitment to the BPO initiative.

These steps are customized to fit the specific needs of an organization. From a planning perspective, in addition to the above-mentioned steps, a business case must address (1) how the initiative team will keep sponsors informed at all times regarding the progress of the BPX initiative; (2) how the initiative relates to other ongoing initiatives in the enterprise; and (3) how the initiative will be managed by an IT governance board or steering committee.

Consider addressing the following four specific activities for the business case:

- **Assessment** (including industry trends) of current business processes and identification of why the organization needs BPX. For external customers, the study of industry trends is an important aspect of establishing a convincing case to make changes in organizational culture and business performance improvement.
- **Common Risks or Threats** that can jeopardize the well-being of the organization, including issues related to time-to-market, competitive advantage, or must-have levels of customer satisfaction. Once the related risks are identified, it is important to consider the root causes of the risks.
- **Opportunity** that a BPX initiative creates for an organization in delivering better solutions or services to customers. This area may emphasize optimizing performance, ease of monitoring progress in the delivery of business value, and improving productivity of employees.
- **Costs and Benefits** are key factors for many C-level executives and must be presented clearly to justify the business case. In many instances, the hidden costs of BPX initiatives aren't revealed until it's too late. In today's economy, it's wise to make a case for incremental funding during multiple stages. This allows executives to review the initiative's progress and make informed decisions about whether to continue further funding.

HOLISTIC APPROACH TO BUSINESS PROCESS TRANSFORMATION

BPX initiatives vary in their nature or complexity. They are not interchangeable. Digitization of business processes leads to:

- better quality of services or solutions;
- improved levels of performance, efficiency, and effectiveness; and
- maximization of customer satisfaction or fulfillment.

Current industry trends and best practices also provide input in a BPX effort. The road map includes various steps, milestones, and deliverables to make BPX initiatives successful.

Once the initiative is underway, it is important to measure, monitor, and manage the initiative to maintain sufficient progress continuously and to ensure that the progress made meets the criteria for further funding. Subsequently, it is important to conduct lessons-learned sessions to capture and share suggestions from current experience for use in future initiatives. After carrying out several BPX initiatives, many organizations recycle lessons learned in building their knowledge capital or in ensuring knowledge transfer to their customers or business partners. In helping

FIGURE 6.3 Formalizing a holistic approach for BPX initiatives.

organizations prepare for BPX initiatives, a holistic approach that allows practitioners to formalize their BPX initiatives is most important. Figure 6.3 presents a basic outline of this.

THE PRINCIPLES OF DIGITIZING BUSINESS PROCESSES

Depending on whether the BPX initiative is intended for internal or external customers, strategic principles may differ to some extent. For internal customers, the impetus is creating the capability to deliver, rather than financial sustainability or the stability of the organization. For external customers, the value proposition involves both functional capability and financial stability.

Many organizations undergoing or considering a BPX initiative are not necessarily well positioned to carry out the associated activities on their own. In most cases, these organizations weigh a number of viable options depending on affordability; the level of interest in pursuing business process change; and the willingness to manage risks, time, and schedule. In general, these options range from formalizing a partnership with an industry leader in the field of BPX or merging with or acquiring an organization with the capability to perform BPX activities. Several leading solution or service providers deliver BPX solutions. As a result, organizations with no prior experience in BPX may find it extremely difficult to enter the market at this juncture.

For the organizations that do deliver BPX solutions on their own or through partnerships with other industry leaders, establishing strategic principles for BPX initiatives usually involves four basic steps:

1. **Proposing a Transformation**

    This step includes the activities involved in making a business case for BPX, as described previously. Most teams working on these BPX initiatives consider four important elements before pursuing a BPX initiative:
    - Justification for the Proposal – a clearly defined set of objectives in considering a BPX initiative and the measurable value to be generated by deployment.
    - Governance of the initiative – well-defined roles, responsibilities, and accountabilities of all parties involved.
    - Making the entire enterprise cognizant of the risks and issues involved.
    - Institutionalizing the metrics to be monitored during the initiative – making the organization responsible for its progress in achieving the desired objectives of the initiative.

2. **Managing the Digitization of Business Processes**

This step involves charting a road map that defines how targeted business processes relate to business impact and how the initiative team can achieve the desired goals or improvements successfully. For many organizations involved in BPO initiatives, this step establishes strategic principles for evaluating and assessing, and also allows the opportunity to select outsourcing organizations, formalize partnerships, and manage expectations in the relationship.

3. **Procedures or Protocols**

This step creates a set of procedures or protocols that define how each initiative should utilize people, process, and technology as part of enterprise governance principles. It also outlines how an initiative team or the enterprise in general plans to overcome any barriers it may encounter during the initiative. In most cases, these barriers are identified as resistance due to resource conflicts, a mismatch of accountabilities or responsibilities, lack of incentives, or simply the unwillingness to comply with organizational culture changes. A governance board or steering committee, under the guidance of an executive, enforces compliance, handles conflicting priorities or accountability issues, and aligns the direction of the initiative with the set goals of the initiative.

4. **Perform the Activities**

Various best practices and lessons learned are published and accepted throughout the industry. Each initiative requires certain guidelines and a set of established frameworks specific to its needs. This step usually describes how the initiative team plans to perform the activities related to a BPX initiative. In a BPA initiative, for example, this step clarifies how business and IT organizations will collaborate, at what level business domain experts will be involved and interviewed, and in how much detail interviews will be documented. This step also identifies known risks and concerns, and prescribes ways of managing such them while performing relevant transformation activities.

Maintaining Transformation

A set of metrics are usually defined to capture, measure, monitor, and maintain the progress of a BPX initiative. This step is primarily intended to establish standards to be followed in managing expectations of stakeholders and customers. In most cases, the initiative teams are responsible for managing the differing expectations of multiple sponsors and therefore are liable to follow conflicting models of the transformation initiative. In some cases, the initiative may suffer from inconsistent guidance of executive sponsors and require multiple assessment or review sessions. To prevent differing models from dictating the transformation, this step lays out a consistent charter for maintaining the transformation initiative. For many organizations, a governance board or steering committee offers a set of guidelines to define various reviews, milestones, inspections, and walkthroughs to be conducted during the initiative in order to maintain consistent progress.

MONITORING PROGRESS

From recent studies, it is evident that many organizations today are involved in some form of BPX. A common observation from most of these studies is that organizations with consistent ways of measuring and monitoring progress have demonstrated a better rate of success with BPX initiatives. It is important to monitor progress of a BPX initiative from its inception to: (1) secure continued funding, (2) assess the organization's capabilities, (3) determine whether appropriate resources are assigned to the initiative, and (4) ensure the ability to deliver results on time and within budget. So now the question becomes, "How do we monitor the progress of BPX initiatives?"

The following steps are useful in monitoring the progress of a BPX initiative:

- Define performance and compliance metrics that gauge the progress of the initiative. These metrics must be well defined and accepted by stakeholders, as well as other parties involved in the initiative. For example, the availability of the right expertise, tools, and technology are questions of resource utilization – which fall into the category of performance metrics – and must be supported by stakeholders and team leaders.
- Identify deliverables, milestones, and checkpoints. Like other IT initiatives, BPX initiatives must be controlled and managed by identifying specific deliverables, milestones, and checkpoints. These decision points help executives monitor progress and subsequent funding prospects.
- Define and enculturate the elements to be measured and how the progress of the initiative will be monitored throughout the organization. This eliminates political barriers and forges relationships among multiple teams or ongoing initiatives.
- Analyze and assess the data collected to measure the progress and exhibit the use of metrics. While collecting metrics data requires time, effort, and the commitment of the initiative team, monitoring does not stop after data has been collected. In order to leverage the value of metrics, the data collected must be analyzed and assessed. Resources must be evaluated based on their performance as exhibited in the metrics.

If the metrics reveal a threat to the health of the initiative, take corrective measures to set progress in the right direction. In many cases, organizations negotiate service-level agreements (SLAs) or trading-partner agreements (TPAs) to outline corrective measures; in some cases, corrective measures involve forfeiture of executives' bonuses or reward points for service providers, partners, or outsourcing vendors.

One approach to monitor the progress of enterprise-level initiatives is active matrix modeling [1]. Initially, this is to manage EA deployments, but the same concept is equally effective and applicable in managing recent BPX initiatives. Active matrix modeling allows practitioners to develop "what if" scenarios in the event of changes in IT risk factors or business driver priorities. Using active matrix models, practitioners can prioritize various activities that must be performed, by weighing the risks and the availability of resources or expertise for a BPX initiative. Active matrix models can also be used in monitoring the progress of all activities of any

BPX initiative throughout its life cycle. Another approach used to monitor the progress of BPM initiatives borrows from the concept of business activity monitoring. But this provides only limited oversight of the activities in most BPX initiatives.

EVALUATING INDUSTRY TRENDS

A great deal of research indicates that a lack of understanding business processes or their inefficiencies severely undermines cost savings, customer satisfaction, and employee productivity [2]. In some cases, business process inefficiencies are the result of solutions or services that are delivered late, or are the byproduct of a business' slow response to a customer request. In others, services fail to fulfill customer needs because of the manual nature of the business processes involved. Thus, many IT industry leaders are getting involved in marketing their BPX solution and service offerings, and product vendors are soliciting suites of products designed to solve BPX-related problems. It also important to consider a comprehensive evaluation of current and desired business capabilities in order to master BPX effectively.

As organizations learn more about BPX initiatives, they should share their experience with the rest of the community. As organizations evaluate industry trends, the following four focus areas are of primary interest:

CAPABILITY ASSESSMENT AND DEVELOPMENT

Many industry standards and best practices are evolving, which indicates the significant need for developing capabilities to resolve BPX challenges. Trends in this area include efficient resource utilization (people, processes, and technology) in legacy modernization and service orientation, as well as offshore development. Many organizations are maximizing their reuse of solutions from other organizations, particularly those dealing with COTS-based packaged applications. Many organizations are also considering mergers and acquisitions to strengthen their capabilities through consolidation.

ORGANIZATIONAL CHANGE

This is a common phenomenon in the changing business environment today that affects the efficiency and accuracy of current business processes. Industry trends in evolving organizational change include (1) engaging business partners and senior executives from the earliest stages of the initiative; (2) developing a sense of ownership and accountability at all levels; and (3) creating a collaborative environment for individuals, teams, and the enterprise during all stages of the transformation.

GOVERNANCE AND MANAGEMENT

Most organizations recognize this area as vital to the successful deployment of BPX initiatives. Common industry trends in this area involve:

- running transformation initiatives within a portfolio of programs with finite goals, objectives, or results intended;

- implementing iterative, incremental phases to capitalize on lessons learned;
- rolling out best practices incorporated from the industry and from internal organizations;
- promoting accountabilities, responsibilities, and ownership with appropriate rewards; and
- ensuring a balanced approach to measuring and monitoring the progress of BPX initiatives.

COMPETITION

This is one of the most critical areas for organizations pursuing BPX initiatives with external customers. Given the openness of the internet, it's not difficult to gather information about organizations involved in BPX initiatives. A organization can effectively use this readily available information to change business models via BPX initiatives if it (1) employs the right expertise (or people), (2) implements the right process, and (3) acquires the right set of technologies that its competitors don't share.

From a business perspective, evaluating industry trends offers practitioners a way to measure the current state of BPX in the industry. It allows them to make informed decisions in choosing an outsourcing partner based on past performance in similar initiatives, such as automating existing business processes that do not mesh with the extended enterprise (an enterprise that connects internal and external business processes or functionalities) or retiring redundant or nonfunctional business processes.

PREPARING FOR PROCESS TRANSFORMATION

Consider both a top-down and a bottom-up approach when beginning a BPX initiative. In a top-down approach, organizations establish BPX principles that meet their strategic goals and vision. Primarily, these principles institutionalize process excellence across the enterprise by formalizing a set of common standards, models, and notations to be adopted across the board.

A bottom-up approach, however, begins at the organizational or (business) functional unit level and passes through approval and refinement processes to become a corporate standard. With either approach, the baseline is the same: it involves people, process, and technology to get started. Using this baseline, practitioners must answer the following questions to determine their organization's readiness for a BPX initiative:

- Who must be involved (i.e., people)?
- When and how do they need to be involved (i.e., people and time)?
- What are the activities that must be performed (i.e., process)?
- How will these activities be performed (i.e., process)?
- Which existing technologies or environments must be considered (i.e., technology)?
- Where and when will all these activities be performed (process, organization, and time)?

This list does not encompass all questions that practitioners may have as they begin an initiative. For some, though, answering these questions helps practitioners get started with organizational readiness. For others, however, readying the organization for a BPX initiative requires further probing into the awareness of an enterprise's capabilities as well as its vision and objectives.

To promote awareness of organizational readiness, practitioners may want to ask the following short list of questions:

What are the business objectives or goals of your organization? From the perspective of a top-down (i.e., a long-term or strategic) approach, this question may relate to prospects of revenue growth, profitability, new customer intimacy, or productivity increases. From a bottom-up (i.e., short-term or tactical) approach, this question may address immediate cost savings or productivity gains.

What are the strengths and weaknesses of your organization? In which business functions or process areas does your organization excel and in which does it fall short? These questions provide an inventory of core capabilities, domain expertise, or technology experience. These questions also expose a lack of experience or expertise within the organization.

Which business processes are critical to achieve your business objectives and which ones are peripheral? This question helps practitioners prioritize their existing or desired business processes and reallocate their resources to optimize efficiency and productivity.

What are the most common barriers or resistance your organization encounters in making a change to how it does business? This question helps practitioners identify risks associated with pursuing BPX initiatives. It also enables them visualize the interactions, interfaces, and dependencies of the BPX initiative on other ongoing initiatives in the organization.

Finally, what are senior executives' and the entire organization's expectations of the BPX initiative? This question leads practitioners to set appropriate expectations and define and track a set of metrics (such as those relating to productivity increase or revenue growth).

Organizations pursue process improvement programs – such as the Capability Maturity Model Integration (CMMI) from the Software Engineering Institute (SEI) at Carnegie Mellon – internally to achieve capability or maturity levels. Some organizations leverage other best practices such as Lean and Six Sigma to improve the quality of products and services and to reduce associated risks.

Furthermore, these process improvement programs are directly connected to corporate objectives and goals such as revenue growth, productivity increases, higher efficiency, and higher customer satisfaction. Overall, these process improvement programs add significant value to the baseline mentioned previously by providing models, standards, methodologies, and guidelines to get practitioners started.

As shown in Figure 6.4, the most commonly observed steps of a road map include (1) preparing the road map, (2) enculturating it into the IT organization, (3) rolling it out to explore business challenges (within an associated business functional unit or across the enterprise), and (4) obtaining buy-in from various stakeholders. As the road map evolves, lessons learned from BPX initiatives are captured to prepare the organization for future initiatives.

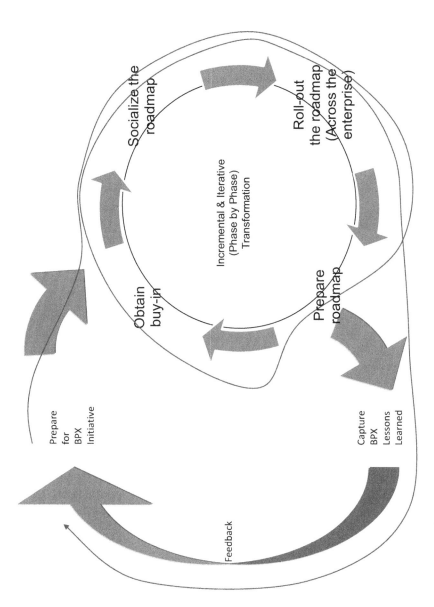

FIGURE 6.4   Building a road map for incremental and iterative BPX initiatives.

This BPX road map continues to improve iteratively. Figure 6.5 presents its various stages, as well as each stage's objectives, steps, and the anticipated level of effort. In preparing this road map, two different approaches are considered: one relates to component-based system integration methodology; the other promotes MDA concepts that originate from the Object Management Group (OMG). This road map is applicable for many EA, portal, and web services deployment initiatives.

From the component-based system integration perspective, the proposed road map constitutes four distinct phases: discovery, gap analysis, mediation plan, and solution or service integration. The following are the primary objectives of these phases:

- Discovery – investigate strategic and tactical business drivers, needs, and organizational or corporate values to make the business case for a BPX initiative.
- Gap analysis – study current business processes to determine the functions that have critical impact on the business and determine the scope of the BPX initiative.
- Mediation plan – recognize the risks, issues, challenges, and CSFs, along with the dependency and interaction of this initiative on others, so that all the associated challenges for the BPX initiative can be mitigated, optimized, or resolved.
- Solution or service integration – determine the viability of build, buy, or outsource options and implement the activities leading to successful integration of business processes under transformation. Subsequently, formal customer acceptance is expected for the transition of existing business processes to new processes.

The road map in Figure 6.5 incorporates three phases in concurrence with the models prescribed by the OMG. These three phases are business process modeling, transformation, and deployment.

- **Business Process Modeling**

    Create PIMs and technology-independent models for current business processes. Meanwhile, identify significant business processes, define the requirements for transformation, and refine the road map based on identified prioritized processes of the initiative.
- **Transformation**

    Develop and monitor various activities using transformation metrics that can track contractual agreements such SLAs and TPAs, dependencies with other ongoing initiatives, and plans for managing risks. This phase facilitates building platform-specific models for functions that are related to business processes considered in the BPX initiative.
- **Deployment**

    Integrate, manage, and maintain implementation-related decision-making activities by employing people, process, and technology imperatives.

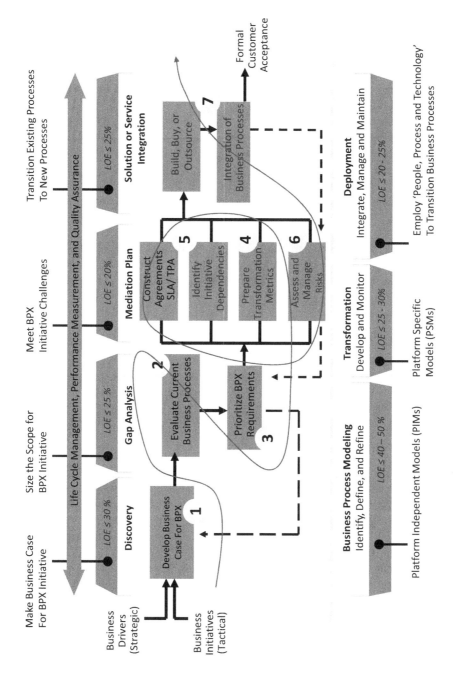

FIGURE 6.5 A road map for an iterative and incremental BPX initiative.

Building a road map for BPX initiatives involves the following seven steps:

1. Develop a business case for BPX to obtain approvals from financial sponsors and stakeholders.
2. Evaluate current business processes to determine their significance and impact on the organization.
3. Prioritize BPX requirements to validate the importance of processes in delivering business value, and plan milestones, schedules, and resource allocation.
4. Prepare transformation metrics for monitoring progress of the initiative and facilitate governance of the initiative.
5. Identify dependencies with other ongoing initiatives and formalize necessary agreements with the parties involved in the BPX initiative.
6. Assess and manage identified risks associated with the transformation initiative.
7. Make decisions to build, buy, or outsource and integrate resultant business processes.

These steps are performed iteratively and incrementally to achieve optimum results. For both internal and external BPX initiatives, a road map can facilitate establishing mutually beneficial relationship between business and IT in all aspects of customers' confidence, intimacy, and level of satisfaction.

BPX initiatives differ in terms of the activities involved and the level of effort needed. For example, a simple organizational reorchestration may not be complex from process viewpoint. However, in a situation in which a business process requires analysis, automation, reengineering, integration, and finally optimization there is a need for rigorous due diligence. Determination of the appropriate extent of due diligence required for the initiatives has to be made on a case by case basis.

SHARING THE EXPERIENCES OF BPX

Successfully implementing BPX initiatives includes sharing practical experience within the organization or transferring relevant knowledge across the enterprise. Although BPX initiatives usually vary in nature, they share commonalities. For example, establishing the evaluation criteria for vendor or partner selection is similar for BPM, BPR, BPA, BPI, or BPO initiatives. Similarly, tools and technology selection for certain BPX initiatives are alike.

An important aspect of knowledge sharing in a BPX initiative is that of understanding existing business processes. For example, in order to establish and implement the strategy for automating disconnected and manual business processes, a team must rely on domain experts' knowledge. Similarly, to streamline a set of business processes inherited from mergers and acquisitions requires collaboration and knowledge sharing among the teams involved.

Many organizations formalize a practice for utilizing organizational or corporate repositories to share BPX-related experience and knowledge between various teams. In some organizations, this approach has been a part of the corporate reuse strategy.

For others, a liaison team is put in place to disseminate information related to BPX across the enterprise.

In the case of a national retail and supply chain industry leader, for example, knowledge sharing has become an essential part of successful implementation of BPX. In the past, the organization had multiple inventory management systems and two completely different order entry systems. Over the years, the organization acquired these systems through mergers and acquisitions. Furthermore, these inventory management and order entry systems did not connect with the financial or transport management systems standardized by the organization. Some of those who operated the systems had used them for so many years that they didn't want change, either.

In order to reengineer, automate, and outsource the associated business processes, the organization formed a team that

- documented the existing business processes,
- recommended training and education for employees involved with the current systems,
- facilitated collaboration between teams to develop one efficient inventory management system and one order entry system, and
- promoted knowledge sharing by rewarding high performers.

Practitioners in any organization can benefit from knowledge sharing in their BPX initiatives. For the retail organization, knowledge sharing has been promoted to roll out various BPX initiatives across the enterprise.

COMMERCIAL VENDORS AND TOOLS

Many IT industry leaders are either actively involved in pursuing BPX initiatives for their own enterprises or are facilitating them for other organizations. Organizations pursuing BPX initiatives for their own enterprises usually survey commercial vendors, tools, and techniques that help support their BPX initiatives. Major questions in this area concern how to find services or solutions for BPX initiatives, including:

- How can an organization select external partners or vendors to support its internal BPX initiatives?
- Are any tools commercially available to use in managing or supporting BPX initiatives?
- How can these tools help practitioners to succeed in their BPX initiatives?

A number of software vendors have focused on building BPX solutions or tools that are based on their existing products or solution sets. Other vendors focus primarily on BPX solutions or services. Most of these can be grouped into four categories:

- Enterprise application integration or EAI-related vendors. These vendors have established their presence in facilitating application development and integration solutions that consolidate multiple applications encompassing primary business processes of an enterprise. BEA, Sun, Microsoft, and IBM are known for their application platforms; TIBCO, webMethods, and SeeBeyond are known for their application integration and middleware solutions; and SAP, Oracle, and Siebel Systems are known for their enterprise application solutions.

- Packaged application vendors. These vendors – which include Documentum, Pegasystems, FileNet, and Intalio – are working toward a set of integrated solutions that can be deployed and fit into other enterprise solutions with little or no customization.
- BPX service providers. A large number of solution or service providers as well as system integrators fall into this category. These vendors – including McKinsey, Booz Allen Hamilton, Accenture, and BearingPoint – provide either a set of tools or specific solutions related to BPX initiatives. They are service providers that help other organizations formulate BPX initiative strategies. Organizations such as Ultimus and MegaStorm Systems offer Microsoft-centric solutions.
- Pure-play BPX-related product vendors. This group of vendors – including Lombardi Software, Fuego, and Savvion – focuses primarily on BPX-related software products. They offer software solutions that are built to manage process change from scratch. Most of these products are quite effective and deliver a wide range of capabilities.

As practitioners survey the landscape for appropriate commercial tools, techniques, or solution partners, we recommend considering the following criteria, among other specific needs:

Ease of use, integration, and the portability of solutions or software tools and techniques allow practitioners to get started with fewer resources, less time expended, and less initial investment of effort.

Ease of deployment and flexibility to accommodate change of business needs allow practitioners to roll out BPX solutions over time and across the enterprise with less customization and leave the initiative team less concerned with meeting business goals and objectives.

The ability to promote collaboration and risk aversion among teams is essential to eliminating risks to organizational culture and minimizing political barriers.

Scalability is also essential to rapid iterative and incremental implementations so that BPX initiatives can be rolled out over multiple phases and funding approval can be obtained in a timely manner.

Additionally, practitioners may wish to consider organizations that provide tools associated with business process modeling and analysis along with the above-mentioned features and capabilities.

DISCUSSION TOPICS

1. What is the importance of BPX within the overall effort of DT in an organization? Why does BPX deserve specific discussion?
2. What are the different types of BPX activities that are undertaken when an organization transforms? Describe with examples.
3. What are some of the ways of transforming business processes?
4. How would you justify/make a business case for BPX?
5. What are the key principles of digitizing business processes?
6. What are collaborative business processes? What is their significance in BPX?
7. Create a road map for BPX within an organization undergoing DT.

NOTES

1 Hazra, T. "Transforming Your Business Processes Effectively." *Cutter Executive Report* Posted March 31, 2005 in Business Technology & Digital Transformation Strategies.
2 Hazra, T. K. "Empowering a Collaborative Enterprise Architecture." *Cutter Consortium Enterprise Architecture Executive Report*, Vol. 7, No. 6, 2004.
3 Based on Logan, J. "Corporate Cholesterol: Business Process Inefficiencies Clog Corporate Arteries." *Business Integration Journal*, Vol. 7, No. 1, 9 February 2005.

7 Digital Transformation and Business Agility

SUMMARY

Agility and collaboration are the two hallmarks of a successful Digital Transformation (DT) of a business. Both these characteristics are crucial in providing customer value. Therefore, the concept of "Agile Business" is discussed in this chapter with the aim of enhancing customer value. The value proposition of DT is based on alignment of organizational initiatives with desired outcomes. The end-result of such an alignment is the ability of the organization to take rapid and more accurate decisions. This enhancement of decision-making is described as "Agility." Composite Agile Method and Strategy (CAMS) has been discussed in the past and so too a corresponding Big Data Framework for Agile Business (BDFAB). These frameworks are referenced here as means to provide ongoing Agility and knowledge synchronization between users and systems.

AGILITY IN DIGITAL BUSINESS

AGILE AS A BUSINESS VALUE

An "Agile" organization has rapid response capabilities to internal and external stimuli. The rapidity of response is based on availability of knowledge and insights for decision-makers and the frontline staff of the organization. Customer value is also enhanced by having a unified, 360° view of the customer without multiple copies of data stored in multiple places. Value for customers is based on providing a unified view of the organization to them. This "Value Stream Mapping" enables a product or service to reach a customer in a unified manner. Digital business enables such an Agile functioning of business by bringing together data science and Enterprise Architecture (EA).

Agile can mean different things to different people. For a developer, Agile is a method to produce a solution – for example, Scrum and XP. For an architect, it is the necessary opportunity for business value through people, processes, and technologies. For a product manager, Agile is a mechanism to develop products and services that enable growth in market share. For a regulator, Agility can be used in real-time transaction reporting for compliance. For business leaders, however, Agile holds the promise of a faster and more accurate response to a changing business situation – and digitization is a means to achieve that.

Business Agility handles change. The business response to an external or internal stimulus depends on how Agile the organization is. The time gap between the change and the organization's response can be considered the "sensitivity" of the organization.[1] The shorter the time gap to respond, the higher the sensitivity. Reducing the transactional gap and increasing the sensitivity is the purpose of any initiative in an organization. Digital Transformation (DT) focuses on aligning initiatives with outcomes and also has the eventual goal of enhancing the Agility of the organization.

Agile is thus the eventual business value, with Big Data adoption the means to achieving that. Agile is also a method to produce Big Data solutions and is described both as a "culture" and "mindset."[2] Thus, the keyword "Agile" has a lot to offer to the discussion on DT and vice versa.

DT brings about new business processes, changes interactions with customers, and demands continuous improvement – all of which are based on organizational Agility.

Agility in the solutions development space enhances product delivery, whereas it enhances operational value in the business space. Changes to the business space – primarily through business processes – require corresponding changes in the solutions development. Agile projects take up the responsibility of developing solutions that enhance the capabilities of the organization to meet business goals.

Thus, the creation of capabilities for the new digital business benefits immensely from Agile techniques. "Scrum"[3] is one of the most popular Agile approaches in the solutions development space; the challenges of scalability in Scrum are handled by SAFe.[4] With the increasing sourcing of high volume, high velocity data coming into the organization, there is further need for a framework that can provide guidance and control in digitizing the business. One example is the Big Data Framework for Agile Business (BDFAB).[5] The starting point for a BDFAB is an Agile mindset. This deals with the psyche of the decision makers. For example, a decentralized, fine granular decision-making process dilutes the power of hierarchical decision-making. This can be unsettling for some users. Similarly, the collaborative and cross-functional nature of Agile teams can also come as a surprise to some business stakeholders.

A holistic approach is possible with a team that is Agile because one characteristic of such a team is cross-functionality. With this, business stakeholders realize they are expected to actively participate in the DT process and in the development of corresponding new solutions. These business stakeholders may discover they are "too busy" running the business to participate on a daily basis in the prioritization and decision-making process. Yet, when quizzed they say they are "totally committed" to Agile. These contradictions are anticipated in DT using Agile principles; skilled adoption champions have to deal with these challenges as highlighted in Figure 7.1.

Business Agility can be understood as a time measure of changes to the operating environment of the business and the time it takes for the organization to respond to the change. An Agile organization is able to quickly respond to a change in the environment; however, as the rate of change of stimuli increases, there is a corresponding challenge to business Agility. An interesting aspect of enterprise Agility is the correlation it has with a Lean organization.[6] Being Lean is a precursor to

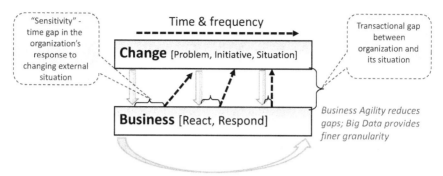

Speed of response is a measure of granularity;
Big Data enables finer granularity of inputs and outputs resulting in an Agile response.
[Additional factors include organizational structure, legal compliance,
technology sophistication, change anticipation and business
collaboration)

FIGURE 7.1 Big Data facilitates organizational Agility by ensuring a very small gap between the organization and the situation impacting it, to enable faster and more accurate decision-making.

becoming Agile – in fact, Leanness and Agility are intricately tied together. Changes to business requirements are considered inevitable and, therefore, welcomed in an Agile organization. Agile principles and methods enable solution providers to cope with changing business requirements.

Agile is a holistic and comprehensive enterprise-wide approach that brings together tools, methods, processes, standards, frameworks, and costs across multiple tiers of an organization, resulting in what is called a "composite approach." This focuses not only on the practices of Agile that are commonly understood as daily standups and user stories, but also on best practices, phases, and deliverables from the planned family of methods. Business Agility stands to benefit from understanding how to apply an Agile culture value system across all organizational functions.

Thus, despite the popularity of Agile in the software development arena, enough care needs to be exercised when it is applied across an enterprise. Consideration needs to be given to the role of Agility in the following examples:

- **Production Systems** – mission critical production systems need to be supported and kept operational. Ongoing iterative releases of a solution can be potentially risky to the operation. Therefore, a balance between the continuity of existing services and introduction of new services needs to be managed.
- **Supported Users** – software releases impact users. Any changes affect one or more users and they need to be supported. For example, if a business process used by a million customers and thousands of branches in a bank has to change to incorporate analytics, then the users of that process need to be trained to successfully implement the change. This support function can take time and effort and it needs to be planned from the outset.

- **Regulatory** – within complex regulatory environments like health, aviation, and financial services, regulatory approvals are a key compliance requirement. Obtaining these approvals can take time to implement and adopt. Therefore, iterative solutions releases may have to be grouped together in a major release that is compliant with regulatory needs.
- **Customer Understanding** – customers often seek stability so they can learn to use the service. Multiple release cycles by vendors are often resisted and need to be planned to keep customer confidence high.
- **Migration** – Big Data adoption requires data and process migrations. For example, the use of NoSQL databases in the background require movement and/or integration of unstructured data with existing enterprise systems. This migration also requires the use of APIs provided by tool and database vendors.
- **Legal** – change often means revisions or entirely new contracts and agreements. From additional vendor services through to customer onboarding, Agility is required but is tempered against necessary legal obligations.
- **Risk Management** – Agility is a counterpart to risk. Every change has an associated risk. The more changes made, the greater the risks and the greater the chance of realization. Conversely, not changing has its own risks. It is the balance of risk management against Agility that is important.
- **Freeze Periods** – whether it is for compliance like the Sarbanes–Oxley Act, audit, or investigations, systems and business operations are subject to freeze-periods where changes cannot be made. These are part of the business environment and need to be accommodated within Agile businesses.
- **Cost** – ongoing iterative software development has costs associated with it. These include those of release cycles, integration with existing data, regulatory compliance, and data migration. These costs need to be considered within Agile.

ADVANTAGES OF AGILITY AND BIG DATA FOR A DIGITAL BUSINESS

Enterprise-wide Agility implies small, cross-functional teams involving customers, users, and producers (developers) of solutions working in short, sharp iterations producing visible results. Once overall deliverables are achieved by the team, it is dismantled and the members revert to a common pool of resources. A composite approach to Agile makes use of a community of practices and knowledge sharing within the organization. Therefore, while self-organizing small, Agile teams implement features in a solution, the larger pool of talent in the organization is nurtured and developed. This occurs through upskilling and socializing team members, and is vital for development of a Big Data skill set within an organization.

Agile is thus a socio-cultural phenomenon across an organization that includes Agile methods, Agile style of working and applying Agility across the organizational space. The advantage of using Agility is that it creates business value rather than software solutions and packages.

ENVISIONING AN AGILE ORGANIZATION

What makes an organization Agile? And what does one look like? First and foremost, an Agile business has an Agile vision that aligns with its digital strategy (or is a part of the digital strategy) and continues to evolve in response to changes in the business environment. Within Agility, fluidity in the vision of an Agile organization is essential. This means that while the vision and mission of an organization is meant to provide direction and guidance for its growth, it is not unchangeable. Figure 7.2 envisions such an Agile organization.

At its core, an Agile organization anticipates, detects, and responds efficiently and effectively to change, both external and internal. This is a collaborative, highly interconnected, and communicative organization that is in sync with the ecosystem (comprising industry, government, and society) it exists in. Providing Agile business value implies transitioning the organization from what it is right now (presumably slow-moving, inefficient, rigid, hierarchical, and disconnected with the environment in which it exists) to one that is well aligned and well connected with its customers and partners. Big Data used in a strategic manner offers significant opportunities to achieve this transformation and eventual business Agility. This is because Big Data analytics highly enhance an organization's ability to detect and respond to external and internal stimuli.

Precisely measuring the level of Agility of an organization, however, is not easy. An Agile organization is much more than the sum total of its individuals and their Agile practices. While "doing" Agile is easier to measure and justify, "being" Agile is "fuzzy" and not easily measurable. But it is being Agile that provides maximum value to all stakeholders. BDFAB works to create synergy between technology, method, people, and business to allow an organization to be Agile.

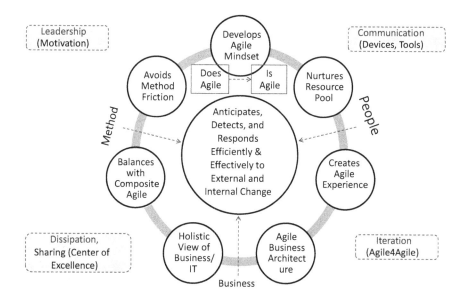

FIGURE 7.2 Envisioning an Agile organization.

Figure 7.2 summarizes some of the key ongoing characteristics of an Agile organization that are embedded in the psycho-sociology of its people, methods of work, and business decision-making. These are the characteristics that facilitate easier and smoother adoption of Big Data and that are, at the same time, provided added impetus from Big Data. An Agile organization:

- **Develops an Agile mindset** by welcoming change across all functions of the organization. This is the starting point for the business transformation process. The Agile mindset is one that is used to spot a problem to solve or an opportunity to grasp. Analyzing the problem (or opportunity) results in understanding business needs, proposing initiatives, and undertaking solutions development projects (including Big Data solutions). Agile becomes a mindset of the organization at all levels, covering needs, projects, alternatives, solutions, validations, deployment, and operational usage. In addition to key customer-centric processes, supporting business functions such as accounts, payroll, HR, and legal are also influenced by the Agile mindset, as they utilize Agile principles of collaboration, conversation, collocation, and visibility amongst others.
- **Nurtures a resource pool** by devoting considerable attention to individuals and their interactions. Agile is preserved, enhanced, and dispersed across the organization by managing and nurturing the Agile resource pool. This results in shared knowledge and experiences categorized into the areas of psychology, sociology, and culture. Cohesion within and amongst groups, understanding the natural resistance to change, helping individuals overcome their biases and phobias, and enabling trust and sharing (by reducing the internal and often wasteful competition and, instead, promoting collaboration) – all result in enhancing the capabilities of the organization's resource pool.
- **Creates an Agile experience** for customers, enabling their collaboration right from the inception of a product or service (e.g., an analytical service). In an Agile organization, there is maximum customer involvement in setting product or service directions. For example, the Net Promoter Score (NPS) can become an integral part of the decision-making process for new products and services. If customers are unlikely to recommend a product or service, then a major debriefing needs to be carried out to ascertain the root cause for potential rejection. Agile is not just confined to the boardroom; is implemented and visible across all levels of decision-making. When the customer-driven experience results in satisfied and supportive customers, it in turn also leads to the service staff of the organization feeling satisfied.
- **Implements an Agile Business Architecture** that enables and supports internal structural changes to facilitate business response to internal and external pressures. Technical (enterprise) architecture can sometimes be stuck in time. This may happen with the good intention of providing stability to the organization. But more often than not, this technologically slow-moving entity and its corresponding organizational structures reduce organizational Agility. Agile extricates an organization from the dungeons

of rigid hierarchy and endless planning and pushes it into the real world, where change is the impetus for every decision.[7]
- **Maintains a holistic view of business** rather than a "siloed," function-driven one. This is important for the EA. Agility as a culture results in a collaborative and communicative problem-solving approach within the projects of the organization. Due to its holistic nature, Agility also helps an organization deal with maintenance, operations, and infrastructure processes in line with desired business outcomes. These non-project activities provide as much contribution in establishing a holistic customer view as the project activities dealing with a solution.[8]
- **Balances with Composite Agile** by ensuring proper utilization of the existing assets of the organization. In non-Agile organizations, planning is the key to reducing risks associated with any change and its impact on the business. A risk-averse organization was once considered a stable organization. This stability was viewed as indicative of the ability of the organization to handle the impact of change. However, flexibility rather than rigid stability is the key to absorbing change.[9] For example, a flexible, flat, and cross-functional internal organizational structure can withstand the impact of government policy changes that result in the opening of a region to global markets, while a hierarchical and rigidly stable organization struggles to adapt. Changes to labor laws leading to shifts in relationships with trade unions is another example where the flexibility of an organizational structure can provide positive value in successively adapting to change. Needless to say, *balance* plays a crucial role in bringing together planned and pure Agile aspects of activities within an organization.[10]
- **Avoids method friction** by giving due attention to the many friction points within the organization.[11] These friction points arise on the project level due to multiple projects, and multiple methods within those (e.g., project management, IT governance, software development methods, and quality assurance), with each stakeholder focusing on their own roles and goals. The fundamental and philosophical differences between Agile and planned approaches add to these friction points. On the organizational level, there are numerous "business as usual" activities that follow their own processes and standards. For example, the architecture, infrastructure, operations, and maintenance disciplines have their standards that are potentially in conflict with project standards – mainly because the latter focuses on delivery of solutions instead of on maintaining stability and optimized operations.

In addition to the characteristics of Agile organizations, Figure 7.2 shows four defining activities of such organizations:

- **Leadership** plays a crucial role in motivating and sustaining change towards Agile. Agile business value is considered strategic and leadership helps maintain focus on that. Big Data is considered an enabler rather than an end-goal in itself, and leadership continues to direct the effort of the organization, keeping that in mind.

- **Communication** in its many different forms, channels, and frequencies is yet another cornerstone of an Agile organization. Big Data adoption needs continuous communication – it must almost become a routine part of every meeting, briefing, and organization-wide update.
- **Mindset** of such an organization is *iterative* and incremental, and therefore uses Agile even in Agile adoption. Whilst the strategy of an organization is clearly set, the way it is implemented changes with the business environment. This alignment with strategy while adopting the implementation is the mindset of an Agile organization.
- **Sharing** and diffusion of knowledge and experiences, typically through a Center of Excellence. Just as organizations have mentoring schemes and specialization support for project managers, so too, it must be with Agile and Big Data within the context of their respective business areas.

It's worth noting that the above characteristics of an Agile organization are fluid. Hard metrics seldom provide correct measures of business outcomes. These characteristics can vary depending on the type of business, size of the organization, and the industry it belongs to. For example, in banking, which is in the service sector, a holistic view of the business is based around business processes and their Agility. In a product-based organization, such as an auto manufacturer, a holistic view focuses on the inventory and supply chain processes. The level of Agility desired by the business can also dictate the level of granularity in its analytics. For example, a government organization, which is bureaucratic by nature, may not aim for fine granularity like a commercial bank might. Bureaucratic organizations, however, need to place special emphasis on avoiding method friction, while a Big Data-based technology organization (e.g., a vendor) focusing on providing Analytics-as-a-Service (AaaS) will have to ensure an Agile EA to facilitate changes to its business policies resulting from analytics.

FUNCTIONING AGILE BUSINESS WITH EMBEDDED BIG DATA ANALYTICS

HOLISTIC, FINE GRANULAR, AND SENSITIVE BUSINESS

Business Agility is less an activity or method and more a value system. This is also an indicator of holistic, fine granular, and sensitive business that capitalizes on the technical and analytical capabilities of Big Data. Composite Agile Method and Strategy (CAMS) plays an important role in balancing such business Agility. CAMS supports formal methods and frameworks (e.g., business methods, governance frameworks, and project management approaches) needed within the organization but also facilitates the application of pure Agile principles and practices in developing solutions.

Understanding the Agile touchpoints within these methods helps the organization reduce "methods friction." Incremental changes are made to the practice of these methods to ensure a balance between the formality of control and the flexibility of Agility. For example, a formal contract (deliverable) mandated by a governance framework is produced through negotiations, but the Agile value of customer collaboration and face-to-face communication is also carried out. Similarly, other elements of a method or framework, such as its roles, tasks, techniques, and practices are examined and adjusted to overcome method friction points.

People issues are considered paramount in producing Agile business value. Not only are individual workers affected when an organization shifts to overall Agility but so also are senior managers and decision makers, whose style of working can be affected by changes to the business methods and processes. Thus, the rate of transition of a business to Agility is continuously adjusted to ensure a high comfort level for people. Dynamicity in terms of skills, attitudes, and the knowledge of individuals is factored in as the organization adopts a composite Agile approach. Formal policies and Key Performance Indicators (KPIs) need to be tied in with risks and leadership to achieve balanced business Agility.

Figure 7.3 summarizes internal and external (dependent) areas for a functioning Agile business that capitalizes on Big Data business strategies to consider. These are grouped into two parts. Those factors that are directly under the control of the organization are shown inside the organizational boundary. The relatively bigger circles are dependent on external collaborations as well and are shown traversing organizational boundaries. Big Data and Agile together bring about fundamental changes to the business. The internal changes to an organization are as follows:

- **Business Policies** – this is forming new business actions and updating existing ones to incorporate Agile values. These business policies elevate the focus of Agility from project-based to organizational, strategic Agility.

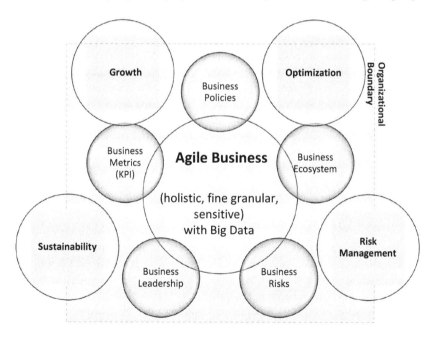

FIGURE 7.3 A functioning Agile business (holistic) capitalizing on Big Data strategies: internal and external impacts.

Business policies play an important role in enabling collaboration between partnering organizations. This is important for Big Data analytics based on wide-ranging data sources.

- **Business Ecosystem** – this considers the change brought about not only in the business with a shift to Agility, but also to the many partnering organizations and their relationships. Techniques such as SWOT and PESTLE analysis are very helpful in ascertaining the impact of collaborations and Agility on the business ecosystem and vice versa. These techniques are also a part of BDFAB as the digitizing business adopts Big Data.
- **Business Risks** – risks associated with changes in internal management structure as Agility is embraced; as well as changes to external relationships. These risks start emerging as soon as an organization makes attempts to inculcate Agile values and behaviors in its interactions – as compared with the original contract-based interactions and relationships.
- **Business Leadership** – this is affected and, in turn, affects Agile changes. Visionary Agile leadership changes the way in which an organization is structured, its culture, and the way in which it operates. Agile as a value system relies more on leadership and less on management. This, in turn, requires changes to the way in which management functions in an organization. Relinquishing control, facilitating sharing of tasks, and accepting informality in reporting are important changes brought about by leadership, not management. These same leadership qualities are required as Big Data is adopted by the organization, as the value derived from Big Data is achieving business Agility.
- **Business Metrics** – this comprises measures and indicators in terms of what constitutes success for an Agile business. KPIs change their focus as a business transforms to Agile – from being purely objective measures to including a certain amount of subjectivity in them. For example, an Agile business will not index employee reward structures merely to an objective measure of customer satisfaction; instead, business metrics for customer satisfaction will include subjective discussions and insights gained from interacting directly with the customer.

Figure 7.3 summarizes factors that are not directly under the control of the organization but are dependent on other external factors and that impact the business Agility of an organization.

- Growth opportunities for the business based on improving customer satisfaction/experience, development of innovative products and services, establishment of collaborations with vendors and business partners, and ensuring value in mergers and acquisitions.
- Optimization of business operations based on innovative problem solving, use of external tools and technologies, process modeling, reengineering and optimization, and establishing decentralizing decision-making through Big Data analytics.

- Risk associated with the business including security and privacy, compliance and documentation, and audits and traceability of transactions. Big Data technologies and analytics help ascertain these risks (both external and internal). However, Big Data adoption has its own risks that need to be handled, by using a formal framework like BDFAB when in undertaking adoption.
- Sustainability that intends to reduce a carbon footprint, enhances carbon metrics and measurement through analytics and used training, and coaching for developing positive user attitude. Successful incorporation of sustainable, environmental considerations within an Agile, holistic business requires collaboration and participation with internal and external entities.[12,13]

BIG DATA ENABLES AGILITY IN BUSINESS DIMENSIONS

While a business aspires for Agility, a number of its functions and organizational aspects undergo change. These business functions are also affected by external and internal factors. Figure 7.4 shows the external factors that affect business Agility (shown on the outside of the box) and the way in which the business responds to these factors internally (shown on the inside of the box). These external and internal factors affecting agile business transformation are discussed in greater detail next.

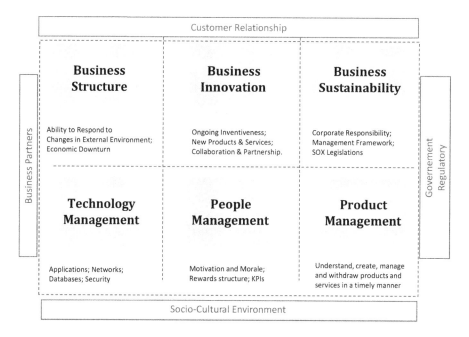

FIGURE 7.4 Business dimensions (external and internal) that enable becoming Agile by incorporating Big Data-driven business strategies.

The external influencing factors in an Agile business transformation include markets, customer relationships, business partners, government and regulatory requirements, and the socio-cultural environment in which the business exists. Many of these manifest through the costs of a business. These factors are discussed next.

Customer Relationships

Agile business transformations impact the customer relationships of the organization. Through Agility, the organization becomes more flexible in its offerings (customer centric). This, in turn, enables the customers to configure their own requirements from the organization. With Agility, customers can also be invited to participate in business decision-making, in terms of product design and service expectation. The transforming organization needs to ensure it aligns Agile changes with its customers. For example, if an organization changes the way in which it offers a product (e.g., making it self-serve), customers need to be made aware of those changes. An Agile bank offering the customer the ability to put together her accounts in different formats that suit her has to educate and align the customer to such an offering. The demographics of the customer also need to be considered when adopting Agility. For example, elderly customers dealing with superannuation accounts may not be able to utilize self-serve analytics (SSA) features and the flexibility that a bank is offering. These customers need to be treated differently than ones who are comfortable dealing with the organization online exclusively.

Business Partners

Collaboration, Agility, and Big Data are closely related. Adopting Agile, especially in its composite format across the organization, implies a definite impact on the organization's business partners. For example, the relationship of the enterprise and its business partners expands based on Agile values of trust and honesty. This has relevance to the way in which it communicates physically and technically. For example, a business process analyzing production schedules of an organization are exposed to a supplier electronically to reduce inventory. An Agile organization will thus have many processes that cannot be executed in isolation. Business partners are affected by the transformation and, therefore, they need to be involved in the very early stages of Agile transformation.

Internet-based communications are the backbone of business processes, which also means businesses are invariably dependent and sensitive to changes in the applications and behavior of their business partners. This is because any change in any business process of an organization has immediate ramifications for the processes of their partners. Starting right from the ubiquitous spreadsheet used by a small business through to the comprehensive ERP solutions used by large corporations and multinationals – sharing information with business partners through ICT plays a core role in business decision-making. Partners influence every aspect of an organization's marketing, management, growth, and expansion. These business partners demand services, implement new technologies, and upgrade their own business processes as a result of Agile adoption by a business. Sharing information with these partners not only avoids issues relating to process mismatches with them, but the partners can themselves provide assistance in enabling a comprehensive Agile transformation (especially if they have adopted Agile values themselves).

Government Regulatory Factors & Sustainability

Adopting Agility at an organizational level requires careful consideration of the legal and regulatory requirements usually external to the organization. While Agility promotes collaboration and open communication, there is still a need to document interactions from a legal viewpoint. Understanding regulatory requirements, ongoing changes to legislations across multiple collaborative partners and their regions, and the impact of these legal requirements on the organization are crucial factors in adopting Agility. Interactions between an organization (especially large and global ones) with governmental structures may have to be documented in detail – to facilitate traceability and audit. Irrespective of the desire of the organization to be Agile, some of these government-business interactions cannot be Agile in the pure sense. A combination of Agile values and corresponding formal documentation is required in dealing with this factor during transformation.

Socio-Cultural Environment

The socio-cultural environment in which the organization exists and operates is immediately affected when Agility is adopted. Similar to the consideration of customer demographics, the social environment requires due consideration in terms of its acceptance of Agility. For example, a business dealing with selling goods online to a teenage audience will find it relevant to investigate social media frequented by these potential customers. Agility at the business level changes the way in which goods are sold online. Collaborative-Agile, in particular, expands the reach of the organization beyond its geographical boundaries. In such cases, proper study of the socio-cultural environment and the way it is affected by Agility is required as a part of an Agile business transformation.

INTERNAL FACTORS AND RESPONSES

Business Structure

The structural flexibility of the business is its ability to change internally to respond to external pressures. The structural model needs to be flexible enough to allow it to respond to external demands. Global economic downturns can come upon businesses without much warning. A flexible business model and associated Agile corporate culture can become capable of handling such sudden external changes. Accompanying the need for structural flexibility of business is the need for the underpinning systems (e. g. HR, CRM) to facilitate such nimbleness. Communications technologies remove duplicate activities, eliminate redundant activities, merge manual processes with electronic and mobile processes, and improve the overall process flow within and across the organization.[14,15,16] BDFAB (the 5th module in particular) aims to integrate these technologies and tools with processes and people, thus paving the path for a flexible business structure.

Business Innovation

Business innovation is the ability of the business to creatively generate new products and services, come up with innovative ways of handling competition, and prioritize its risks.[17] An Agile business creates many opportunities within itself to be creative and innovative. Enabling this approach to business often calls for changes in business practices, operations, and culture. These changes are facilitated by keeping Agility in mind during Big Data adoption. Agility understands the type of business, the domain in which it exists, its available resources, and its strengths and weaknesses, as well as offering a supportive culture. Conversely, the need to foster an innovative culture is also high in Agile business transformation, which enables people to experiment with processes and technologies to improve and optimize them.

Business Compliance

Business compliance is the need for the enterprise to develop capabilities to meet regulatory compliances. The external demands for government and regulatory requirements alluded to earlier need to be satisfied by businesses internally reorganizing. An Agile internal business structure is able to respond easily to ever-changing legislation. Consider, for example, SOX legislation, which provides shareholders and the general public protection from fraudulent practices and, at the same time, pins the responsibility for internal controls and financial reporting on CEOs and the CFOs.

Agile transformation enables the business to carry out this accountability and responsibility through changes in the internal processes, updating ICT-based systems to enable accurate collection and timely reporting of business data, and changing the attitude and practices of senior management. Another example of the need for the business to comply is the rapid implementation of regulations related to carbon emissions. This requires businesses to update and implement their carbon collection procedures, analysis, control, audit, and internal and external reporting.

Technology Management

Technology management in Agile adoption involves handling changes to underlying technologies that support the business and its processes. Challenges in managing technologies include changes to wired and wireless networks, service-oriented applications, distributed data warehouses, and complexities of security as the organization transforms to an Agile one. Businesses rightfully aim to capitalize on the connectivity accorded by the ubiquitous internet.[18] This ICT-based communication results in an enhanced customer experience and improved internal business efficiency.

For example, an Agile organization wants to provide services to a customer at his/her location. This requires the organization to be flexible in its customer service processes and be able to move those processes around by utilizing its mobile networks. Corresponding data relating to the customer also has to change to accommodate the context and changing mobile contents.

People Management

Adopting Agility impacts the people within an organization. Managing employees and other contract staff within an organization, keeping motivation high, and keeping abreast of changes are crucial ingredients of successful Agile adoption.

In adopting Agile across the organization, careful attention needs to be given to the career aspirations of individuals, their personal job satisfaction criteria, and their attitude toward Agility. Large, global organizations employ people in numerous ways, including permanent employment, contract labor, and in consulting/advisory roles. The approach to each of these engagements differs when Agile is adopted as an organizational culture. For example, a permanent employee will be interested in finding out what happens to his/her next promotion if the tasks to be performed are "shared." Contract employees may be happy to share tasks but would like to index their contract rates to quality and time. HR systems and processes supporting these engagements need to be flexible and capable of handling these differences and changing scenarios. Agile business transformation investigates, updates, and ensures a flexible approach to resourcing people, managing them, motivating them, and enabling them to provide their best to the organization and its customers.

Product Management

Product management refers to the need to develop new products and services and to continue existing products with improved parameters (such as time and cost). Agility changes the way the organization captures data related to products, analyzes it, and incorporates the output into product development and deployment. For example, an Agile organization eschews long-winded analyses of product feedback, but, instead directly collaborates with the customer to derive instantaneous updates on product feedback. This information is immediately made available to decision makers through internet-enabled collaborative systems. With the adoption of Agility, the processes for product development change, as do corresponding supporting ICT systems. While the organization develops consistency across its various product lines and its development and deployment activities, collaborative Agile also offers opportunities for "mass customization" (i.e., the ability to produce customized products for each customer, but on a mass production scale). This occurs in an Agile organization due to reduced touch points during the production process. Disposal of used products and withdrawal of a product line in a timely and coordinated manner are also a part of product management. The new Agile organization has a Lean inventory, reduced paperwork, and continuous change incorporated in its product lifecycle management (PLM).

CAMS: BALANCING AGILITY WITH FORMALITY IN BIG DATA ADOPTION

CAMS facilitates the application of methods at various levels of an organization depending on their relevance, principles, and practices. In bringing the business planned and Agile behaviors together, technology and the operational views of an organization need to unite based on "balance."

Leadership from all collaborating organizations should focus attention on competencies and frameworks that go beyond commonly known software development life cycles. Thus, the use of psychology and sociology, and bringing in innovative techniques to overcome cultural differences become important functions in such outsourced projects.

For example, with the overwhelming focus of Agile on face-to-face communication, outsourcing parties are naturally inclined toward holding physical meetings at least before the initiative begins – even if it is not possible to do so on a daily basis as specified in Agile methods. Effective global outsourced contracts are based on a balance between electronic and physical communications – the latter going a long way in overcoming the socio-cultural differences and in developing much better working relationships.

AGILE PRINCIPLES IN PRACTICE

Big Data solutions development includes database design, modelling algorithms and applications, and eventually their coding and testing. Many of these solution level activities can occur in an outsourced environment. Agile principles at the solutions development level can be kept in mind for their uniqueness in an outsourced environment. Following are the four groups of Agile principles[19]:

Customer-Centric – these principles focus on the external aspect of a project and encourage provisioning value to the end user. In outsourced contracts, the client side can find these principles valuable and apply them to their own customers in their markets. The customers of the client can be invited to be a part of the outsourcing initiatives to make it easier for the vendor to understand their core needs. These principles apply particularly well where the solution is indeed a customer-facing one. For outsourced infrastructure and maintenance activities, the role of these customer-centric Agile principles is limited to gathering requirements for enhancements and fixing errors.

Developer-Centric – these principles are focused internally on a project and enable team members to function effectively and efficiently. These present an immense opportunity to be applied by the vendor of an outsourcing arrangement in arriving at the solution. These Agile principles, however, are more tactical than strategic in nature, are more suitable for product development, and are derived from pure Agile methods.

Architecture-Centric – these principles provide the basis for work that offers stability and ongoing improvement in the product, as well as in the working style of the team. These Agile principles, revolving around technical excellence and design, are applicable more on the vendor side of an outsourcing arrangement but with substantial inputs from the client side. They express a strategic, long-term view of the environment in which a solution operates.

Management-Centric – these principles enable the team to focus on organizing itself to reduce administrative overheads of time and effort and, at the same time, on enhancing its working style. These Agile principles, including acceptance of changes and self-organization of teams, play a crucial role in BPO and knowledge process outsourcing (KPO) work.

COLLABORATIONS AND INTELLIGENCE AS FUNCTIONING AGILE

In order to understand the evolving complexities of processes, they are categorized as individual (carried out by a user), organizational (carried out by multiple users), and collaborative (occurring across an organization). Technically, they can also be categorized as physical (occurring through face-to-face and paper-based interactions), electronic (occurring through the internet-based communication mediums), and mobile (occurring independent of location).

This categorization is based on original work by Unhelkar (2003)[20] and later by Unhelkar and Murugesan (2010),[21] wherein a finer categorization is attempted. Figure 7.5 shows the evolving complexity of Agile organizations from a business as well as technical viewpoint. The increasing levels of complexities from business process viewpoints (starting with broadcast processes and going up to full collaborative processes) are shown on the left. The right side of Figure 7.5 shows the evolving complexities of information technologies (starting with data and going up to intelligence). The types of collaborations and the evolving complexities of a collaborative-Agile business are discussed in greater detail next.

Reaching Collaborative Intelligence in Agile Business

Collaborative Intelligence (CI) was discussed by Unhelkar and Tiwary,[22] where CI was shown to facilitate the sharing of intelligence across a group of collaborative organizations. CI is achieved through an incremental rise in technologies and complexities starting with data, then information, process, knowledge, and intelligence. SSA on the Cloud enables collaboration at all levels within and across the organization (see sidebar).

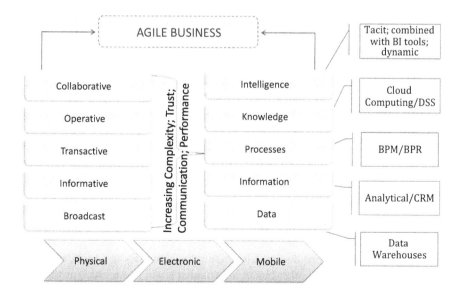

FIGURE 7.5   Agile businesses make substantial use of business intelligence at all levels.

Collaborative Data and Agility

Collaboration in the electronic form starts by sharing data with well-connected, reliable, and trustworthy partners. This allows greater opportunities to reuse data and provide solutions that are based on a variety of data sources. For example, demographic data of a customer, such as her name and address, usually stored by another organization (e.g., a telephone company) need not be stored by the bank. Instead, the source for this data is made available through a collaboration with a telephone company under contracts. Such basic collaborations reduce data storage overheads and contribute towards Agility.

Collaborative Information and Agility

This is the next level of sharing – that of information, in a generic way so that the customer behavior is also personalized. For example, the bank now provides information on the demographic behavior patterns such as spending styles, income groups, and geographical nuances (e.g., beach or hills or next to a large sporting arena) to the telephone company – once again under contracts. Sharing of information creates opportunities for timely services and new products, thereby enhancing the Agility of the organization.

Collaborative Process and Agility

Collaborative approaches aim to model and share business processes across multiple organizations. This collaboration of processes amongst businesses is the natural evolution after sharing data and information. For example, there are opportunities to share the process of opening an account in a bank through a commonly created process-model by a third party. Alternatively, the process of account opening from a bank can collaborate with the process of verifying the details of a person or can reuse the basic "name, address, phone number" data and related information from yet another service provider. While the variation in each of these processes is accepted, many fundamental processes in modern businesses are streamlined. There is limited value in businesses trying to reinvent processes now routinely known in respective sectors, such as banking, airline, and hospital.

The collaborative advantage comes from reusing and sharing the processes across multiple organizations. Collaborative business processes are built on electronic and mobile communications and, as such, enable businesses to put together new customer-centric processes that they would not be able to do on their own. Creating process-models for commonly known processes and making them available across organizations provide many advantages to collaborating organizations – the most important one being their enhanced ability to respond to changes or, in other words, Agility.

Collaborative Knowledge and Agility

This level shares knowledge about an individual or a group of customers/users across multiple organizations. For example, location information about a mobile customer (person) is correlated with other bits of information about them – such as their buying history – to produce knowledge about that customer and, additionally, about that customer group. This knowledge is invaluable in designing new products and services dynamically, as opposed to going through a full iteration of market research, prototyping, and customer feedback.

Collaborative Intelligence and Agility

This is a fully mature implementation of collaboration by a group of organizations within and across multiple industrial sectors with a common goal of enhancing customer experiences. Conversely, a group of organizations at this level could also be the customers, acting in a collaborative manner to achieve higher value. What is most important in a CI environment is that not only are the aforementioned data, information, process, and knowledge being shared, but that it is also made available at the right time and place for participating organizations. Right from data hubs and warehouses through to operational processes and new product development, CI is a positive influence on business Agility. The real advantage of CI comes from having a strategy for multiple organizations to share these elements in a timely and succinct fashion.

REACHING COLLABORATIVE BUSINESS PROCESSES

Collaborative business processes were discussed earlier as a part of the evolving complexities of collaborative Agile business processes. The entire process discussion itself is made up of five increasing levels of complexities – as shown on the left in Figure 7.5. These are the broadcasting, information, transactive, operative, and collaborative processes employed by an Agile business. It should be noted that these business processes themselves may not be exclusive to each other, but may co-exist within a business as it strives for Agility through collaboration. However, understanding each of these types of businesses can also help understand the approach to collaborative business.

Broadcasting Business Processes

This is a unidirectional aspect of the business that provides large-scale broadcasts of its products and services. Physical broadcasting is through print media, including newspapers and brochures. Electronic broadcast includes advertisements and related marketing material on professional and social websites. At a very basic level, it is scanning the organization's product brochures and putting them up on the internet, resulting in what has been known as the "brochureware." Mobile broadcasts are messages that appear on individual users' handsets. They are the most convenient way to reach globally dispersed customers that may be on the move. The increasing importance of social media has to be factored in as well.

Informative Business Processes

This informative aspect of the internet (e-information) encompasses providing information to known or registered parties. Alternatively, information can be put up in the public domain for users/customers to pull as required (as opposed to the aforementioned "broadcast," which is "pushed"). For example, this aspect of business includes providing basic company contact details like the phone number, email and physical address. As a result, the informative aspect has minimal maintenance and security requirements.

Transactive Business Processes

The transactive business is what is commonly referred to as "e-commerce" or "trans-actionware." This is the beginning of collaboration. The earlier EDI (Electronic Data Interchange) has now evolved into internet-based financial transactions involving multiple parties. Transactive business on the web involves the ability to send and receive messages – and thereby conduct business transactions – by communicating with multiple businesses behind the web interface. Examples of these include bookings and reservations, posting feedback, buying goods, and seeking services (the last two being paid for using another collaborative party, such as a credit card provider).

Operative Business Processes

This is shifting the operational aspect of the business to the internet. Physically, this used to involve detailed administration of business operations. Electronically, this is the shifting of HR, timesheets, payroll, and personnel systems to the web. Furthermore, internal production and inventory processes are also moved online. Operative business results in close alignment of the business to its customers, suppliers, and – internally – to its employees. As a result, there is a large component of B2B transactions in operative businesses.

Collaborative Business Processes

Collaborative business encompasses the previous four levels but further expands it for multiple organizations. Electronic communications facilitate data, information, process, knowledge, and intelligence to be shared across many organizations – as and when required. This sharing can result in broadcasting marketing material, providing information, conducting multi-party financial transactions, and also sharing the operational aspects of each other's businesses. This is a truly collaborative business scenario, with the customer being the eventual beneficiary.

ONGOING KNOWLEDGE SYNCHRONIZATION IN A LEARNING AGILE ORGANIZATION

HOLISTIC CUSTOMER – THE ULTIMATE GOAL OF BUSINESS AGILITY

A holistic, single, 360° view of a customer can only be supported by a highly synchronized, unified, and minimal-friction organization. While Big Data is an enabler, its ultimate value is in business Agility. This Agility, however, has to result in a holistic, 360° view of (and for) a customer. Figure 7.6 shows this.[23] The view itself is holistic but the various business functions and systems enabling it are themselves continuously changing. For example, the underlying Master Data Management (MDM)[24] initiative of an organization needs to continuously update itself based on data sourced from the customer.

An Agile organization is not a static one but, instead, is one that is continuously changing, evolving, and learning. Such a "learning" organization augments its capabilities with Big Data technologies and analytics. Figure 7.6 shows the need for continuous updates to customer profiles, billing information, products, and services, and for monitoring the usage of solutions by the customer, to result in a unified view.

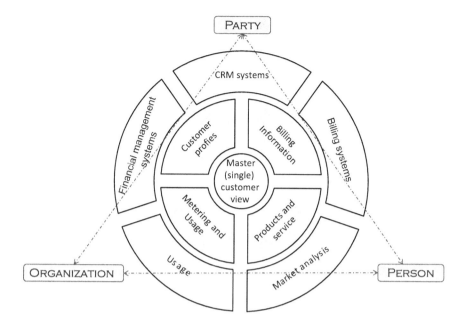

FIGURE 7.6 Holistic customer view resulting from the implementation of BDFAB in practice.

These aforementioned activities are further supported by CRM systems, market analysis, billing systems, usage statistics, and financial management systems. The parties involved in this holistic exercise are the individual and the organization – whose capabilities are enhanced by Big Data analytics and technologies. An important part of this is the knowledge synchronization and usage resulting from Big Data. The users and the organization have to continuously share and enhance their knowledge.

DISCUSSION TOPICS

1. Why is it important to consider Agility in the discussions on DT?
2. Describe the practical ways in which leadership, communications, iteration and dissipation play a role in enabling an Agile organization? Why are each of these important for incorporation of Big Data in DT? *(Hint – because Big Data is an enabler of Agile business)*
3. How does the vision of an Agile organization fit in with that of a digital business? Discuss how each factor influencing business Agility can benefit and utilize Big Data?
4. How does data become intelligence? Discuss the transformational process based on Agile and Big Data utilization.
5. Why is Composite Agile Method and Strategy (CAMS) as a balancing act more appropriate than a pure Agile method in developing Big Data solutions? And why does such a balancing act need good leadership? *(Hint – because it is dynamic)*

6. What is meant by a collaborative holistic 360° view from both customer and internal staff? Describe with examples.
7. What is the importance of Master Data Management (MDM) in a digital business?

ACKNOWLEDGEMENT

This chapter is based on the co-author's earlier work in *Outcome Driven Business Architecture.*

NOTES

1 Unhelkar, B., (2013), *The Art of Agile Practice: A Composite Approach for Projects and Organizations*, CRC Press, (Taylor & Francis Group/an Auerbach Book), Boca Raton, FL. ISBN 9781439851180.
2 *Agile in Practice: A Composite Approach*, Cutter Executive Report, January 2010, USA. Vol. 11, No. 1, *Agile Product and Project Management Practice.*
3 https://www.scrum.org/resources/what-is-scrum accessed 2 April, 2020.
4 SAFe - https://www.scaledagileframework.com/ accessed 2 April, 2020.
5 Unhelkar, B., (2017), *Big Data Strategies for Agile Business,* CRC Press, (Taylor & Francis Group/an Auerbach Book), Boca Raton, FL, (Hardback), Foreword Prof. James Curran, USFSM, FL, Authored ISBN 978-1-498-72438-8.
6 Unhelkar, B., (2014), *Lean-Agile Tautology*, (Cutter Executive Update, Vol. 15, No. 5, Agile Product & Project Management Practice), Boston, MA.
7 Unhelkar, B., (2010, January), *Agile in Practice: A Composite Approach,* (Cutter Executive Report, USA. Vol. 11, No. 1, Agile Product and Project Management Practice), Boston, MA.
8 See Note 6.
9 Murugesan, S. and Unhelkar, B. "A Roadmap for Successful ICT Innovation; Turning Great Ideas into Successful Implementations." *Cutter IT Journal*, Vol. 17, No. 11, 2004.
10 Unhelkar, B., (2013), *The Art of Agile Practice: A Composite Approach for Projects and Organizations,* CRC Press, (Taylor & Francis Group/an Auerbach Book), Boca Raton, FL, USA. ISBN 9781439851180.
11 Unhelkar, B., (2012, August 20), *Avoiding Method Friction: A CAMS-Based Perspective,* (Cutter Executive Report, Vol. 13, No. 6, Agile Product and Project Management Practice), Boston, MA.
12 Unhelkar, B., (2011, April), *Green ICT Strategies & Applications: Using Environmental Intelligence,* CRC Press (Taylor & Francis /Group/An Auerbach Book), Boca Raton, FL, Authored ISBN 9781439837801.
13 Unhelkar, B., (2010, December), *Handbook of Green ICT: Technical, Methodological and Social Perspectives*, Edited, *IGI Global,* Hershey, PA.
14 Unhelkar, B., Abbass, G., and Houman, Y., (2009), *Collaborative Business Process Engineering and Global Organizations: Frameworks for Service Integration*, (IGI Global), Hershey, PA, ISBN: 978-1-60566-689-1; 323 pp.; (c) 2010.
15 Ghanbary, A. and Unhelkar, B. "Collaborative Business Process Engineering (CBPE) across Multiple Organisations in a Cluster." *Proceedings of IRMA Conference. IRMA 2007*, Vancouver, Canada, 19–23 May 2007. ISBN 0-978-159904930-4.
16 Unhelkar, B. "Understanding Collaborations and Clusters in the e-Business World." *We-B Conference,* (www. we-bcentre. com; with Edith Cowan University), Perth, 24–25 Nov, 2003.

17 Murugesan, S. and Unhelkar. B. "A Roadmap for Successful ICT Innovation; Turning Great Ideas into Successful Implementations." *Cutter IT Journal,* Vol. 17, No. 11, 2004.

18 Arunatileka, S., and Ginige, A. "The Seven E's in eTransformation: A Strategic eTransformation Model." *Presented at IADIS International Conference — e-Society 2003,* Lisbon, Portugal, 2003; Ginige, A., (2002), "A New Paradigm for Developing Evolutionary Software to Support E-Business." In *Handbook of Software Engineering and Knowledge Engineering,* Vol. 2. Edited by S. K. Chang. World Scientific, pp. 711–725.

19 Unhelkar, B., (2013), *The Art of Agile Practice: A Composite Approach for Projects and Organizations,* CRC Press, (Taylor and Francis Group/an Auerbach Book), Boca Raton, FL. Authored ISBN 9781439851180.

20 Unhelkar, B., (2003), *Process Quality Assurance for UML-Based Projects,* Pearson Education (*Addison-Wesley*), Boston, MA; (394 Pages + CD. Foreword by Vicki P. Rainey, Raytheon Corporation, USA). ISBN 9 780201-758214.

21 Unhelkar, B., and Murugesan, S., (2010, May/June), *The Enterprise Mobile Applications Development Framework,* Computer.org/ITpro, IEEE Computer Society publication, pp. 33–39.

22 Unhelkar, B., and Tiwary, A., (2010, June), "Collaborative Intelligence" In *Cutter IT Journal* Edited by Dave Higgins' Business Intelligence 2010: Delivering the Goods or Standing Us Up?- Vol. 23, No. 6.

23 Based Tiwary, A., and Unhelkar, B., (2018), *Outcome Driven Business Architecture,* CRC Press, (Taylor & Francis Group /an Auerbach Book), Boca Raton, FL.

24 Loshin D., (2009), *Master Data Management,* (Elsevier/Morgan Kaufmann), USA. pp. 1–28, pp. 87–101, pp. 177–199.

Part C

Leveraging the Value of Digital Enterprise Architecture

8 EA as a Practice in Digital Transformation

SUMMARY

Enterprise Architecture (EA) as a practice offers significant opportunities for practitioners, within and outside an organization, to apply their skills as a business unit in itself. This chapter starts with a brief review of the realities of an EA practice. Once the senior leadership of the organization directing the Digital Transformation (DT) accepts the idea in an EA practice, a business plan for it is created within the overall digital strategy. This chapter outlines how to create such an EA practice, to gain support and sponsorship to establish it, and to ensure it becomes part of the fabric of the organization. This chapter also explains the "why" and "how" of running an EA practice like a business entity. The EA practice utilizes standards, frameworks, guidelines, reference models, and measures to deliver business value. The steps necessary for substantiating EA as a practice and how to get it started are discussed. Qualitative and quantitative value generation and measurements, as well as Key Performance Indicators (KPIs), are outlined as integral to the EA practice.

WHY CONSIDER EA AS A PRACTICE IN DIGITAL BUSINESS?

Given the criticality of Enterprise Architecture (EA) in Digital Transformation (DT), it is important for organizations to have complete readiness of those functions. The EA function can be provided in multiple formats, including having it in-house – which can serve a specific organization – or as an external consulting practice that provides EA as an effective service. Having EA as a practice makes it a semi-independent activity that provides continuous support during and after DT.

A vital reason to consider the EA function as a practice during DT is that the actual architecture itself changes and also enables change *while* the organization is in operation. This requires a specialist, holistic viewpoint that makes EA as a practice ideal. Establishing and managing the EA practice is important for DT to succeed.

Digital strategies and measurable business value arising from the implementation of such initiatives across the enterprise is a daunting task. The EA is tasked with delivering effective results on an ongoing basis. It needs to be owned and handled by a well-defined and consistent process and requires a team of expert resources with core competencies that can orchestrate the use of digital technology and tools. An EA practice captures the business goals of an organization – from strategic vision and business requirements to capitalizing on measurable results to deliver effective solutions or services. The EA practice involves business organizations and its leadership as participants. The endeavor of building the EA practice can be an effective conduit for integrating "silo" organizations and their disparate business applications.

Benefits of running the EA practice like a business extend beyond the functional boundaries of any specific organization. It enables multiple federated business organizations to take advantage of the business-like operations of the EA practice and to coexist.

Major benefits of establishing and running an EA practice like a business within an organization include:

- Creating repeatable processes, frameworks, and best practices for the entire organization.
- Recognizing the ongoing nature of the change in transformational business needs.
- Supporting strategic, as well as tactical, initiatives to maintain business operations.
- Engaging business organizations from the beginning, while demonstrating relevant cost benefits.
- Following a business-driven approach to achieve specific, strategically aligned goals.
- Collaborating to identify and describe the right digital business requirements.
- Evolving EA bottom-up from the application-level and enabling it to become more of a strategic initiative.
- Creating a foundation that encapsulates the blueprints of enterprise business processes and helping execute operations.

The objectives of an EA practice from the point of view of its own success are:

- Achieving return on existing technology investments.
- Reducing the cost of deployment and operations support.
- Extending business capabilities to serve a larger customer base.
- Managing complexities of various roles, responsibilities, and accountabilities.
- Owning EA tasks and assigning them to the correct resources.
- Creating a set of metrics to measure the contributions of the EA practice (resources, process, and technology).
- Governing EA initiatives.
- Supporting organizational culture change through effective deployment of technologies in business processes.

THE REALITIES OF EA PRACTICE

DT includes the modification, redesign, and integration of business applications. However, replacing the entire enterprise and its infrastructure is difficult – especially if the organization is operating during the process. The most common practical initiatives include modernizing legacy applications, rationalizing existent business applications, and transforming some of them to web services. Most importantly, though, EA as a practice works on collaboration and teamwork during the delivery of customer and user value from the digital business.

The realities of EA practice include benefits, as well as challenges and issues. All these activities reduce chaos and enhance the productivity of the organization:

- Impact to the financial well-being of the organization as a key strategy contributor – with its oversight and focus across the enterprise's IT spending, an EA practice can be directly responsible for delivering information and making business decisions.
- Influences on leveraging relationship elements for the evolving organizational structure and for cultural change – most EA practitioners are passionate about the orderly and effective delivery of a solution or service, which helps a business utilize a global workforce and streamline organizational culture in the event of the consolidation of multiple functional units (or during mergers and acquisitions).
- Improvement factors in overall productivity and in achieving both strategic and tactical business goals – an EA practice assimilates (or consolidates) and rationalizes various business applications and functions; offers liaison between multiple initiative teams; and aligns business and IT visions and goals.

An EA practice enables professionals to strengthen their foundations and allows them to manage the key focus areas and associated functions of their EA initiative. As shown in Figure 8.1, the key EA practice focus areas can be classified under four categories:

1. EA management,
2. EA governance,
3. infrastructure support, and
4. operations support.

- EA management primarily facilitates business and IT collaboration and alignment, offers strategic guidance and technical directions to ongoing IT initiatives and prospective teams, and helps review current projects or programs.
- EA governance formalizes a set of corporate-level architectural principles and guidelines, and asserts compliance by reviewing and certifying individual projects.
- The infrastructure and operations support areas concentrate on architectural qualities related to business operations and the enterprise infrastructure.

Specific functions involved in these areas are discussed later. These focus areas delineate the roles and responsibilities of various resources associated with the EA practice and the process itself alleviates many challenges of enterprise initiatives. The EA practice also engages business organizations and sponsors in resolving many challenges from the beginning.

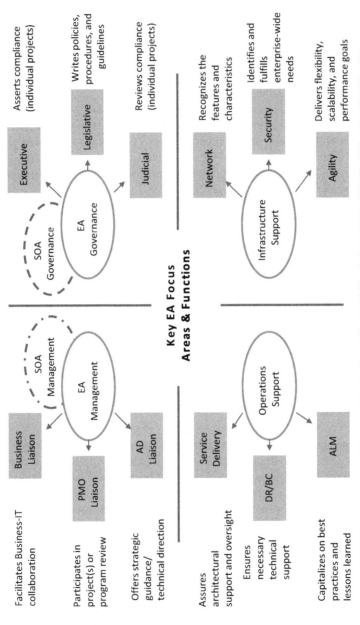

FIGURE 8.1 Foundation of the EA practice – key focus areas and associated functions.

SEVEN PRINCIPLES OF RUNNING EA AS A PRACTICE

While understanding the realities of EA practice is essential, it is equally important to follow a set of principles to get started. A holistic approach is most helpful for running the EA practice like a business.

These principles (see Figure 8.2) include:

1. Define a life cycle that is comprehensive to all initiative team members and also provides a result-oriented, performance-driven delivery map.
2. Capture practices that are not just "best" but also "effective" and widely used by practitioners in the field,
3. Recognize existing investments in people, processes, and technology, so that plans can be put in place to achieve the associated ROI.
4. Publicize a "call to action" across the enterprise and motivate key players to take charge.
5. Develop requirements for a set of metrics that can help business sponsors measure and manage, as well as control, the schedule and budget.
6. Capitalize and catalyze industry trends into the organization through gentle influence.
7. Identify corporate-wide governance policies and procedures, and monitor the compliance of individual initiatives to imposed mandates and relevant government regulations.

These principles, when applied continuously and iteratively, support overall business and IT strategies, improve the organization's effectiveness in solution or service delivery, and subsequently empower business and IT alignment. The EA practice as a business also considers strategic business goals and the IT vision as a mission statement for charting the course of the practice, and so constantly refines it based on evolving requirements or changes.

THE LIFE CYCLE OF A CONSISTENT EA PRACTICE

Model-Driven Architecture (MDA) is an innovative approach to constructing an EA. It visually represents architecture models.[1,2,3,4] MDA can be used to define a road map for delivering EA initiative life cycle activities. The intention behind using the MDA approach is based on the idea that models are the most convenient medium of interaction between business and IT teams. An MDA streamlines the visualization or modeling of life cycle activities and various interactions involved between them and associated tasks.

Activities are organized under different categories in the model based on their commonalities. The key points are the level of interaction between business and IT functions and how these lead to running the EA practice like a business.

There are three common sets of jobs performed concurrently during any EA initiative life cycle:

a. Business-IT collaborative tasks.

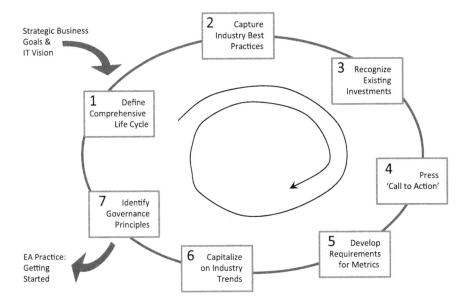

FIGURE 8.2   Running the EA practice like a business – seven principles of a holistic approach.

    b. Model-driven activities.

    c. Enterprise IT common tasks.

In each of these, business stakeholders must be involved with IT teams, despite differences in responsibilities and accountabilities. For business-IT collaborative tasks, business organizations play a key role and become actively involved in decision-making. The ownership of tasks and accountabilities are shared equally by all the teams and the executives managing them.

    The activities related to MDA, performed primarily by IT resources, culminate in reviewing various EA models with the business functions, whose roles and responsibilities shift from active involvement to participating as reviewers. IT organizations own the models and are directly answerable to executives involved in making business and IT decisions for the organization, including the CIO, CTO, and CFO.

    The third set of activities are the tasks common to multiple IT organizations across the enterprise. In this case, these organizations are responsible for performing the tasks under guidance and advice from business organizations and for delivering quantified results incessantly.

    The life cycle approach integrates various activities involved in the EA practice so that a set of finite deliverables can be defined and the progress made can be measured, monitored, and managed.

    The EA life cycle approach constitutes four distinct phases – strategize, organize, socialize, and institutionalize.

During the first phase (Strategize), the business vision, mission, goals and objectives are identified and captured in a consistent form for the EA practice. Based on these available facts, corporate documents, and strategic principles, a business plan is generated. In a sense, this plan also acts as a charter of the practice moving forward.

The next phase (Organize) entails capitalizing on existent resources, processes, technology, best practices, and compliance requirements to formalize a blueprint for integrating the enterprise. This phase organizes the practice to prepare for the anticipated ROI and the total cost of ownership (TCO), while delivering the associated financial impact to the bottom line. As a deliverable, this phase produces a project plan for enterprise-level application integration that is refined over the course of next two phases and that will continue to deliver specific features of the EA periodically.

The third phase (Socialize) extends the plan developed in Phase 2 and prepares the entire enterprise for the EA rollout. The developed plan is socialized across the board to make sure that specific needs of different business organizations are captured appropriately.

Once the final phase (Institutionalize) gets started and certain best practices and policies are captured, the EA rollout plan is delivered to the entire organization. This phase focuses on refining the plan while deploying and delivering the target EA for the organization. While Phases 2 and 3 require less active involvement of the business organizations, the first and last phases promote significant engagement of the business teams.

FOUR FOCUS AREAS

In order to clarify the business value proposition for the EA practice, four focus areas (shown in Figure 8.1) estimate effort needed to establish a collaborative environment for the EA practice and to promote teamwork during EA initiatives.[5]

The first focus area involves translating the business needs to EA goals – it obviously emphasizes capturing business strategies and goals in the early phase of the EA practice life cycle and modifying EA goals during the remaining phases. This focus area also provides special attention to identifying risks, issues, and Critical Success Factors (CSFs) of the EA from the business organizations' perspectives and recognizes the obligations and financial accountabilities of the practice to senior management.

The second focus area offers a blueprint for transforming existing business functions to target EA elements. During the process of transformation in the third focus area, practitioners utilize various industry frameworks and reference models for the EA, while incorporating best practices, policies, and regulatory mandates into their initiatives. This focus area spans the last part of Phase 1 and the rest of the phases.

The third focus area directs efforts toward transitioning existing system components to new ones and guarantees return on investments in existing technologies and resources.

The fourth and the final focus area addresses learning and awareness issues of the EA practice. This area helps existing resources transcend to a new level of awareness and acquire skills necessary to successfully execute their duties for the EA practice. A number of formal and informal educational activities are spread across the life cycle to take advantage of lessons learned, past performance, and core competencies, with advanced technologies and tools.

ACTIONS BY EA PRACTICE IN DIGITAL TRANSFORMATION

The four specific actions by the EA practice in DT, shown in Figure 8.3 and further broken down in subsequent figures, are as follows:

1. Translate business needs to EA goals (Figure 8.4).
2. Transform existing business functions to target EA elements (Figure 8.5).
3. Transition existing system components to new system components (Figure 8.6).
4. Transcend existing and new resources to a novel level of awareness and skills (Figure 8.7).

Various activities are involved in each of these steps. These are iterative steps that have resource, project schedule, and deliverable dependencies. The curves associated with each of these steps (Figure 8.3) indicate the level of effort necessary for each one of them throughout the EA life cycle. These steps support all the activities presented in the road map earlier and address all the challenges.

These steps also provide business sponsors with an opportunity to oversee IT activities during the charter of an entire EA practice. They also ensure that all the stakeholders affected by the EA are included in the decision-making process. Separating each step also helps create a framework for innovation and business transformation in the business-IT relationship as part of the EA practice.

These steps improve the execution capabilities of the transforming organization as follows:

- The excellence of execution is accomplished only when business organizations capitalize on the best practices, processes, and relevant frameworks proposed by the EA practice and are not overwhelmed by the technology skills or expertise of the EA practitioners.
- The engagement of business teams from the beginning in managing the EA practice can eliminate many risks, as well as governance and collaboration issues, and can accelerate the progress in achieving business goals.
- A set of metrics can be easily established and utilized to measure the progress of an EA initiative, and corrective actions can be taken swiftly if necessary.[6]
- Business organizations spend money on IT investments; their direct supervision, readiness to make business decisions, and prompt cooperation must be reciprocal to achieve ROI and associated benefits.

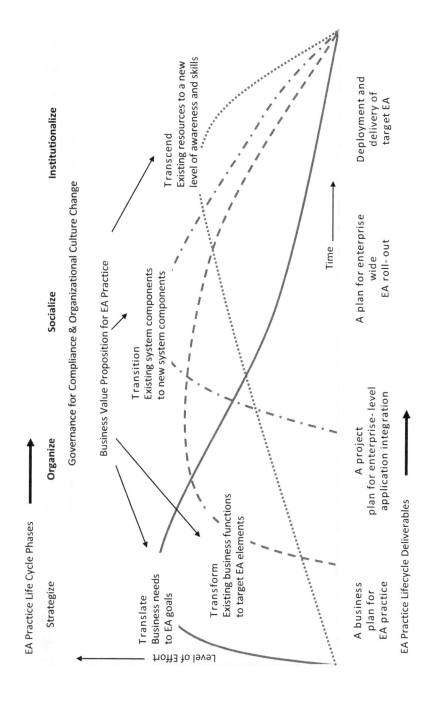

FIGURE 8.3 EA practice lifecycle – phases, deliverables & business value proposition.

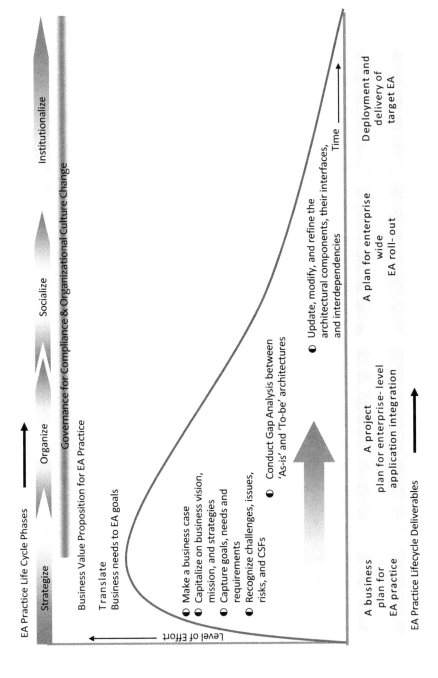

FIGURE 8.4   EA practice lifecycle phases and deliverables – 'Translate' activities.

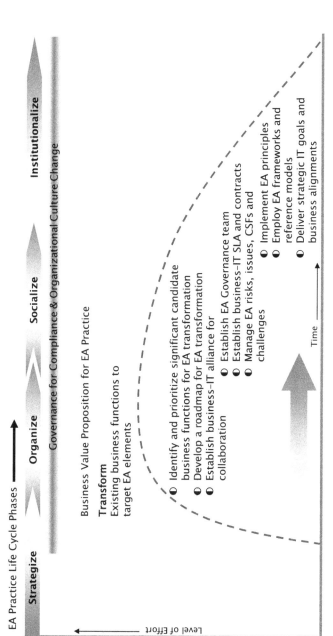

FIGURE 8.5 EA practice lifecycle phases and deliverables – 'Transform' activities.

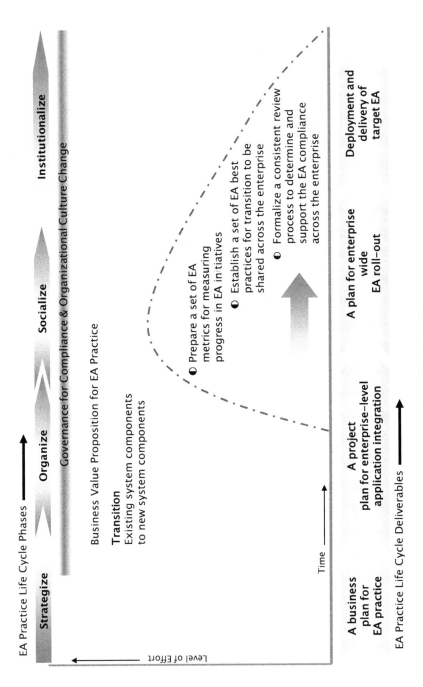

FIGURE 8.6   EA practice lifecycle phases and deliverables – 'Transition' activities.

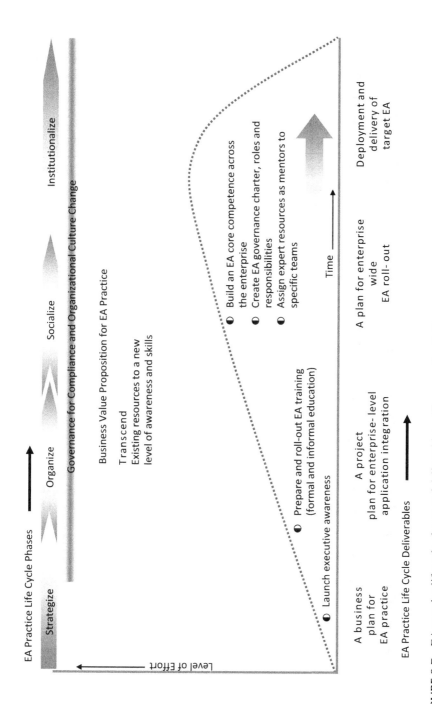

FIGURE 8.7 EA practice lifecycle phases and deliverables – 'Transcend' activities.

Managing the EA practice like a business can result in the following advantages from the technologist's perspective:

- The EA team or enterprise architects can add tremendous value with their forward thinking ("not living in an ivory tower" attitude) and incorporating the advancements of technology accepted by industry leaders into their internal organizations
- The EA team can facilitate EA governance for their business sponsors and influence compliance to specific government and industry mandates by recommending best practices, industry standards, and proven frameworks, as well as reference models.
- The EA team can also act as the proactive liaison between the business and IT teams in employing consistent processes, utilizing global resources (as part of sourcing efforts), and monitoring, as well as reporting, various deficiencies and discrepancies of the ongoing EA initiatives.

MANAGING EA AS A PRACTICE

Business transformation, execution, and innovation play a significant role in delivering tangible value and must be connected with a common foundation that can also link associated business processes of the organization. This common foundation is the EA, which embraces the business goals of an organization more closely than its IT strategies. Therefore, managing the EA practice is a business in itself.

IT is an enabler that empowers business. EA offers a structural framework to align IT with business. Hence, the EA practice must be run like a business. Key EA focus areas and functions are directed primarily towards meeting the business user needs and promoting business-like accountabilities.

SYSTEM INTEGRATION LIFE CYCLE ROAD MAP

A road map for the system integration life cycle is necessary when building collaborative EA and enterprise portals.[7,8] This road map (shown in Figure 8.8) takes a step back to offer a high-level view of the four phases of an EA initiative. The figure exhibits these four self-explanatory phases: Discovery, Gap Analysis, Mediation Plan, and Solution.

It is not possible to over-emphasize the significant need for strategic directions from senior executives, thought leaders, and business sponsors to successfully run the EA practice as a business. In order to deploy the EA well, the business must be engaged from the start of the DT exercise. This means that IT practitioners must empower their business counterparts and help their sponsors assume leading roles in driving EA initiatives from the get-go. As shown in Figure 8.4, during the Discovery phase, IT teams help business organizations consider their strategic and tactical drivers to identify primary EA requirements.

As a part of this facilitated exercise, business and IT teams together discover and document most assumptions, CSFs, associated risks, and concerns relevant to the EA initiatives.

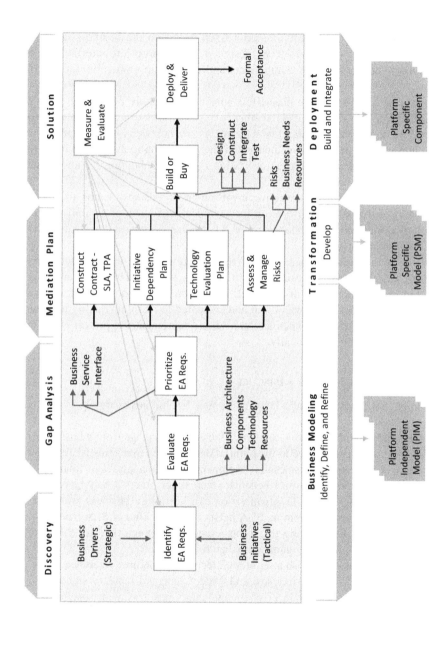

FIGURE 8.8 A high-level system integration life cycle road map.

In the next phase, Gap Analysis, previously identified EA requirements are evaluated on the basis of their potential impact on the business architecture, existent technology, and available resources with desired skills and expertise to make the changes necessary (from the current "as-is" architecture to the target "to-be" one). Once, the current architecture and its various components are inventoried, the suggested EA requirements are prioritized based on the business functions they affect, necessary services to be designed, and appropriate interfaces to be created between the new EA components and the business operations they will support.

During the Mediation Plan phase, four major activities are performed – two of them are technology-oriented and the other two are business-driven. The latter activities include constructing contractual agreements such service-level agreements (or SLAs) and trading partner agreements (or TPAs); evaluating associated business, organizational culture, or resource utilization risks; and planning for appropriate measures.

These activities require the active involvement of business teams to achieve anticipated results. While performing the technical activities, particularly for the technology evaluation and vendor selection, IT teams get business teams engaged in the decision-making process.

Finally, at the Solution phase, the IT teams take the lead in constructing and delivering EA solutions for business organizations – while the business teams sign off on the formal acceptance of the new EA solutions. Throughout the life cycle of the initiative, each activity is measured and evaluated to maintain quality in results delivery. Complexities arise when an iterative and incremental approach is applied to deliver EA solutions periodically.

MAJOR CHALLENGES IN EA AS A PRACTICE

Four major challenges and issues involved in most EA initiatives are:

- **Organizational Culture** – recognize the cultural change from a business-IT alignment perspective to the point of defining and managing SLAs. For many organizations, business-IT alignment involves analyses of financial, operational, and competitive benefits; whereas for others it may be recognizing how closely the IT organization can best align business priorities with IT investments. From an SLA perspective, the kind of SLAs, or contractual agreements, to be put in place and their monitoring are the two challenges that impact organizational cultures most.
- **Best Practices** – establish a set of architectural guidelines, reference models, frameworks, key principles, and widely accepted industry standards. While this is primarily an IT challenge, many business teams play a significant role in selecting the processes and tools used to integrate business applications and the EA.
- **Collaboration** – prepare an environment with the right tools and techniques for business and IT teams to work together. This challenge involves

recognizing existing business processes, or lack of thereof; prioritizing those that must be monitored and managed; and engaging the business teams continuously in most decision-making processes.

- **Execution** – create a model to support the operations of a business and expedite the delivery of results. The word "execution" is overused in the industry. In this context, the challenge of execution involves considering strategies for efficient business operations and implementing them using advanced technology, geared towards delivering measurable results and making business organizations Agile to cope with new or changed requirements in the long run.

All of these challenges require readying business and IT organizations from the "people, process, and technology" perspective. These challenges also necessitate specific focus areas that deserve special attention to be managed effectively.

EA PRACTICE MATURITY

Five Simplified Levels of EA Practice Maturity

EA practice can be aligned to a number of levels or stages in a maturity model. Most of these models are consistent with the Capability Maturity Model (CMM) or Capability Maturity Model for Integration (CMMi), originating from the Software Engineering Institute (SEI) of Carnegie Mellon University (CMU) and advocate five stages. A high-level simplified view of the five stages of this maturity model is presented in Figure 8.9. These are:

- **Level 1: Start Up** – at this level, practitioners usually create an EA awareness program for their organization and primarily educate their customers.
- **Level 2: Beginners** – at this level, practitioners usually get started with the fundamental concepts of an EA practice (upon obtaining approvals from their business sponsors).
- **Level 3: Prepared** – this level denotes the establishing of the EA practice, as practitioners realize the business needs for it.
- **Level 4: Organized** – this level marks the point of governing the EA practice through influence, as practitioners get their business counterparts involved and help them comply with the EA governance principles.
- **Level 5: Managed** – this level helps practitioners achieve their desired ROI via reuse of established frameworks, standards, and best practices in multiple EA initiatives.

According to many practitioners currently using this standard to rate their own EA practices, potential benefits of the practice are directly related to the levels mentioned above. These levels also demonstrate the commitments made by the teams involved in their EA practice to support their business organizations.

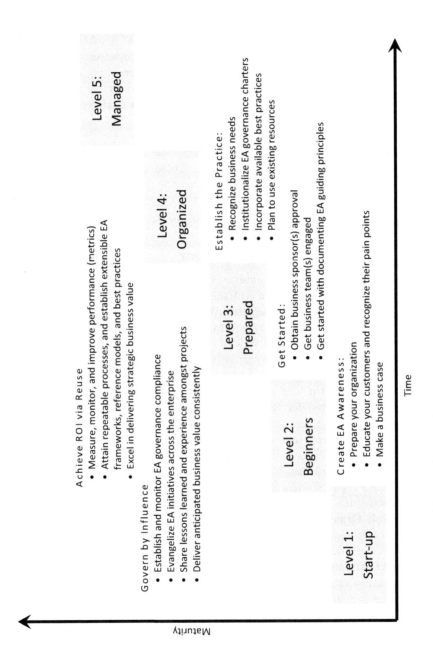

FIGURE 8.9 Five simplified levels of EA practice maturity.

EMPOWERING THE PRACTICE – SEVEN ESSENTIAL STEPS

While cultivating maturity levels, there is a list of seven essential steps (please see Figure 8.6), closely connected to ongoing EA initiatives, that can be performed iteratively as appropriate during the EA practice life cycle.

As presented in Figure 8.10, these steps are:

1. Defining architectural guiding principles to obtain formal acceptance of the EA practice and then to employ them consistently across the organization – these principles also include an initial set of EA governance and management policies.
2. Recognizing EA initiative road maps that define various interactions between multiple ongoing enterprise-level initiatives and that provide an account of specific deliverables, milestones, and complexities therein.
3. Assigning expert resources that can first guide various business and IT teams in understanding and employing the EA guiding principles and then help these teams comply with the principles and other regulatory or governance mandates.
4. Adopting project life cycle methodology to substantiate the importance of business value delivery and to ensure business organizations keep the focus on performing "on time and within budget" activities so as to achieve measurable results.
5. Assessing technology options, as appropriate, to utilize existing investments in resources (including technology, people, and processes) and to provide time for the initiative teams to learn from their previous experiences, as well as advances in business and technology concepts.
6. Measuring, managing, and controlling change to enhance the quality and improve the performance of ongoing EA initiatives, as well as the end results delivered for business organizations.
7. Cultivating best practices in employing EA guiding and governance principles to catalyze the incorporation of changes from the industry as well as the lessons learned in the organization. Although they are presented in a sequential arrangement in the figure, these steps can be performed either in a sequence or in parallel. These steps must be considered in alignment with the EA practice life cycle phases, while keeping deliverables in mind. For many organizations, available EA experts create a critical mass for the core competency and the number of such experts makes or breaks the success of the practice.

DISCUSSION TOPICS

- How will you chart the course for an EA practice to be established in your organization in order to support DT? *(Business Agility; EA is not an IT affair – it must offer business organizations the ability to be flexible in their operations. The EA practice must have a charter that makes itself an ongoing initiative.)*

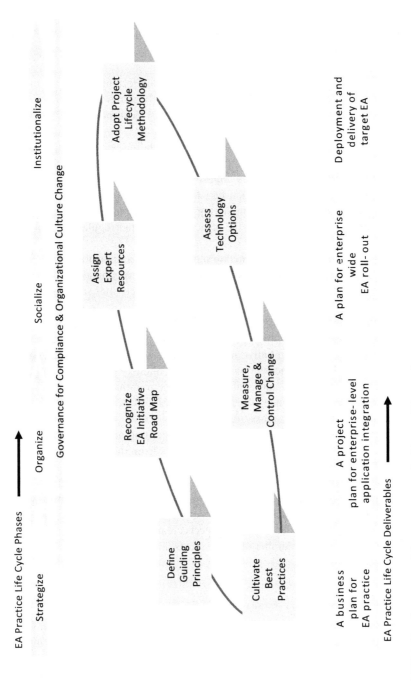

FIGURE 8.10   Seven essential steps to succeed with your EA practice.

- What would be a typical business plan for your EA practice? *(It will differ from the organizational plan for DT but will keep that plan in mind. Besides, it is important to treat the EA practice like a business, and therefore it must have a business plan that justifies its existence and credibility.)*
- How do you envisage the EA practice impacting DT? *(Draw a "big picture" view of your enterprise – to help teams see how their functions impact overall business goals and how they must interact to build a consistent and effective enterprise.)*
- What will be your strategies to ensure the EA provides maximum value to business in its DT efforts? *(Engage business from the start – as mentioned, business organizations play a key role in building the EA and business sponsors provide the funding – they must be engaged and actively involved from the beginning to mitigate potential risks.)*
- How do you plan to control and continuously improve your EA practice and its impact on DT? *(Establish a governance structure – a model that works. To make consistent measurable progress, a set of policies must be complied with – waivers are approved by the governing body to make room for exceptional cases.)*
- How can an EA practice ensure it remains legally viable? *(Comply with government regulations and mandates – to make an organization part of the vertical industry it belongs to, a set of binding regulations must be followed by practitioners. Compliance adds to the Agility of the business.)*
- What are the key actions that can ensure an EA practice continues to provide ongoing support to a Digital Business after its transformation? *(Measure, monitor, manage, and maintain performance. To deliver business goals and quantifiable results effectively, each and every step involved in the EA practice must be tracked, validated, and verified with a set of flexible metrics.)*
- Discuss the need for measuring the maturity of an EA practice. *(Consider scenarios where the EA practice itself has no measures of maturity.)*

NOTES

1 Hazra, T. K., *MDA Brings Standards-Based Modeling to EAI Teams*, Application Development Trends, 101 Communications, May 2002.
2 Merriman, T. "MDA in Action: An Anatomy of a Platform-Independent Model." *Enterprise Architecture Advisory Service Executive Report*, Cutter Consortium, Vol. 6, No. 1, January 2003.
3 Rosen, M. "Understanding and Evaluating Modeling and MDA Tools." *Enterprise Architecture Advisory Service Executive Report*, Cutter Consortium, Vol. 6, No. 5, May 2003.
4 Welsh, T. "MDA: What's Real, What's Illusory, and What's in the Works." *Enterprise Architecture Advisory Service Executive Report*, Cutter Consortium, Vol. 7, No. 11, November 2004.
5 Hazra, T. K. "Empowering a Collaborative Enterprise Architecture." *Enterprise Architecture Advisory Service Executive Report*, Cutter Consortium, Vol. 7, No. 6, June 2004.

6 Hazra, T. K. "Getting Your Enterprise Architecture Metrics Right." *Executive Report*, Vol. 9, No. 9, Cutter Consortium, September 2006.

7 Hazra, T. K. "Employing Web Services Technologies to Deploy Collaborative Enterprise Architectures." *Cutter Consortium Enterprise Architecture Executive Report*, Vol. 6, No. 9, September 2003.

8 Hazra, T. K. "Empowering a Collaborative Enterprise Architecture." *Cutter Consortium Enterprise Architecture Executive Report*, Vol. 7, No. 6, June 2004.

9 Measuring EA in Digital Transformation
Metrics, KPIs, and Risks

SUMMARY

Architecture (EA) and their impact on Digital Transformation (DT). Metrics defined in EA can demonstrate tangible business value resulting from DT. This starts with defining and identifying a set of metrics and key performance indicators (KPIs). Standards, frameworks, guidelines, reference models, and best practices are all helpful in measuring, managing, and governing EA. This chapter offers a holistic, comprehensive, and consistent approach for demonstrating the value of EA in DT. The practical concepts, steps, and challenges of establishing EA metrics are discussed. The discussions in this chapter are based on "how to" leverage corporate culture, organizational structure, customer-oriented strategy, and adaptive business goals to develop and govern EA metrics.

ESTABLISHING ENTERPRISE ARCHITECTURE METRICS

Metrics and measurements are invaluable in any new initiative but more so in Digital Transformation (DT). This is because the transformation of a business while it is in operation is a challenging exercise. Metrics provide a measure of the success in undertaking such an exercise. In fact, metrics and measurements can provide the necessary impetus to start the DT effort in the first place. Furthermore, industry-wide metrics also provide a benchmark for organizations undertaking DT.

The value of Enterprise Architecture (EA) is evident in both government agencies and commercial sectors globally. IT practitioners recognize the need to adopt and adapt to industry standards and apply best practices while formulating their strategies. Customer-focused EA metrics and Key Performance Indicators (KPIs) are integrated into these strategies to achieve the goal of customer satisfaction.

Establishing the EA metrics is a large undertaking that requires significant investment of time, energy, and resources.[1] The DT business case needs to include EA metrics and provide opportunities for them to evolve in an iterative and incremental manner. A road map that visualizes the "big picture" of the enterprise and how various business applications, business processes, business functions, interfaces, digital partners, and devices connect and integrate with each other is most helpful in the development of EA metrics. Furthermore, organizational cultures also impact how well most architectural guidelines, best practices, and principles are accepted by employees. EA metrics, therefore, need to keep pace with needs and the changing people and their work environments during DT. A set of well-defined guidelines and best practices while also promoting a consistent organizational culture is advantageous in capturing and adopting the changes in metrics. Considering EA metrics as a technology affair only is risky in DT, wherein business measures outweigh technology ones.

Metrics measure the success – or lack thereof – in the effort made by the organization. For most enterprise-wide DT initiatives, the key to effective metrics is the establishment of the right models that create and collect relevant data and maintain various parameters of the EA. Significance of the impact of the EA on digitization is crucial in formulating EA metrics.

At the start of the DT effort, identify, capture, and start managing a set of relevant metrics. These provide data and information on company-wide activities that integrate business applications and systems, reengineer business processes, and provide customer value. EA metrics provide a benchmark for the productivity, efficiency, and performance of the entire enterprise. With the help of EA metrics, an organization can ascertain whether its DT efforts have succeeded or not. EA metrics deliver a value proposition for everyone involved via (a) inherently correlating the KPIs of the enterprise, (b) defining responsibility, accountability, and flexibility of practitioners involved, and (c) assessing the capability of relevant process areas and the maturity of existing technology investments.

Figure 9.1 shows elements of EA that form the basis for EA metrics in DT. These aspects are discussed as follows:

- The organizational management element enables the measurement of enterprise-wide organizational culture and associated changes, to assimilate an extended enterprise (including business and technology partners) and demonstrate how the organization incorporates best practices and industry standards that can support implementation of DT.
- Business drivers form an element that directly relates to features or characteristics of user access, customer confidence, expectation levels, and the technical solutions impacting these drivers that need to be measured and promoted. The EA, architectural frameworks, reference models, and a set of core services are included in these measures.
- The business value element encourages the enterprise to fulfil and exceed customer expectations through various integrated and transformed business processes. Utilizing resources prudently and delivering within time and budget is showcased by the metrics and measurements in DT.
- The KPIs element promotes estimating qualitative as well as quantitative measures periodically to determine if the right EA is developed and also if it is developed right. These metrics help justify the role of EA in DT.

FIGURE 9.1   EA elements as the basis for metrics.

The EA elements highlighted above work in conjunction with the fundamental characteristics of any organization: people, process, and technology. These characteristics offer the means to execute rhythm, rigor, and reality in an enterprise. Metrics and measurements build synergy among the aforementioned three characteristics in order to achieve effective results during and beyond DT.

From a people perspective, the need for EA metrics arises from the global nature of the workforce today and the demand for interactive collaboration therein. The only way to track the effectiveness and seamless collaboration of the workforce is to measure the rate of success delivered by connection, communication, coordination, and commitment elements of the people in a teamwork-oriented environment.[2] The people perspective also includes cultural diversity and personal perceptions of business value for individual team members.

From a process perspective, there is no silver bullet or "one size fits all" approach to utilizing processes for enterprise integration initiatives. Organizations also focus more on system integration than "pure play" software development during DT. This means EA metrics need to critically focus on processes, integration of interfaces of various business applications, and embedding of analytics within business processes. EA metrics provide support to each of the ongoing application integration initiatives.

From a technology viewpoint, it is evident that companies are progressing from the phases of "legacy modernization" and "web enablement" to "application rationalization" and "service orientation." Technologies described in Chapter 2 have their impact on EA and DT. Metrics to measure the complexity, security, and impact of technologies on transformation are integral to the success of DT. In particular, digital transformational change is characterized by leveraging a federated approach for applications and processes over a distributed technical environment. A federated approach also offers autonomy to business units while maintaining their allegiance to corporate directives, vision, and business goals. A distributed environment enhances the capability of technology as a service enabler and ROI facilitator in promoting strategic investments.

EA metrics facilitate measuring, monitoring, and managing performance in all aspects of the enterprise. Various elements of EA metrics can be utilized in different forms of reports (i.e., balance scorecards or weekly status reports, etc.) and used effectively in corporate decision-making processes. Thus, EA metrics play a significant role in:

- achieving consensus of involved stakeholders in business- or technology-driven issues and acceptance of resolutions thereof;
- developing a set of measures (i.e., balanced scorecards) to evaluate or assess the value proposition and/or performance indicators related to any specific set of business functions;
- ensuring implementation of appropriate technology or techniques through cohesive collaboration of involved teams; and
- improving the alignment of information technology with operational programs or business functions.

These activities also heavily impact the morale and performance of employees and associates in an enterprise.

MAKING A CASE FOR EA METRICS IN DIGITAL TRANSFORMATION

The complexity and enormity of DT is common because it brings about changes in every function of the organization. Metrics play a crucial role in helping with the estimation of the effort, managing risks, and providing proof of the value delivered. Consider specific needs in developing the business case for EA metrics. Three specific contexts of an enterprise strategy, while doing that are:

- Handle most EA complexities by (1) evaluating high-risk and significant reward-based criteria, (2) eliminating built-in organizational bias toward technology or deployment techniques, and (3) creating highly dynamic and motivated teams and team environments.
- Establish cross-organizational support in order to manage, monitor and maintain the EA metrics as a set of multiple perspectives or viewpoints. These metrics are continuously improved, in terms of their quality, through multiple uses of standards and policies.
- Facilitate a set of periodic events or a sequence of activities using an Active Matrix Monitoring Model(discussed later in this chapter) and help senior leaders and executives in making informed decisions.

IDENTIFYING EA METRICS PARAMETERS

What should the right parameters for EA metrics be? And how can they be improved as changes take place? How should they be revisited during DT? The following five steps are most commonly used in identifying the right parameters for EA metrics in any organization pursuing DT:

- **Get the Right Stakeholders Involved from the Beginning** – this is an absolutely essential step – the primary stakeholders always play a key role in defining which EA metrics are important for the business and how closely they must be monitored.
- **Formalize Gathering and Tracking the Right Business Requirements** – this step is extremely useful for EA initiatives where multiple teams are involved.
- **Prioritize Requirements Based on Associated Risks and Business Impact** – this step usually follows associated cost benefit analyses performed on identified requirements and their impact on business goals.
- **Derive the Right Parameters from Both the Strategic and Tactical Goals of Business Users** – this step emphasizes the relevance of strategic and tactical business goals and how most parameters identified really impact achieving them.
- **Refine the Parameters with Change in Requirements, Business Environments, Competition, or Economic Climate** – this is usually performed concurrently with all the previous steps.

RELEVANCE OF EA METRICS TO DIGITAL TRANSFORMATION

DT is a "work in progress" as the typical iterative and incremental approach continues to change and improve the organization for years to come. Therefore, EA metrics are developed keeping the business vision, goals, and requirements of DT in mind. Business stakeholders are engaged from the beginning and the EA is founded on a "big picture" view for digital business. Project management related to digital capability development falls under the auspices of a portfolio management office (PMO). Formalizing business and technology projects helps in their measurement at a holistic, organizational level.

Portfolio management adds a new dimension to the Agility of the organizational structure. This is so because the portfolio view enables corporate business leaders to understand the importance of EA and DT on the entire organization. The portfolio view of DT is the preferred mechanism to cope with ever-changing corporate cultures. Strategic moves such as mergers and acquisitions (M&A) and outsourcing are also well supported by a portfolio, holistic view.

Proactive measures throughout the EA life cycle can boost the rate of progress for an enterprise in its business application integration initiatives. Flexibility in EA helps leverage ever-evolving technology and business environments, as it makes provisions to accommodate changes in one environment and its impact on the other. A flexible

EA allows suitable and sensible variations in a standard set of architectural guide-lines or principles, and architectural blueprints that encompass industry-strength frameworks, reference models, and a set of common core application services.

The aforementioned enterprise-level architectural principles, practices and measures provide control and understanding of the core values delivered by DT. These principles also help IT teams embed operational efficiencies in their digital business processes. Architectural practices and principles create the foundation of EA metrics.

GETTING THE EA METRICS RIGHT

A DT initiative needs to identify, determine, and establish the right parameters to get EA metrics right. Starting with a set of architectural principles is an effective way to identify the right parameters. This is followed by developing a road map to establish and follow the right metrics.

Once the metrics are established, it is essential for an enterprise to plan how to successfully incorporate the governance of EA metrics in practice (discussed in Chapter 10 in greater detail). The intention in establishing the governance is to share practical lessons learned on how to leverage corporate culture, organizational struc-ture, customer-oriented strategy, and adaptive business goals to develop and govern EA metrics.

WHAT SHOULD EA METRICS HAVE?

EA metrics represent a set of standards for measuring progress in EA activities and associated business goals, and objectives. EA metrics present a conduit to deliver effec-tive business solutions in rhythm, rigor, and reality. "Rhythm" refers to the consistent approach of periodic review of the metrics, "rigor" translates as the meticulous due diligence exerted to manage and maintain the metrics, and "reality" correlates to the results obtained at any given point of time. As a result, productivity, efficiency, and per-formance of the entire digital enterprise are positively affected by the use of EA metrics. EA metrics primarily deliver a value proposition for everyone involved via (1) inherently correlating the KPIs of the enterprise with the EA metrics, (2) defining the respon-sibility, accountability, and flexibility of practitioners involved, and (3) assessing the capability of relevant process areas and the maturity of existing technology investments.

EA metrics impact different aspects of strategic as well as tactical business goals or objectives of an enterprise, but are not always transparent to business services or operations. As a result, in many cases, these metrics may be too intangible for busi-ness and IT executives to recognize or appreciate. This can create a challenge for practitioners in making a business case for establishing or managing EA metrics. Particularly, in order to obtain appropriate sponsorship or funding approval of the senior management or executives, practitioners must consider a well-thought-out EA metrics awareness initiative before developing a set of consistent EA metrics.

FORMULATING EA METRICS

EA and portfolio management practices, along with consistent processes, facilitate integrated business applications. An enterprise must measure, manage, and improve its flexibility as it undertakes DT. This requires coalescing various aspects of data collection for developing a set of metrics and using them to deliver predefined business values of a company. Therefore, it is difficult to strategically align IT-based activities and initiatives using one unique set of metrics in measuring DT. Furthermore, the complexities involved in collecting and managing elements of EA metrics increase with the size and organizational structure of a company.

Small companies usually involve a simplified version of EA. In some cases, EA metrics may not be well defined and organizational structures not well-established enough to share responsibilities and accountabilities consistently in establishing and managing the data relevant to the metrics. Small companies are also constrained by limited resources (including appropriate expertise) as well as existing tools and technologies to manage the metrics.

For medium and big companies, EA usually deals with various business issues, challenges, and problems associated with enterprise-level initiatives. Complexities of such initiatives influence the scope and focus areas EA metrics must encompass, including organizational alignments such as responsibilities and accountabilities of various resources, to deliver quality business solutions or services that incorporate industry best practices.

MODEL FOR ESTABLISHING EA METRICS

There are four major areas that usually contribute to the strategic architectural principles of most companies while building the foundation of the EA metrics model (Figure 9.2). These four major focus areas – corporate IT strategy, corporate

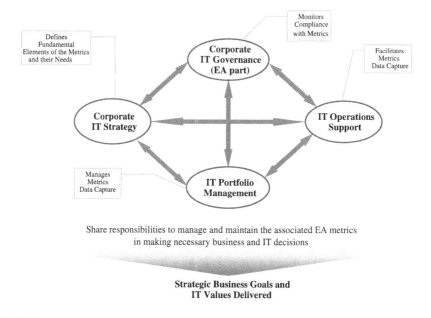

FIGURE 9.2 A commonly observed model for establishing EA metrics.

IT governance, IT operations support, and IT portfolio management – act as IT functional counterparts with the business units and collaboratively share responsibilities to establish and maintain associated EA metrics while making necessary business and IT decisions for delivering strategic business goals and IT values. During this process, these focus areas also interact with each other and support their functionalities.

- The "corporate IT strategy" focus area defines the basic principles for identifying EA metrics primarily to match up with the corporate business objectives. This means that practitioners involved in recognizing the corporate IT strategy usually agree upon a set of business goals that must be realized by the EA metrics. Once established, these metrics are subsequently tracked throughout the life cycle of enterprise-level initiatives to measure the progress of an enterprise in meeting business goals.
- A part of the "corporate IT governance" focus area monitors the compliance of relevant initiatives to EA metrics. These are recognized based on their impact on achieving enterprise goals and their significance in terms of funding and resource needs. The governance also allows or authorizes exemptions or waivers to individual initiatives if necessary.
- The "IT operations support" focus area facilitates capturing metrics data relevant to a specific set of IT operations that encompass a number of initiatives. In some cases, a lot of metrics data is shared across multiple business application integration initiatives in an enterprise, while providing network- and infrastructure-related operational support. Hence, in turn, specific elements of EA metrics data are also utilized in IT operations support.
- The "IT portfolio management" focus area manages metrics data for specific initiatives at project, program, and portfolio levels. In this context, an enterprise-level initiative consists of several projects, a number of which are associated to a program, and a few programs build a portfolio. This focus area also participates with other areas in defining the metrics data capture process, to formalize updates and changes and to manage or coordinate review of the metrics data for their validity.

Corporate IT strategy and corporate IT governance focus areas direct their attention towards supporting the business, whereas IT operations support and IT portfolio management concentrate on managing IT initiatives and supporting operations, while aligning technology imperatives and business goals. Team members involved in each of these focus areas also perform other roles and responsibilities besides actively participating in the process of establishing EA metrics. For example, the EA team responsible for setting the technology direction of the enterprise also focuses on building a set of architectural principles, architectural frameworks, reference models, and a set of standards to be adopted and supported across the enterprise.

EA metrics during DT focus on IT spending, ROI on existing technology and resource-related investments, compliance with government regulations, latest industry standards, and corporate policies and procedures.

Circumstances Surrounding EA Metrics Formulation

EA metrics are formulated under following three circumstances:

- **Precaution** – as a safeguard to deal with uncertainties and unknowns of DT and integration initiatives. IT and business teams engage early in the DT and recognize possible risks, issues, and critical success factors (CSFs). Initial qualitative metrics are subsequently validated with quantifiable parameters. For example, a team starts with a set of metrics first to determine how important the concurrent user access to a particular application via corporate portal is. Later they substantiate the metrics with a numerical range of concurrent users for which the corporate portal can provide support while they access a specified application.
- **Prevention** – as a mechanism to manage or avoid unwanted outcomes during DT. These results relate to a range of goals like attaining financial benefits, minimizing cost impacts, or maximizing ROI. This is a situation where initiative teams are constrained by certain technology selections or senior executive sponsorships, or where CSFs are hampered due to inavailability of expert resources. In this case, EA metrics are monitored consistently to eliminate adverse effects on enterprise-level initiatives. For example, an initiative team prepares a set of metrics dealing with system performance to provide timely response time (less than 30 seconds wait time) to customers.
- **Promotion** – as a way to recognize the prospects and potential of IT. In these metrics, a set of IT assets and business processes are monitored for gradual replacements, upgrades, or improvements. This is a case where an enterprise may have redundant business processes, applications, or systems due to mergers or acquisitions, which need to be streamlined. As a result, the enterprise adopts a new set of strategies, best practices, and governance principles, and establishes a set of EA metrics to monitor and manage compliance with them. Additionally, the organization considers a similar set of EA metrics to review the compliance to technology standards and techniques. For example, a company decides to create a set of EA metrics while identifying the most accessed application, and later develops a service (using Service-Oriented Architecture) to access the application over the network.

Practicalities of EA metrics from the above-mentioned situations are as follows:

- EA metrics are initially business driven, so most parameters in EA metrics are at first focused on meeting identified business requirements. As the requirements are further analyzed during the life cycle of an enterprise business integration initiative, parameters are substantiated with measurable values.
- EA metrics are essentially valuable to both management and technical teams and, as a result, metrics parameters are ultimately measured and monitored to serve both parties. Companies may allow different teams to

manage metrics independently and then share results under a single dash-board or separate metrics charts. Hence, one set of EA metrics may be reviewed under financial dashboards to recognize financial impacts, and the same data may highlight necessary corrective measures for resource allocation.

- EA metrics are more widely accepted across the enterprise as the EA model evolves and matures. This leads to more visibility of corrective measures across the company and enhances the potential for consistently delivering business values in the future.

ACTIVE MATRIX MONITORING MODEL

An Active Matrix Monitoring Model forms the foundation for creating and main-taining EA metrics correctly. This model represents a set of evaluation and decision criteria that can be modified to meet the specific needs of an enterprise. The Active Matrix Monitoring Model helps (1) identify critical areas of their EA, (2) define the logical or statistical significance of critical areas, and (3) monitor the metrics con-tinuously. This model usually allows practitioners to scrutinize "what if" situations and change any contextual views of the EA metrics if necessary.

Figure 9.3 exhibits a simplistic view of the Active Matrix Monitoring Model. In this example, associated risk factors and priorities are weighted based on their signif-icance to the enterprise from the perspectives of IT imperatives and constraints, as well as strategic business drivers. Subsequently, the overall weighted measures can help an enterprise align their IT efforts with strategic business goals. This model is active in the sense that it is used in a "live" manner when managing EA metrics con-tinuously throughout the life cycle of an enterprise initiative. This model has been used with modifications for many service-oriented and collaborative EA projects.[3] There are major benefits of using this model when creating a business case for devel-oping EA metrics because it is easy and interactive to use, and can help practitioners evaluate different "what if" scenarios based on their situations.[4]

A road map for establishing collaborative EAs employs four phases: discovery, gap analysis, mediation plan, and solution. This same road map is used in multi-ple strategic level EA initiatives. In developing a collaborative EA practice, a list of common activities usually performed through the life cycle of an EA initiative are compiled. These activities help define EA metrics or essential parameters. A repre-sentative set of such activities, arranged under above-mentioned four incremental and iterative phases of a collaborative EA initiative life cycle, are shown in Figure 9.4.

During the discovery phase, practitioners usually focus on activities that are impor-tant to making a strong business case for embarking upon an EA initiative. Decision makers usually explore all business drivers as well as the strategic goals of their organi-zation. While documenting identified requirements, special attention is usually directed toward recognizing parameters that are relevant to the set of desired EA metrics. For example, most risks, issues, and concerns pointed out by executive sponsors are vali-dated and then tracked as significant EA metrics parameters from the beginning.

At a strategic level, where one corporate-wide EA initiative influences other EA-related or influenced projects across multiple organizations, roles for a number

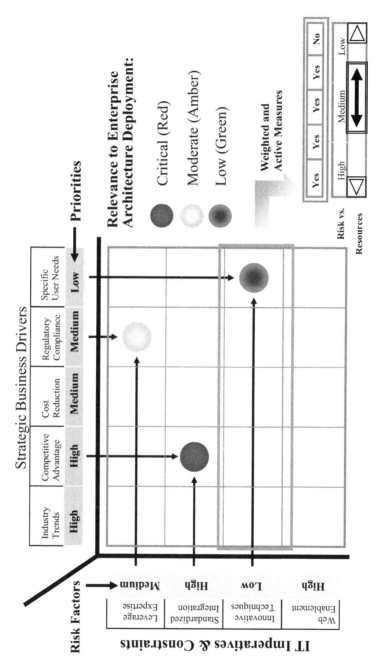

FIGURE 9.3 A simplistic view of the Active Matrix Monitoring Model.

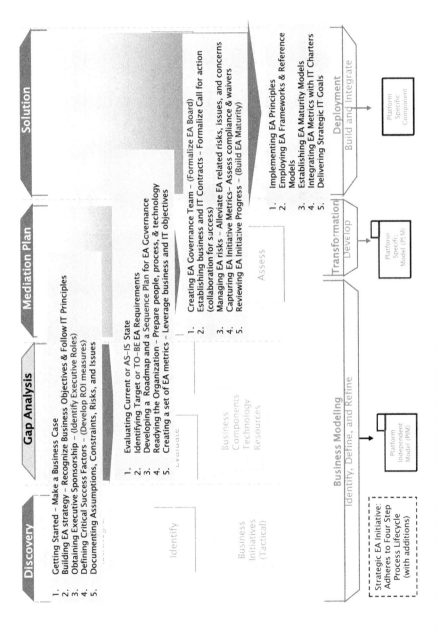

FIGURE 9.4 Common activities in strategic EA initiative life cycle.

of senior executives who will assume specific responsibilities or authorities are identified and ROI measures are defined through working sessions during this phase. Additionally, many companies consider putting together a set of principles related to ways of collecting EA metrics data and preparing a set of policies and procedures that will be followed throughout the process of gathering data for metrics or obtaining waivers from it. This phase primarily sets the stage for the involved teams to understand from the stakeholders and executive sponsor's perspective the parameters important for creating the EA metrics.

During the gap analysis, the primary focus of the practitioners involved shifts from obtaining the approval of executive sponsors to recognizing organizational challenges, issues, and concerns. Technical, operational, and sourcing challenges add further complexity to the approved process. As a result, associated parameters for EA metrics that need to be considered relate to activities such as (1) inventorying the current state of the EA (including existing technologies, frameworks, reference models, processes, and standards, as well as best practices) and (2) capturing business requirements for the target or future EA. Subsequently, these two activities help define the size, scope, and cost-control-related parameters for EA metrics. For a strategic EA initiative, these three activities enable understanding "as-is" and "to-be" states of the enterprise and how to develop a sequence plan to promote EA governance. Other activities such as readying an organization and formalizing an awareness program facilitate the creation of a set of basic EA metrics that leverages business and IT objectives.

During the mediation plan phase, activities that can help deal with identified risks, issues, and constraints for EA initiatives are identified. They usually start with instituting a charter for the EA governance team that includes representatives from both business and IT functions. This may mean formalizing a corporate EA governance board as a subset of the corporate IT governance board. A formal business and IT contract lays out required roles and responsibilities, accountabilities, and ownerships for the teams involved. As a result, elements in the EA metrics include architectural features and qualities to be supported, how they then satisfy different business requirements, and how business team members can be engaged in supporting the goals or objectives of the respective EA initiatives. This phase also involves periodic reviews of the progress made in the EA initiative based on a corporate-level maturity model for the EA. Most of these reviews are directed towards determining how processes can improve EA features and qualities, whether they can support existing and new EA frameworks, what the direct impact of established processes are on the strategic goals of the organization, and how processes can help initiative teams capitalize on open industry standards while satisfying all or most business requirements. The EA metrics present a set of qualitative and quantitative measures for these reviews.

The solution phase is all about the practical implementation of EA principles. Existing or new EA frameworks and reference models are employed. This effort also includes incorporating best practices, organizational or corporate policies and procedures, and following open industry standards as appropriate. As a result, most EA metrics collected or measured throughout the previous three phases are tested and validated at this time. Operations may establish EA maturity models and integrate EA metrics with their corporate IT charters at this point. EA metrics are essentially improved based on delivery of the initiative or the results produced during this phase. "Lessons learned" sessions improve the quality of EA metrics during this phase.

All activities involved in these phases are evaluated and measured for quality management purposes. As a result, the EA metrics created during these phases become an inherent part of the EA initiative life cycle. The details or in-depth presentation of parameters in the EA metrics usually vary depending on their intended audience. For example, most of the information relevant to executive sponsors or corporate leadership is summarized in an executive scorecard or dashboard. Some of the EA metrics data is presented in different forms to different target audience or users. For example, information related to the cost benefits involved in EA initiatives are presented to the finance and operation management teams differently, based on their needs.

While the activities involved in the above-mentioned EA life cycle present a general approach to creating EA metrics correctly, most companies struggle to identify the right parameters for their EA metrics. The following five steps help identify that:

1. **Get the Right Stakeholders Involved from the Beginning** – this is an absolutely essential step – the primary stakeholders always play a key role in defining which EA metrics are important for the business and how closely they must be monitored. This step is also significant from the perspective of making a strong business case for EA initiatives and obtaining the appropriate approvals from sponsors.
2. **Formalize Gathering and Tracking the Right Business Requirements** – this step is extremely useful for EA initiatives where multiple teams are involved, from when a set of requirements is abstracted to when it is reviewed and finally documented in a traceability matrix.
3. **Prioritize Requirements Based on Associated Risks and Business Impact** – this step usually follows associated cost benefit analyses performed on identified requirements and their impact on business goals. Metrics related to total cost of ownership (TCO), ROI, and maintenance-cost changes are recognized as part of cost benefit analyses.
4. **Derive the Right Parameters from Both the Strategic and Tactical Goals of Business Users** – this step emphasizes the relevance of strategic and tactical business goals, and how most parameters identified really influence achieving these goals. For many companies, when it comes to recognizing relevant parameters, organizational complexities, interdependencies between multiple initiatives, and political barriers take higher priority than the ones derived from the technical challenges experienced.
5. **Refine the Parameters with the Change in Requirements, Business Environments, Competition or Economic Climate** – this step is usually performed concurrently with the above mentioned steps. While practitioners in many companies find it difficult to identify the right parameters for their EA metrics initially, in most cases they manage to improve them as changes take place and as they are revisited over the EA life cycle.

GOVERNANCE OF EA METRICS

Establishing the governance for EA metrics is important to successfully incorporate them in EA initiatives as depicted in Figure 9.5.

The exercise of creating EA metrics is complex and requires significant energy, time, and resources to capitalize on the best practices for identifying right parameters and creating consistent metrics. Accordingly, it is essential for companies to set up an appropriate enterprise infrastructure that can support multiple initiatives while practitioners are utilizing any information from the data collected, for the EA metrics.

A structured EA life cycle during DT needs to be complemented by governing the EA metrics. The governance must address who, what, when, and how to get EA metrics right. These four focus areas form the foundation of EA governance:

WHO – THE EA TEAM

The EA team is the "who" primarily responsible for creating, socializing, and enforcing all relevant elements of EA metrics. Subsequently, this team is also responsible for influencing adoption of the metrics across the organization. EA begins with a focus on the business vision of a company. The key to having an effective and business-aligned EA is an EA governance structure that maintains visibility through the cross-section of management and leadership. The governance structure has to include all key stakeholders within the organization. In general, the business organization management aligns the EA process with the mission, vision, and overall strategy of the organization. The governance structure has to include the appropriate oversight boards and steering committees with executive participation. EA metrics

Who
- ▪ **Responsible: Enterprise Architecture Team**
- ▪ **Accountable: EA Governance Board**
- ▪ **Participant: Entire Enterprise, including Application Development and Business Operations Teams**

What
- ▪ **Qualitative**
  - ➤ Critical Success Factors
  - ➤ Productivity Improvement Goals and Objectives
- ▪ **Quantitative**
  - ➤ Key Performance Indicators

When
- ▪ **Throughout Enterprise Architecture Life Cycle**
  - ➤ Kick-off and Lessons Learned Sessions
  - ➤ Periodic Walkthroughs, Reviews, and Inspections
  - ➤ Enterprise Architecture Awareness

How
- ▪ **Continuous Measurement (Mostly Web Enabled)**
  - ➤ Reported on Executive Dashboard
  - ➤ Often Escalated to Organized Events, if necessary

FIGURE 9.5 Who, what, when, and how to get EA metrics right.

can then be collected from member participation. Obviously, participants will include quality assurance, configuration management, system architects, and business and technology managers. The responsibility of the EA team must start with getting business organization(s) engaged early in the initiative. Furthermore, the ownership as well as accountabilities for creating and managing EA metrics must span business and IT organizations equally. The EA team is structured in a very organized way to form a consistent matrix. The responsibilities of all team members are usually well defined, including:

- establishing EA metrics;
- incorporating industry best practices, technical standards, and corporate policies;
- complying with various government regulations and mandates while establishing relevant data for the metrics.

For small and medium business (SMB) entities, the distinction between various teams involved may not be so prominent – in fact, team members usually participate in multiple virtual functional organizations while supporting EA governance activities.

WHAT – QUANTITATIVE AND QUALITATIVE MEASURES

The second focus area for the practitioners in establishing EA governance is to decide "what" the most relevant information – whether qualitative or quantitative – to be collected as part of the EA is. EA metrics also offer relevant information for other measures such as financial planning, performance measurement, program management, and executive sponsors' approval processes. From a qualitative standpoint, recognizing CSFs relevant to organizational or enterprise-level initiatives and how EA-related activities impact them is most helpful.

It is vital to identify productivity improvement goals and objectives set as overall enterprise strategy by the company's senior executives and leaders. For most service or solution providers, productivity improvement is an ongoing effort and draws significant attention from executive management teams. Hence, collecting productivity improvement related data becomes a key element in establishing EA governance. From a quantitative view, productivity improvement leads to enhancing the performance of a function or the entire enterprise. Additionally, KPIs become an essential part of the equation when determining the requirements for performance measurement metrics. For most companies KPIs become the connecting link between performance measurement and EA governance.

WHEN – TO PERFORM GOVERNANCE ACTIVITIES

The next focus area most practitioners consider while establishing the governance of EA metrics is "when" to conduct various associated activities in order to best deliver effective results. Governance activities are performed with other activities associated with strategic and tactical projects. However, they require the undivided attention of responsible senior executive sponsors as well as the reporting of the project status to them. For example, the CIO may usually chair the management review of the overall IT governance board and report significant IT decision-making steps to the board of directors. In general, governance activities are spread throughout the EA life cycle, from the project kickoff or initiation to periodic walkthroughs, reviews, and inspections to post-project "lessons learned" sessions. An important step for most companies to consider in this regard is the institutionalizing of an EA awareness program. This must be tracked at a project level and should be directed to deliver a specific set of results for a particular initiative and in long run to the company.

How – To Capture the Metrics

In order to decide "how" to capture the EA metrics-related information for governance, practitioners utilize different approaches. Without making the governance process a barrier or a roadblock to delivering anticipated project results, practitioners may use a two-pronged approach in collecting and disseminating EA metrics data across the enterprise. With most web-enabled project management tools, dashboards, and scorecards, executives and associated project team members alike can be kept abreast with the decision-making activities they must be involved in, participate in, or monitor. Governance activities culminate in periodic events organized to discuss the status of various projects and action items, as well as to review specific challenges associated with related decision-making by executives. A number of collaboration tools and technologies are made available through corporate portals to make all relevant information readily available to all parties involved throughout the EA initiative life cycle.

CHALLENGES IN APPLYING EA METRICS IN PRACTICE

EA metrics can provide more effective results in terms of delivering business needs of the end users, making both business and IT human resources more efficient and productive, and helping senior executives make more informed decisions in order to achieve strategic business goals and objectives. This does not mean that no confusion exists amongst practitioners about the effectiveness or intention behind establishing the EA practice. Hence, the need for employing EA metrics in practice. Challenges or issues experienced in establishing EA metrics correctly are as follows[5,6]:

- **Lack of Executive Sponsorship** – senior executives in many companies may still believe that they are already doing everything possible to support enterprise-level initiatives and that the cost of incorporating a separate EA practice may be an extra burden to the company. The EA must be treated as a live, ongoing, strategic practice and must be operated concurrently as an integral effort with all other enterprise-level initiatives. The challenge for practitioners is making a convincing business case to get senior executives to sponsor the practice. Another difficulty for practitioners in this kind of situation is that not too many published "lessons learned" or "success stories" are readily available to support such undertakings. It is important to establish a set of achievable benefits that the EA practice can deliver, in collaboration with other initiative teams and organizations.

- **Results Provided by EA Metrics are Vague** – this scenario primarily occurs when results are too premature to be examined or when the EA practice in place is still in the infancy stage. This also happens when executive sponsors do not perceive the precise value proposition derived from the EA metrics. Many practitioners recognize that EA metrics include both qualitative and quantitative measurements. EA metrics spread across organizational boundaries to support multiple decision-making activities such as business-IT alignments, performance measurements, productivity improvements, and return on existing technology investments, as well as resource utilizations. As a result, it may be difficult to extract and absorb all the results easily – not to mention the complexities that an enterprise may experience from the number, size, scope, interdependencies, and the constraints of the multiple projects it may have going on at any given point of time. Setting expectations for executive sponsors early in the process and progressively adding to the scope of the EA over time is very important.
- **The EA Team is Detached from Reality** – this is mostly the case for the companies where the EA team does not communicate well enough with the rest of the organization. The EA team needs to be extremely efficient in its communication efforts in order to perform three of its primary responsibilities – (1) developing EA guiding principles that focus on meeting business needs and that must be socialized across IT organizations; (2) creating a road map for implementing guidelines in conjunction with various application architecture teams and readying organizations to employ EA metrics and collect relevant data; and (3) reviewing, as a part of EA governance, the compliance of various EA initiatives with industry standards and the guidelines developed earlier. Finally, it is essential for the EA and various application integration, deployment, and delivery teams to coordinate while capturing best practices, frameworks, and reference models that can deliver effective results for the enterprise. EA teams must recognize that their success is entirely dependent upon the success of their business counterparts and associated IT organizations. The challenge is to assign the right experts and leaders to guide EA teams in establishing the metrics and in helping rest of the IT organizations adopt the metrics and associated guiding principles (as appropriate).
- **Disengaged Business Stakeholders** – this is a situation where IT organizations are either yet to demonstrate their ability to reduce risks, costs, or times of development, to increase end user satisfaction; or yet to improve operational efficiencies for business organizations. In other words, business organizations do not trust IT organizations enough to believe that the EA practice and metrics will help them achieve their strategic goals. Often, it is also the case where IT organizations did not successfully articulate the benefits of establishing the EA practice to their business counterparts or executive sponsors, thereby generating no interest from business functions.

The challenge is to create an appropriate value proposition that can deliver specific business use. The focus should be on understanding both strategic and tactical business goals. The EA team must connect with business executives and propose the EA solution set that can efficiently deliver prioritized business functions. This makes a business case for the EA practice. Subsequently, a practice can be established incrementally and iteratively as different elements of EA metrics can be adopted by the practice over a period of time. The results produced by the metrics will allow business organizations to recognize the need for more active engagement with the EA practice.

- **The EA Governance Charter is Too Political to Deliver Quantifiable Results on Time** – Too often action items captured during reviews or walkthroughs in EA governance meetings are not followed up to ensure that EA initiative teams can deliver a set of measurable outcomes to business organizations. In most of these cases, political barriers are to be blamed for creating a situation of non-compliance or for not imposing corrective measures where guidelines presented by the EA practice are not being followed adequately. In many cases, the EA practice charters are not well defined and as a result, the interactions between various organizations or teams are not formalized. This harbors ongoing "silo" mentalities already existent in many business and IT organizations. The challenge is to build a lean governance structure that can be strong enough to lead the enterprise and that can also gather key executives to make quick, effective decisions. Executives need to be proactive and involved in running governance activities like a business. They should insist that the results of EA efforts are measured, reviewed, and communicated across the enterprise effectively and in a timely manner.

- **The Use of the EA Metrics Do Not Add Up** – this is yet another version of "we are already doing it" syndrome. Many executives claim that performing an exercise to create EA metrics may not add substantial value to customers and hence it is not of interest to their function. In general, EA initiatives must start with studying the current "as-is" state of an enterprise, its existing business applications, how these are connected to each other, and how well they support specific business functions and processes. It must be followed by capturing the target "to-be" enterprise – that is, what end users would like their business organizations to have in the future. Once the gap between the current and future enterprise-level architectures is analyzed, a road map is developed to outline various activities of the EA life cycle that must be considered. Additionally, a set of blueprints that presents various frameworks, reference architecture models, industry standards, and best practices that may be used is developed. In order to create a reasonable set of EA metrics, it is necessary to (a) start with visualizing or modeling a business architecture that presents both the current and future states of business, and (b) address how well the EA metrics can help implement business strategy and goals without impacting current business operations. Additionally, in a situation like this, practitioners must organize the delivery of results obtained from EA metrics on a period basis. Practitioners must also make every effort to keep executive sponsors well informed regarding the value EA metrics offer throughout the EA life cycle. This also means that a set of processes must be followed and that expert architects must be dedicated to the projects.

- **EA Metrics Needs are Not High Enough on the Priority List** – this may be a situation where (a) previous attempts to build an EA practice or associated EA metrics may have failed to deliver promised results, (b) the practice did not meet the expectations of business organizations or executive sponsors, (c) the metrics created by external consultants were not socialized across the enterprise, or (d) it simply takes too long to make the changes necessary to indoctrinate the EA principles to the current organizational culture. Primarily, risk factors must be considered; challenges or issues should be addressed; CSFs associated with the EA metrics need to be identified in the early stages of enterprise-level initiatives; and, most importantly, how EA metrics can impact the delivery of business results must be explored. This sets expectations for the company. Most companies still need to consider a consistent EA awareness program to improve their readiness. Managing the IT experience and the relationship between business and IT organizations becomes important. It is important to convince executive sponsors and business organizations that by employing the right set of EA metrics, projects can be delivered on time and associated risks can be reduced early. EA metrics can improve the Agility or flexibility of the business in addressing new requirements. This is one way EA metrics become higher on the priority list for businesses, so that they seriously consider establishing an EA practice.

ESTABLISHING THE "RIGHT" EA METRICS

There is a seven-step approach in getting EA metrics right. This approach (Figure 9.6) reiterates how the issues or challenges mentioned above can be addressed consistently. Figure 9.6 shows two streams of activities or steps performed in getting EA metrics right. One set relates to business and IT joint operations and are usually carried out on an ongoing basis to support all enterprise-level projects. These include establishing enterprise level portfolio management, building a knowledge capital repository on technology, standards, and regulatory mandates, and conducting various awareness programs to ready the enterprise or specific organizations. The other set of seven steps is specific to the EA initiative and requires constant business-IT collaborations for establishing EA metrics successfully. During the overall process, a road map is developed for transforming the current "as-is" enterprise to the future "to-be" collaborative enterprise. These steps in formulating EA metrics are described here:

1. **Define a Business Case for an EA Practice with a Focus on the Target EA** – as discussed throughout this book, this a step to recognize the need for establishing the EA practice and securing sponsorship. This where assumptions, constraints, CSFs, and risks are explored. A detailed discussion on this step

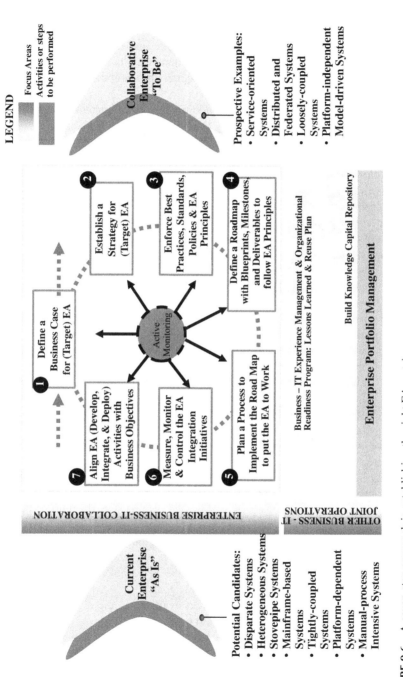

FIGURE 9.6 A seven-step approach in establishing the right EA metrics.

has been made in earlier chapters. During this step, practitioners must address a number of the following questions in order to prepare a business case:

- How will the EA initiative help IT organizations meet existing customer satisfaction and exceed their expectations?
- Can the EA initiative expedite "on time and within budget" project delivery for one or more IT organizations simultaneously?
- Does the EA initiative imply a major change in the existing organizational culture of the company?
- Does the EA initiative require additional core competencies to be built inside the company or do they need to be acquired from outside?
- Finally, can practitioners estimate the size, scope, and cost factors for the initiative to exhibit real benefits of the EA practice and metrics?

2. **Establish a Strategy for Implementing and Deploying the Target EA** – a step to prepare a "business first" approach and formalize architectural principles that can support business objectives while measuring the impact enterprise-level initiatives may have. This is the step where the basic criteria of the EA metrics are identified. Here are a few questions practitioners must consider:

- Does the strategy offer opportunities to integrate cultural changes while delivering a portfolio of projects?
- Does the strategy consider factors such as return on existing technology investments and achieving the anticipated TCO from enterprise-level initiatives?
- How does the strategy address issues such as controlling the delivery cost, reducing the cost of deployment, reusing existing resources, and mitigating risks associated with these issues?
- Can the strategy support the specific business goals of the enterprise?
- How does the strategy formalize a set of best practices, standards, frameworks, and reference models to be adopted across the enterprise?

3. **Enforce Best Practices, Standards, Policies, and EA Guiding Principles** – a step that initiates building a governance structure for the EA practice and that influences various application development teams to implement best practices, standards, policies, and EA guidelines. This is the step where compliance to the EA metrics is addressed. At this step, the most common questions are:

- Do chosen best practices, standards, and guidelines impact the organizational culture of the company?
- Do the organizations or the enterprise as a whole have experience in aligning best practices with business goals?
- Are there enough expert resources available in the organization(s) to incorporate and comply with best practices?
- Can a governance model that already exists in the company be modified to serve the purpose of the EA initiative? If not, what needs to be put in place?

4. **Define a Road Map with Blueprints, Milestones, and Deliverables to Follow Formalized EA Principles** – this is a step where enterprise

architects work closely with different technical architects from the various IT organizations involved to define a road map and identify how these organizations can utilize the EA practice recommendations in a timely manner. This is where ground rules for reviews, walkthroughs, and inspections are put in place. Common questions that arise during this step are:

- Did the IT organizations involved in EA initiatives use a road map before that employs similar best practices and blueprints defined by the EA practice?
- What kind of help and resources are needed to build a road map, and does the organization have previous experience or capability in delivering measurable EA solutions?
- Can the organization interact with their business customers and the EA team to define measurable benefits of the EA, plan to transition the current architecture to target architecture, and define risks of employing new technologies, tools, and techniques?

5. **Plan a Set of EA Processes to Implement the Road Map for Putting the EA Metrics to Work** – a step that helps various IT organizations plan for allocating the right resources, technology, and processes to implement the EA-recommended architectural frameworks, reference models, technology standards, and tools. This is a step where EA metrics are fully mapped with identified business requirements, and where IT organizations start collecting information relevant to EA metrics. Major questions in this step include:

- Do the IT organizations have a process in place or do they have previous experience with a process to support the proposed EA activities?
- Can the defined process help achieve desired EA features and qualities?
- Can the process support the IT organization in adopting the prescribed architectural frameworks?
- Can the process empower business teams to get actively involved?
- How can the cost and performance factors be measured using the defined process?

6. **Measure, Monitor, and Control the EA Integration Initiatives with the EA Metrics** – a step that helps the EA governance review various EA activities, assess the compliance to the policies and guidelines, and approve the status of ongoing projects for various IT organizations to their respective executive sponsors. This is a step where periodic meetings to review the individual projects occur. Primarily, the questions most practitioners consider in this step are:

- How does the EA practice conduct reviews, inspections, or walkthroughs of EA activities? What are the periodic intervals between such activities?
- What are the primary architectural qualities and features that impact identified business goals?
- What are the factors that impact overall enterprise solutions, manage security of the specific business solutions, and help IT organizations reuse frameworks and core EA services?

- How do IT organizations provide information that can be reported to the governance board? What are the steps in place for the approval process for ongoing or future EA activities?
- Can the EA metrics developed during the enterprise initiatives be verified and validated by independent authorities?

7. **Align EA Activities with Delivering Business Objectives at All Times** – a step that helps practitioners keep EA activities aligned with business goals as part of their primary focus. This is a step that spreads across the life cycle of EA initiatives and helps refine and modify EA metrics, as well as make changes to pertinent EA initiative activities. During this step, most practitioners pose the following questions:
   - Do IT and business organizations have available competencies, technologies, and resources to collaborate?
   - What architectural changes need to be made to support business-IT alignment efforts?
   - Can the EA metrics measure the impact of utilizing a global workforce in various enterprise initiatives?
   - What are the roles and responsibilities of an EA practice while acting as a liaison for enterprise initiatives?
   - Do the IT and business organizations currently work together in eliminating project risks or minimizing identified defects?

The above-mentioned steps are generally performed in conjunction with various activities carried out at the project- and program-management levels. Furthermore, some of the elements considered part of EA metrics are directly applicable to project- or program-management activities. As a result, the EA practice usually works closely with their program management office to own responsibilities and accountabilities of managing their EA metrics.

DISCUSSION TOPICS

1. You are in charge of the DT of an organization. You have a budget and you are about to start putting your team together. Is this also the right time to start thinking about the EA metrics discussed in this chapter? Why or why not?
2. What would be your approach to formulating EA metrics for DT? How would you apply the discussion on precaution-prevention-promotion of EA metrics?
3. How relevant is the Active Matrix Monitoring Model for your organization? Discuss in a practical way.
4. Outline your views on the who-what-when-how of governance and EA metrics as applicable to DT.
5. How do you separate EA management activities from EA governance?
6. What are the key challenges in *applying* EA metrics? And what would be your strategies in overcoming those challenges?
7. Discuss the seven-step approach to establishing the "right" metrics in your organization.

NOTES

1 The Practicalities of Enterprise Architecture Metrics- By Tushar H. Posted January 9, 2008 in Business & Enterprise Architecture, Business Technology & Digital Transformation Strategies.
2 Hazra, T. K. "Employing Web Services Technologies to Deploy Collaborative Enterprise Architectures." *Cutter Consortium Enterprise Architecture Executive Report*, Vol. 6, No. 9, September 2003.
3 Hazra, T. K. "Empowering a Collaborative Enterprise Architecture." *Cutter Consortium Enterprise Architecture Executive Report*, Vol. 7, No. 6, June 2004.
4 Hazra, T. K. et al. "Building a Collaborative Enterprise: Harnessing the Power of Portals and Web Services." *Business Integration Journal*, Vol. 7, No. 6, July/August 2005.
5 Hazra, T. K. "Getting Your Enterprise Architecture Metrics Right." *Meta Group and DCI EA Conference*, Orlando, FL, March 8–10, 2005.
6 Hazra, T. K. "Getting Your Enterprise Architecture Metrics Right." *Executive Report.* Vol. 9, No. 9, Cutter Consortium, September 2006.

10 EA Governance in Digital Transformation

SUMMARY

This chapter focuses on the practical concepts of governance, risk management, and compliance (GRC) in the contexts of Enterprise Architecture (EA). The steps followed in establishing an EA governance charter include setting roles and responsibilities of professionals involved, defining processes to manage activities involved, and defining a structure of virtual organization in delivering appropriate business value while incorporating corporate policies and procedures, as well as industry mandates and regulations. The values of ITIL, COBIT, and other industry-recognized service frameworks are correlated to help strengthen the importance of governance, risk management, and compliance in the world of digital business. This chapter offers a strawman governance model that professionals involved in Digital Transformation (DT) can customize or modify to fit their needs.

EA GOVERNANCE AND DT

Enterprise Architecture (EA) governance exists in some form or the other in most organizations, as part of corporate IT governance. The roles and responsibilities of an EA governance have a significant impact on the progress of the Digital Transformation (DT) initiative. Formalizing the charter of EA governance is an important step in the success of DT. It also provides control and direction for EA metrics. The EA is a provider and supporter of an enterprise-wide governance function, as it presents a model of complexity and challenges in large, globally dispersed organizations. The fundamentals of EA governance and making the most effective use of it are integral to DT. EA governance brings together the EA practices, tools, and techniques, and applies EA metrics to them. The "Agile" aspect of development as well as business are accepted in EA governance. EA governance requires keeping solutions development approaches (e.g., Scrum within Agile) in mind; therefore, it must be flexible, nimble, lean, scalable, and innovative in its application.

EA governance is also a potential engagement model when it comes to the use of external consulting practices in DT. This is so because this governance model also provides a comprehensive context to assess, design, and implement DT. EA governance aims to answer five specific questions (summarized in Table 10.1) when

TABLE 10.1

Five Specific Questions in Developing EA Governance

Questions	Responsibilities

Who	Responsible:
	  • EA team
	Accountable:
	  • EA governance board
	Participants:
	  • Entire enterprise and application development, infrastructure, and business operations teams

What	Qualitative:
	  • Critical success factors
	  • Productivity improvement goals and objectives
	Quantitative:
	  • Key performance indicators

When	Throughout EA life cycle:
	  • Kickoff and lessons learned sessions
	  • Periodic walkthroughs, reviews, and inspections
	  • EA awareness

How	Continuous measurement (mostly web-enabled):
	  • Reported on executive dashboard
	  • Often escalated to organized events, if necessary

Where	Locations
	  • Within the business processes
	  • During development and deployment
	  • For audits and compliance

developing a DT road map that can be leveraged for making effective use of the EA. These are:

- **Who** is involved with EA governance?
- **What** are the mandates for EA governance?
- **How** are EA governance activities conducted?
- **When** are specific EA governance activities performed?
- **Where** is EA governance to be used – and where can it be waived?

In order to answer these questions, the EA governance model is sub-divided into four foundational elements as shown in Figure 10.1.

1. **Organization** – focuses on leveraging the virtual yet Agile structure of architecture governance and associated IT governance bodies, review boards, and subcommittees across the organization, as well as interactions of individuals within the organization. Decentralized and streamlined control with the decision-making authority is an ideal foundational element for EA governance.

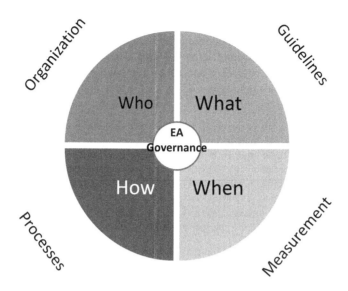

FIGURE 10.1 Four foundational elements of EA governance.

2. **Guidelines** – focuses on addressing various mandates, guiding principles, compliance, reference guides, and solution catalogs, as well as architectural guides or architecturally significant standards considered at all levels: business, data, application, and infrastructure. The intention is to involve minimal bureaucratic roadblocks and expedite the leveraging of emerging technology trends to empower business operations with swift and also sustainable transformation.

3. **Processes** – focuses on addressing various review and approval processes relevant for architecture governance and providing Agile sprint teams with a comprehensive understanding of the timeframe, work flow, approval gates, and review milestones associated with the EA governance. The approval processes aligning with the IT portfolio and program management office, as well as the relevant funding decision processes involving senior leadership, global networks, and regional as well as corporate IT operations, are part of this foundational element of EA governance.

4. **Measurement** – focuses on elaborating various measurement approaches associated with the architecture governance effectiveness, EA alignment, and risk management. Primarily, the objectives of various measurement elements include providing guidance to manage and maintain EA compliance, to establish EA governance effectiveness, and also to track architectural risks, issues, and concerns as well as exceptions and potential waivers.

The EA as a discipline, is responsible for the overall "big picture" representation of enterprise elements and interfaces. This inclusive definition requires that EA consist of the relevant views of the elements of the enterprise, along with their static and dynamic interfaces. However, the key distinction in the value creation and delivery of EA governance lies in the excellence in delivering business Agility – one sprint at a time. EA governance delivers discreet and tangible value during each iteration of the Agile development, integration, and deployment delivery cycle.

One of the most important aspects of EA governance is the governance of the EA work itself.

> For many companies, the concept of EA adds a new dimension to the agility of their organizational structure. With this improved agility, corporate leaders help the business and IT organizations to cope with the ever-changing corporate cultures. The agility also allows the entire company to focus on issues related to mergers and acquisitions (M&A) and outsourcing or, subsequently, to align IT initiatives to meet strategic business goals and demands. Practitioners, however, must always make every effort to measure, monitor, and manage their EA development-, integration-, and deployment related activities to sustain the enterprise agility, or flexibility.[1]

Making a business case for EA starts us down the road towards effective, measurable governance of the EA program. The three key aspects of a business – people, processes, and technology – can all be improved with better information, and better organized information. The architectural understanding of business is what EA is all about.

In a world of Agile enterprises, and Agile EA, service-level agreements (SLAs) and other metrics can be very tricky. There is a common perspective in the technology entrepreneurial world that fast failure is a sure-fire way to succeed. The idea behind the lean startup[2] movement is to conduct controlled or instrumented experiments in the marketplace, monitor the adoption rate of alternative products and services, and be ready to pivot into a different strategy as soon as the data can be analyzed. Mature companies are not often in a position to try such entrepreneurial strategies. However, a robust EA can help simulate various business strategies, The success or failure of those strategies can provide a metric for the successful use of EA itself.

An EA provides navigation and traceability through a rigorous information structure for a framework that starts from facilitating strategies and objectives of the business, all the way down to deploying applications, data stores and flows, and both business and IT capabilities.

All participants in the enterprise are potential beneficiaries of a well-executed, integrated view of the enterprise. These beneficiaries range from associate trainees, who can get a quick orientation to their new surroundings, all the way to the most senior and seasoned decision makers. The EA clearly shows these stakeholders the context and implications for proposed changes to the enterprise. The EA governance framework embraces all functions of an enterprise, from strategy to operations, from marketing to accounting, legal, and human resources, as well as the IT infrastructure.

It is important to make the distinction between "governance" and "management" in setting the context for EA in an organization. Governance differs from management in that the former is primarily about protecting a business through policies and procedures, while the latter is more about growing the business. Governance focuses on issues of "how we do things around here" and keeping a balance among competing interests. Management is about driving initiatives so that the company can operate and flourish, while governance is focused on maintaining coherence and avoiding chaotic conditions.

THE BUSINESS SITUATION

An EA and its governance play a crucial role in an organization's DT journey. This is because of an EA's ability to enable "customer centricity" as a sustainable position in the overall functioning of the business. This represents a departure from a focus on operational technology that manages business processes remotely and inundates customers with information-saturated interactions.

The EA is also crucial in enabling an organization to function on the basis of Return on Assets (ROA) rather than Return on Investment (ROI). This approach to governance provides motivation to keep the level of assets as low as possible, so that ROA is maximized. Part of this strategy is to subsume IT into the operating expense (OpEx) category, thereby creating a perfect opportunity for Cloud Computing, Mobility, and integrated API package deployment during digitization.

ADVANTAGES OF GOVERNANCE, RISK MANAGEMENT, AND COMPLIANCE IN EA AND DT

There are many business benefits that can be realized through a robust EA governance, beyond the obvious features of maintaining coherence in IT architecture.[3] A few of these business value propositions include:

- **Cost** – includes the investment during development and integration initiatives, as well as the spend in running the business operations.
- **Revenue** – relates to the goals and benefits of a business, is obviously measured in ROI, and includes both new and existing revenue generation.
- **Innovation-to-Market** – often starts with a disruption or change of direction and relates to finding new ways to solve a problem or challenge – and monetizing that effort.
- **Strategic Linkage** – almost always ties in with strategic vision. Establishes a correlation to defined or identified business goals and objectives, as well as desired outcomes.
- **Mergers and Acquisitions** – provide a yet another aspect of establishing parameters essential to managing the integration and consolidation of various business functions.
- **Migration** – provides a path to the improvement of business processes as well as associated IT enablers that directly impact the ability of an organization to deliver desired business value.
- **Digital Transformation** – incorporates a major shift from the traditional business approach where the end-users participate and interact with the systems or business applications, and hence support the design of communication channels.

In order to enable Agility in business, EA and its governance structure also prepare solutions development teams to incorporate an Agile, Lean, and adaptive approach that encompasses all aspects of the foundational elements.

The organization of EA governance (the "**who**" element) is influenced by the levels of involvement required by the EA governance in IT-decision domains across the enterprise. It is recognized that EA governance must be directly involved in specific decision-making activities. In other cases, the EA governance may have less or no involvement. Most decision-making efforts where EA governance is currently engaged are primarily in the areas of IT investment and technology selection processes. Typically, the CIO's office is engaged in an ongoing effort to establish, maintain, and support an integrated IT investment analysis and decision-making environment.

In order for the EA governance to substantiate the CIO's effort, it must be able to actively perform necessary requirements, including duties and responsibilities. The governance organization will have stakeholders who may be involved in articulating their expectations and needs during governance meetings or who may submit their requests via written documents. EA governance requires the organization's stakeholders to operate in a timely manner with a specific set of roles and responsibilities. The charter and associated roles and responsibilities of the Architecture Review Board (ARB) and stakeholders is discussed later in this chapter.

EA governance processes (the "**how**" element) leverage the overall EA process, including its conceptual foundation, to integrate the governance mechanism with an Agile, Lean, and adaptive EA. Additionally, the governance processes also recognize portfolio and program management quality gates as well as Scrum-based "Agile" methodology practices. Strategic planning processes for DT incorporate best practices and lessons learned from various industry experts and the core team members involved.

Guidelines (the "**what**" element) considered in EA governance serve as guiding principles for decision-making. They eliminate possible solutions that are not consistent with corporate and regional business goals and objectives of the organization. EA guidelines are derived from the organization's core values and, in conjunction with governance processes, help steer solution planning and investment activities. Most guidelines pertinent to EA governance are aligned with major areas of focus for the organization's EA – enterprise, business, data, application, technology, and infrastructure.

The measurement program and metrics (the "**when**" element) help determine the different impact various architecturally significant decisions will have on the functions of the organization. As a result, EA governance considers a set of measurements for the assessment as well as management of architecture-related activities, primarily focusing on IT and business strategies of the organization both at the management and project delivery levels.

Major measurement parameters and metrics associated with the strategic and tactical aspects of the organization as an enterprise are as follows:

- **EA Alignment** – to substantiate the alignment of current IT assets with industry mandates and corporate policies defined by the organization and transformational architectural framework, currently under development.

- **Governance Effectiveness** – presents a comprehensive account of the number of architecture oversights and the inherent value proposition it offers to senior leadership, strategic planning, and other architecture-related reviews.
- **Issues and Risk Management** – focuses on various issues, exceptions, deferrals, and associated corrective measures to establish an effective architecture across the entire organization.

KEY FACTORS IN EA AND GOVERNANCE

Here are a few key factors that an organization needs in order to get started down the road toward establishing an effective and useful EA governance:

- **Leadership Vision and Motivation**
  1. Executives must feel a need for more effective governance across the various ongoing programs and business innovations.
  2. Only a recognition of the complicated challenges of the business will be able to justify investment in a robust EA program.
- **The Ability to Leverage Existing Programs and Initiatives**
  1. The organization needs to have a very robust program and project management process. With its 57 quality gates, backed up by detailed templates and role assignments, the process is well positioned to underpin the EA governance as it reaches up into the business decision-making level of the transforming organization.
- **Access to EA Tools and Repositories**
  1. Tools and techniques are important investments of a transforming organization. EA tools provide the means to create and link navigation elements of the organization (see Figure 10.5 later). They also provide extensibility features to support Agile EA features the organization requires.
- **Technology Adept Professionals**
  1. Enterprise architects require a balance between business knowledge and IT expertise.
  2. EA practitioners with certifications and proper training, as well as academic education.
- **Service-Oriented Perspective**
  1. EA provides the special service of governance at the enterprise level. The service-oriented approach is ideal both at the business and the IT level.

The above-mentioned fundamental concepts and assessment of the current state of an organization lead to the starting point of EA governance. The following key steps and activities are followed in order to set up the overall governance structure:

1. **Pre-Project Start-Up Phase** – this is a project readiness phase and the activities include (a) getting familiar with the Agile, Lean, and adaptive EA governance framework; (b) getting to know the roles and responsibilities

of each member involved in the "Agile" Scrum team; and (c) recognizing architectural principles, guidelines, and standards.

2. **Project Initiation Phase** – it is important to identify the communication plan to leverage assigned role, responsibilities, and accountabilities, and to define the frequency of architectural reviews to be implemented during an Agile sprint. Depending on the project life cycle and the scope, EA governance can be short (with one or two key reviews), long (multiple reviews or decision points), or not needed at all. Architecture reviews may be formal or informal. It may require a session request for ARB (with key stakeholders and sponsors engaged) to make specific technology-, process-, or standard-related decisions.

3. **Interim and Project Closure or Transition Phase** – as the project proceeds from one sprint to another, or moves from one iteration to another, a more comprehensive architecture review is recommended. This may require a set of formal review requests and specific sign-offs to incorporate new technologies, tools, processes, infrastructure, or Cloud services.

ORGANIZATIONAL STRUCTURE

The EA governance function focuses on the selection, deployment, and maintenance of IT tools, standards, and processes. Typically the IT governance function is handled by the program and project management process. This process was initiated together with the development and operational support for IT systems, using a system of release folios and quality gates. The EA governance model accentuates IT governance and also enhances and accelerates the DT program and corresponding project management activities.

In terms of the organization structure, there is a need for flexibility as well as responsiveness layers to be integrated with the overall governance model. This acts as a liaison between the business and the project management process. As shown in Table 10.2, an EA governance structure has levels and responsibilities corresponding to those levels:

Based on the above-mentioned prospective of an organizational model, a simplistic and pragmatic governance model is presented in Figure 10.2 and outlined below:

- **Level 0** – Sprint-level Scrum
- **Level 1** – Architecture Review Boards
- **Level 2** – EA Governance Board, and
- **Level 3** – Corporate IT Governance Board

These four levels have specific roles and responsibilities, as well as accountabilities, associated with them. The higher levels are more strategic in nature whereas the lower ones are more tactical/operational.

Four levels in this model delineate organizational decision levels:

- **Level 0** – Sprint-level decision-making is the first and foremost step in the governance model. While the intention here is to reduce time and effort spent resolving specific technology-related issues, our plan is to extend a comprehensive and consistent set of principles to the Sprint teams.

TABLE 10.2

Architecture Governance Hierarchy

Level of Architecture Governance in a Digital Organization	Description of Responsibilities in Governance
Technology Decision Board	Highest level responsibility for project architecture governance
	Empowered to make final decisions, acting on recommendations from Architecture Review Board
Architecture Governance Review Team	Resolves architectural issues escalated from project and enterprise architects
	Develops Corrective Action Plans
	Plays an "enabling role" for the next level of escalation in documenting alternatives and making recommendations, for architectural issues with significant cost, schedule or organizational impact
Enterprise Architects	Responsible for enterprise view of architecture and supporting project architects on decisions and deliverables
	Ensures that project approach is aligned with domain strategies and visions
	Identifies deviations from EA and relevant EA artifacts
	Resolves architectural issues with the project team and determines which unresolved issues are escalated to the next level
Project Architects	Responsible for day-to-day architecture leadership and deliverables for a technology project
	Lead project architect is the primary interface between project teams and EA team
	On less architecturally relevant projects, the project architect is the project lead responsible for alignment to technology strategy and EA
	Work with the assigned enterprise architect to resolve architectural issues

The architecture lead will be empowered to influence as well as make architectural decisions in collaboration with the Scrum team lead.

- **Level 1** – ARBs for project architecture-level governance, concentrate on dealing with the "Agile" sprint-level architecture, technology standards, and IT asset management issues. Only architecture issues that have enterprise-level implications or exception that cannot be resolved at this level are escalated to the higher level via a Scrum-based Change Control Board (CCB). Architectural issues that are either significant or have cross-project impacts are also addressed by the EA governance review board.
- **Level 2** – EA governance deals with a set of architecturally significant issues related to the EA. At this level, architecture governance entails both management as well as solution or project review activities. Architecture governance requires active the involvement of multiple organizations such as infrastructure, data, business, and application as well as security and business sponsors. Strategic planning teams also get

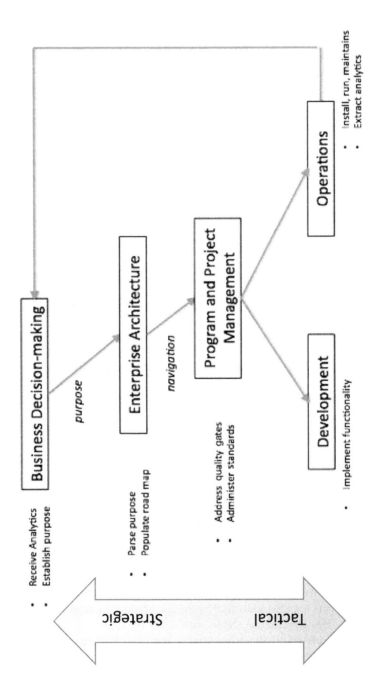

FIGURE 10.2 An EA program forms the basis for EA governance.

involved to conduct its operations. The architecture governance handles cross-project impact analysis, exception management, and corrective action plan development. It also offers support to corporate investment control and funding decisions, as well as reporting processes. This architecture governance escalates architectural issues that have significant IT impacts on the overall business mission of the organization to the corporate IT governance board.

- **Level 3** – executive-level corporate IT governance deals with architectural exceptions that cannot be resolved at Level 2. Exceptional resolution at this level is conducted by a decision team that includes the CIO and IT leadership of the organization. While the CIO acts as the point of contact for the EA governance (from Level 2), he/she also provides oversight to activities involved in this level.

Figure 10.3 further shows the corporate governance, EA governance, and architecture review boards. The architecture decision-making on par with the Sprint schedule indicates the application of governance to development-level activities in the sprints.

CHARTER FOR EA GOVERNANCE

The ARBs shown in Figure 10.3 are themselves governed by a charter. The outline of a charter for an EA as a governance mechanism are discussed here.

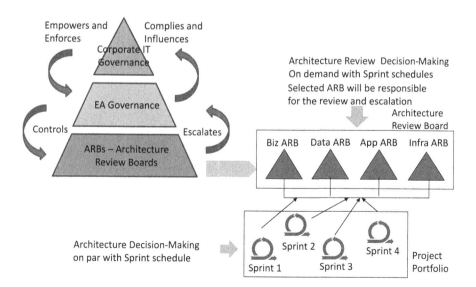

FIGURE 10.3   The structure of EA governance.

ROLES AND RESPONSIBILITIES

An Agile, Innovative, Digital Enterprise Architecture (AIDEA) relies on distributed participation throughout the enterprise in the architecture effort. Many individuals in the organization need to understand which of the following duties they are responsible for in the context of AIDEA.

- Propose projects and initiatives.
- Determine positioning within the enterprise.
- Document the state of a project.
- Create model snippets that reflect each project.
- Compare project models to joined-up model
- Highlight impact on the business (what's being added, what's being replaced).
- Maintain the joined-up road map.
- Determine conformance to principles, guidelines, and standards.
- Allow waivers.
- Escalate requests for waivers.
- Teach EA skills across the organization.

An RACI (Responsible, Accountable, Consulted, and Informed) matrix is also very helpful in assigning the charter within the ARB.

PRINCIPLES, GUIDELINES, AND STANDARDS FOR EA GOVERNANCE

Architectural principles, guidelines, and standards are necessary to maintain coherence of the enterprise in the face of Agile and innovative change. The development and enforcement of principles, guidelines, and standards are based on the following areas:

- Guiding Principles
- Business Principles
- Application Principles
- Data Principles
- Technology Principles
- Security Principles
- Operations Principles

Figure 10.4 highlights the seven steps for successful EA governance. In the context of DT these seven steps are interpreted as follows:

1. **Get Business Engaged Early** – enables business stakeholders to understand the complexity and limitations of an EA at a very early stage.
2. **Create a Consistent Communication Plan** – will benefit both technology and business.
3. **Create a Small Set of Business Initiatives** – part of an Agile approach to EA and DT.

FIGURE 10.4   Seven steps for successful EA governance.

4. **Reuse Principles, Policies, and Experts** – without reinventing the wheel.
5. **Start with a Comprehensive Measurement Plan** – part of the EA governance metrics discussed in previous chapter.
6. **Validate KPIs for Business & IT** – enables their significance and reliability during DT.
7. **Review EA Governance and Management Processes Frequently** – part of Agile EA (discussed in Chapter 1) to ensure those processes are current.

EA FRAMEWORK AND GOVERNANCE FUNCTION

One of the key contributions of the EA discipline is its ability to capture and navigate lower-level details of business knowledge and IT projects and investments. In any large enterprise, the level of complexity is daunting. The starting point for considering a framework for EA representation can be seen as a rich index or set of navigation concepts that tie changes to the business back to business decisions made by the executive management of the organization along the customer-centric DT. This is also a framework to organize the history of architecture decisions, both in business and IT.

Navigation Elements

Figure 10.5 shows a minimal set of elements that provide essential linkage from business purposes (goals, objectives, etc.) through processes and capabilities, and into application and data structures that support the business vision and goals.

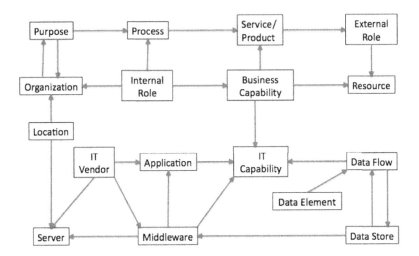

FIGURE 10.5 Navigation elements.

NAVIGATION ELEMENT DEFINITIONS

The key navigation elements proposed in Figure 10.5 are listed and described in terms of how they can be related. The benefits provided by the elements and their relationships are also discussed briefly.

Business Elements

Business elements provide the context for understanding and classifying initiatives and projects. The most important and useful business elements are listed and defined below:

Purpose

Business goals, objectives, mission, vision statements, and the like form the deepest underpinning of any EA. Linkage to these statements of purpose and intent provide the answers to questions that ask, "Why are we doing this?"

Business Services/Products

The outputs from the company consist of various forms of services. Certain services are performed at a distance, without company intervention. These special kinds of services are called products.

Core business processes either perform services or create products (which in turn perform services). Supporting processes, as well as all IT, need to be understood and evaluated in the context of the relationship to products and services.

Processes

Business processes create products and services, or support production and performance. For a process-centric or process-oriented business, processes are key to understanding the overall EA.

Business Capabilities

Business capabilities represent the abilities of the enterprise. Processes are based on capabilities. Multiple business processes can use (or invoke) the same capability. At the same time, any process will inevitably consist of multiple capabilities that are brought to bear in some kind of sequential fashion.

IT capabilities support business capabilities, and capturing information about this linkage is one of the most direct ways of understanding and clarifying how technology supports the business.

Internal Roles

Roles are important to capture as navigation elements, because they have capabilities, perform in processes, and are supported by IT. Internal roles are performed by the organization's personnel.

Such roles include:

- Drivers
- Dispatchers
- Cement creators
- Concrete mixers
- Procurement

External Roles

External roles constitute the parties and entities that the organization does business with. They include:

- Customers
- Suppliers
- Distributors
- Software vendors
- Consultants
- Building architects
- Engineering firms
- Construction companies
- Government agencies
- Non-governmental organizations
- Construction professionals
- Host communities
  - Youth
  - Disadvantaged groups

Organizations

Most organizations consist of groups or roles and role-players in the business. Organizations have a budget, so it is important to understand how they are supported by technology, which roles benefit, and how the benefits adhere to processes that create products, perform services, and support the core purposes of the organization.

Resources

Many resources are required to support the performance of business processes.

Locations

The organization has a strong need to identify geographic locations among key navigation elements. Countries and regions form the core of location concerns in the organization. These elements underpin organizations, and therefore differentiate versions of processes, roles, and capabilities.

IT Elements

IT elements provide the technical context for understanding and classifying initiatives and projects. The most important and useful business elements are listed and defined below.

Data Stores

Data stores represent data at rest, which, in turn, provide sources of stored data for purposes beyond the processes that captured, manipulated, and stored the data for downstream usage.

Data Elements

Data elements represent the meaning of data, which indicate what is produced and consumed by applications, and in turn roles and processes.

Data Flows

One of the most important things to understand about architecture in the software world, and especially as applied in the sense of an enterprise, is the emphasis on interfaces. Data flows represent specific explicit interfaces among applications, between applications and data stores, and by extension between and among organizations and role-players.

Applications

Applications represent software that is put into use by the business for specific purposes. They support role-players in performing their capabilities in the context of processes.

IT Capabilities

As mentioned above, IT capabilities exist to complement or support business capabilities. This is the key navigation point between the business architecture and the IT architecture, both sides being needed for a complete understanding of the EA.

Servers

The term "server" here simply denotes an identifiable unit of hardware infrastructure. From an EA point of view, this represents a direct tie between the IT world and the world of physical or virtualized locations, such as a company data center, or some form of the Cloud.

Networks

At an enterprise level, the link between networks and data flows completes the picture of all-important interfaces, which forms the essence of architecture.

Middleware

For completeness, the enterprise navigation might dip into middleware, which can provide certain key capabilities.

IT Vendors

A key linkage point in the IT navigation structure is the relationship between IT elements and vendors where the IT products and services are obtained.

The Navigation Repository

The navigation repository provides the context for all projects. When projects are indexed by key navigation elements, the redundancies, gaps, and overlaps are very easy to see.

Methods and processes of EA governance comprise a minimal set of navigation elements and describe the reasons for this particular conceptual structure. Business process modeling tools are invaluable in tying EA strongly to the business. Such tools need to be evaluated in terms of support for the minimal set of navigation elements. Despite the complicated patterns, tools should be able to essentially join everything to everything via extensions. This will require careful consideration before undertaking the work of refining the key navigation elements.

PRAGMATIC EA GOVERNANCE STRUCTURE

While the focus areas discussed above provide a road map to practitioners in terms of getting started with their EA governance, it is important to revisit the governance structure. This is essential in order to plan how to successfully incorporate organizational governance of EA in practice. A pragmatic IT governance model – and subsequently an EA governance model as a part of it – is always founded on principles defined by people, process, and technology elements in an enterprise.[4] The significance of these three prime elements and their associated complexities intensify with the size, organizational culture, and interdependencies of business and IT functions in a company. The people element addresses different roles and responsibilities distributed across the organization to capitalize on the business needs of the entire company while establishing an EA metrics. A process is a driving force that runs underneath the surface of a project or an initiative – synergistically orchestrating its execution, delivery, and deployment activities. The technology set is an enabler to delivering effective business results and helps practitioners coordinate and deliver EA solutions.

Figure 10.6 shows a high-level view of the EA governance structure as it builds upon the corporate and organizational culture to deliver corporate business value. In order to effectively utilize the power of the EA governance structure, practitioners expand from "doing the right things" strategic principles to actually "doing things

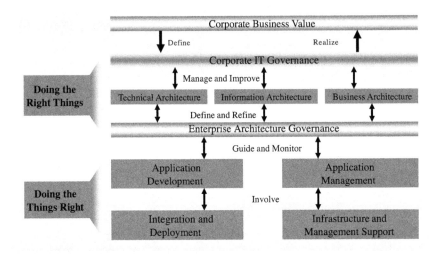

FIGURE 10.6   Incorporating an organizational governance structure of EA in practice.

right" in their business operations. From a strategic point of view, inherent corporate business value and goals drive the primary focus of corporate IT governance, which, ultimately, helps a company realize its perceived business value. Corporate IT governance offers direct oversight on all three architecture areas such as technical architecture, information architecture, and business architecture, to manage and improve the use of technical standards, disseminate information across different business organizations and functional operations, and capitalize on business needs and the expectations of users.

These architecture areas contribute towards defining and refining the EA governance. The purpose is to chart a course for doing the right things and to assimilate a set of best practices, standards, reference models, and architectural frameworks to be used across the enterprise. EA governance also helps practitioners do things right. It starts from setting the ground rules for business-IT alignment and creating an effective EA awareness program that allows practitioners ready their organizations. It also sets expectations right for executive sponsors and business functions, as well as associated partners and vendors. EA governance guides and monitors application development and management activities. Subsequently, these activities involve both integration and deployment, and infrastructure and management support functions. Program management offices (PMO) performing various application development and delivery operations work closely with these functions to resolve EA-related challenges.

As the IT community continues to recognize the significance of the EA in delivering IT solutions and services, the roles and responsibilities of EA governance are bound to change. These can include:

- creating EA awareness,
- formulating EA management policies and procedures,

- incorporating industry standards and best practices,
- preparing various architectural guidelines to use various patterns, frameworks, and reference models, and
- helping organizations comply with EA governance principles and leverage them while making changes to infrastructure and operational supports.

The EA governance structure is primarily a reflection of the IT governance in place.

Luftman and Pukszta offer extensive views and accounts of various elements significant to structuring IT organizations of the future.[5,6] As Service-Oriented Architecture (SOA) solution delivery becomes a prominent mechanism for IT to enable business counterparts, the roles and responsibilities of the EA governance will intensify further – meaning a closer look to the federated or distributed structure of the EA governance will be essential for practitioners.

Efforts in service orientation across commercial and government agencies will enhance the significance of EA governance. Combined with that is the fact that most EAI vendors already support SOA efforts and many focus on the EA governance with their tools and technologies. Practitioners should realize that these advancements emphasize the importance of defining the roles and responsibilities in the EA governance structure for companies involved in using EA metrics in practice.

EA governance must be managed efficiently beyond all the hype. It has to be tightly controlled, financially, to deliver reciprocating results for all companies in the near future. EA governance will continue to enforce the need for complying with industry standards and best practices for architectural success.[7]

ARCHITECTURE REVIEW AND GOVERNANCE BOARDS

As mentioned earlier, the Architecture Review Board (ARB) functions according to its charter. The core of ARB is shown in Figure 10.7. A few key points about the ARB charter are summarized here to complete the picture of EA governance:

- There are four key perspectives for architectures that require review:
  1. Business architecture
  2. Data architecture
  3. Application architecture
  4. Infrastructure architecture
- The charter documentation for these review boards include:
  1. Purpose and Mission
  2. Process and methodology
  3. Roles and responsibilities of maintaining and utilizing the various architectures
  4. Administrative involvement of RACI parties
  5. Scope of responsibilities
  6. Key Activities:
     i. at the enterprise level
     ii. at the project level
  7. Decision tree

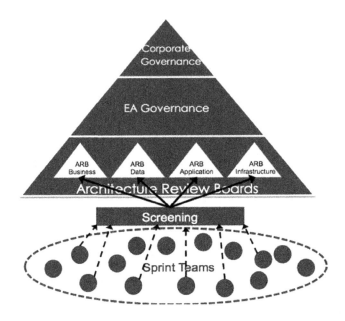

FIGURE 10.7   Architecture Review Boards – ARB.

8. Escalation process
9. Domains of governance for boards

DISCUSSION TOPICS

1. What are the four fundamental elements of EA governance and how would you apply them to a DT exercise?
2. What are the five specific questions you should ask when developing EA governance?
3. What are the key advantages of having EA governance in DT?
4. What are the challenges associated with having EA governance in DT?
5. Create a brief charter for EA governance with roles and responsibilities for your organization.
6. Outline the application of the seven steps for successful EA governance.
7. Discuss the tools and techniques that can be used in EA governance.
8. What is an ARB? Create a real-life ARB based on your experience.

NOTES

1 Hazra, T. K. "Getting Your Enterprise Architecture Metrics Right." *Executive Report*, Vol. 9, No. 9, Cutter Consortium, September 2006.
2 Ries, E., *The Lean Startup*, Crown Business, 2011.
3 https://www.cutter.com/offer/12-compelling-value-propositions-ea.
4 Hazra, T. K. "Getting Your Enterprise Architecture Metrics Right." *Meta Group and DCI EA Conference*, Orlando, FL, March 8–10, 2005.

5 Luftman, J. "Organizing IT: What's the "Right" Structure?" *Cutter Consortium Business IT Strategies Executive Update*, Vol. 7, No. 8, April 2004.
6 Pukszta, H. "Quo Vadis IT? Structuring the IT Organization of the Future." *Cutter Consortium Business – IT Strategies Executive Report*, Vol. 7, No. 12, December 2004.
7 Westerman, G. "EA Governance: From Platitudes to Progress." *Cutter Consortium IT Journal*, Vol. 16, No. 7, July 2003.

11 Business Architecture Practice

Case Study in Healthcare Domain

SUMMARY

This chapter presents a case study on establishing a Business Architecture (BA) for DT. While this book focuses on EA, as discussed earlier, the BA forms an important part of the EA as it focuses on the business functions, their relationships, business processes, and people. This chapter is based on the lead author's practical experience in establishing the BAP at a healthcare IT business – Health-Is-US. The challenges most businesses in healthcare or any other field encounter today when establishing their BAP are very similar. The BAP is critical to business and IT alignment, as it influences the strategy on one hand and builds efficient operational solutions on the other. Most business leaders and IT executives today realize the value proposition of the BAP. However, it is still important to note that a well-governed and fully functional BAP relies on the maturity of the enterprise in embracing the BAP and overcoming the growing pains of the BAP across the organization. This case study provides insight into practical aspects of how a "consulting assignment" can be run for a client undertaking Digital Transformation (DT). The case study includes various practical issues and challenges faced.

BUSINESS ARCHITECTURE

Business Architecture (BA) is a familiar proposition to many business and IT professionals.[1] It represents the blueprint or visual model(s) of any enterprise in the context of its business functions – primarily focusing on "what" the enterprise does and "how" it executes its functional capabilities to deliver tangible business value. As the Business Architecture Working Group (BAWG) of the Object Management Group (OMG) defines it – "A Blueprint of The Enterprise That provides a common understanding of the organization and is used to align strategic objectives and tactical demands."[2]

The BA is always founded on a set of business models. Initially, these models capitalize on the processes inherent to a business and its drivers including strategy, goals, and objectives. Subsequently, they are enhanced to leverage the mission of the business along with other architectural domain models to deliver tangible business solutions or operational goals. The structure and dynamics of the enterprise is documented within the BA and the governance structure, business processes, and business information is continuously validated and refined. Business functions including customer management, sales, marketing, production, inventory, finance, and HR are provided formal models and management through the BA.

The BA promotes a business focus during Digital Transformation (DT) and fosters integration between business and IT. A practical BA consists of business process models, a business capability matrix, concept of operations, and a maturity model in addition to a self-assessment process to evaluate the level of maturity for each business process and to prepare for future modifications. In practice, like in the case of CMS, the BA gradually evolves and matures and adds significant value to the entire enterprise as a key component of its Enterprise Architecture (EA) and beyond.

Business-driven architecture or business system architecture dates back to the early days of EA planning[3] and the Zachman Framework. The Open Group Architecture Framework (TOGAF) and Federal Enterprise Architecture Framework (FEAF) also offer substantial information to help professionals getting started with BA initiatives. In the National Institutes of Health (NIH) Enterprise Architecture Framework, the BA plays a significant role as a driving force of the EA. A number of standardization efforts are underway to establish modeling languages and notations. However, for many professionals – both in the public and private sectors – questions still remain about the availability of tools for modeling as well as building the BA and how well commercially available tools support activities relevant to establishing the BA.

From practice, it is observed that many schools of thoughts exist when it comes to understanding the position of the BA in an enterprise. The BA is a prime element within EA that facilitates digital strategic planning as well as business transformation. It is business driven and customer focused – the former to help business and IT leaders in their strategic planning, and the latter to make the business transformation happen to meet customer needs. In 2004, Whittle[4] and Myrick[5] positioned the BA as the formal link between strategy and results.

A BA can help professionals realize the void that exists in their enterprise behavioral pyramid.[6] It specifically focuses on creating and validating the customer-centric value streams of an enterprise for the business world. The BA is described as an element linked to other enterprise elements to collectively form a structure focused on the customer.[7] Ulrich has also argued for why a BA matters to business executives and how it can be leveraged in business transformation.[8] It enables professionals to establish a common vocabulary, a shared as well as forward-thinking vision, and a blueprint to capture the current state of their business.

A BA provides value in DT by establishing a baseline and a structure of the business at an enterprise level and also by setting the digital business vision. A Business Architecture Practice (BAP) helps the business handle architectural issues from a business viewpoint, just as the EA practice does for the entire enterprise, including its technologies. The BAP has its own nuances and life cycles, as discussed next.

The Value Proposition

The BA plays a significant role in defining the primary value proposition for the EA. It instills the foundation within the EA for building a mature and robust enterprise. A BAP commonly constitutes a set of processes, principles, and expertise pertaining to the BA at the enterprise level. Collectively, the processes and principles pave the way for creating a comprehensive business-centric blueprint or "big picture" model of any enterprise.

Creating an effective BAP is a daunting task for many professionals. It is essential to recognize the value it brings to an organization or an entire enterprise to begin with. Identifying the tangible value of a BAP happens with continuous application – starting with the models and the blueprint for a digital business at the enterprise level. A BAP does the following:

- Describes business functions independent of organizational structure or culture, while carefully depicting the operational dependencies between two or more business units.
- Provides a foundation for information, application, and technology architecture models as they are either related or connected to core business functions.
- Facilitates the impact analysis of changes to business and IT systems from both the strategic and tactical perspectives.

In a typical scenario, a BAP is primarily created under the organizational auspices of an EA practice. In some cases, the practice is sponsored by business executives with an intention to create a liaison or partner that can support them in their business and IT alignment efforts.

As presented in Figure 11.1, a BAP normally provides a conduit for business and technology initiative teams to collaborate at both the strategic and tactical levels. While business strategy is the driving force behind this practice, BAP also holds

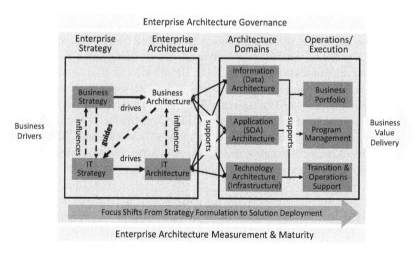

FIGURE 11.1 The position of the BAP in an enterprise.

the responsibility of influencing business strategy. On the other hand, in conjunction with the IT architecture, the BAP directs the information, application, and technology architecture domains, and builds efficient operational solutions for the business transformation. Additionally, governance and management are the two other key components of the EA that leverage the value proposition of the BAP. They influence, support, and leverage each other in visualizing the "big picture" business model of an organization or an agency in terms of its IT strategy, functional capabilities, operational processes, and organizational structure.

A set of fundamental principles that can address the challenges in business environment while establishing the goals or objectives of the BAP include:

- Business and IT teams must first embrace and cultivate relevant industry best practices to define a set of quantifiable goals that can help them cut cost in their operations.
- A "business first" focus can expose and subsequently resolve most risks, issues, and concerns involved in business operations – hence why the BAP always starts with capitalizing on the business functions iteratively and incrementally.
- A business transformation always needs a change agent – the BA provides the foundation of this. It incorporates business capabilities, processes, and other related components and their models.
- A BAP must streamline operational support factors in terms of associated costs for identified services, applications, technology, and the data flow. Ultimately, it must deliver optimum efficiency to business users. Operational structures that transcend functional and organizational boundaries are directly impacted by strategic and tactical imperatives that the BAP drives. Therefore, the BAP must consistently measure the value of operational support.
- A BAP not only creates efficiencies and non-redundant, cost-effective services for internal business functions, but also extends this to customers, suppliers, and external systems that interact with the business. In reality, BAP principles, standards, and blueprints provide the foundation for business portfolio prioritization and drive program management functions to focus on operational efficiencies.
- BA initiatives require transition and operational support from business portfolio and program management functions and can be quantified effectively at these levels of a business unit or the enterprise. It is important to ascertain where a BAP can drive operational efficiencies and effectiveness in terms of business benefits, faster time-to-market, reduced hardware and software spends, and significant reduction in overall labor costs.

Finally, the overall value proposition for a BAP is truly realized in operational savings and efficiencies, and the return on investment (ROI). It may not be visible immediately and multiple challenges can derail or delay the realizing of benefits. It is highly recommended to utilize a set of carefully crafted metrics to track the progress and benefits of the BAP from its inception. In the next section, a real-world BAP has been introduced. Subsequently, an account of the BAP life cycle has been presented. Finally, all the associated processes encountered in establishing this particular BAP are discussed.

THE BA PRACTICE

Consider a US-based healthcare business, Health-Is-US[9] – a multimillion-dollar public sector organization with more than 60,000 employees, serving the citizens of the nation for more than a decade. Health-Is-US had four business units – Clinical Decision Support (CDS), Health Informatics (HI), Public Health Affairs (PHA), and Enterprise Health Solutions (EHS). The organization faced many challenges and the impact of various standardizations, regulations, and reforms, while also weathering the economic climate. Some of the challenges were strategic and had long-term impacts, while others were tactical and had short-term or small impacts with regard to delivering the business objectives of the organization. This organization was trying to expand its current operations with a new set of solutions and services for patient-centric care delivery and clinical decision-making. It was also embarking upon US public-sector health information exchange (HIE) and electronic health records (EHR) initiatives. It planned to support government agencies in the field of health and human services. In addition to its four key business units, this organization had acquired two technology firms that provided security and business intelligence (BI) solutions to US federal healthcare agencies and a training organization that specialized in healthcare delivery.

The management planned to create a BAP with a mission to help its business operations achieve desired goals through reusing collective resources, processes, and services. It certainly had the ability to adapt, with flexible ways to encounter and embrace rapid business transformation and change. The organization and its executives had gone through a series of changes – the reorganization of the company; the modernization of key business processes and existing IT applications; and HIPAA-compliance efforts, just to name a few. The leadership team proactively decided to build a more flexible and collaborative enterprise with a brand new BAP. The primary mission of this BAP was to reflect on the design decisions for processes, resources, and associated logistics in architectural blueprints, to maximize business value and minimize overheads for the organization. The executive sponsor of this initiative considered the BAP an integral part of the EA. However, available EA information and artifacts were moderately structured and not quite sufficient to define actionable architectural plans. Business drivers for creating the BAP included:

- Gathering well-defined and sufficiently structured business-focused information that could help both business and IT executives make architectural plans actionable. The goal was also to create a set of strategic principles that could empower business units to execute these actionable plans in order to control the information, resources, and the associated workflow of the enterprise.
- Embracing emerging web technologies to enable business units achieve a competitive advantage, while supporting the ongoing adoption of Service-Oriented Architecture (SOA) across the enterprise. The goal here was to

establish reusable, loosely coupled, modular, and Agile services that could be provided as part of new service offerings to multiple customers with a hope that these services would generate a new revenue stream for the organization.

- Reengineering and transforming business processes inherent to current business functions, to help identify a number of common services and enable a business unit to create or acquire and then provide its services to the rest of the organization. It was also anticipated that the BAP would drive activities to identify redundancies as well as gaps across the enterprise after its mergers and acquisitions.
- Analyzing relevant business processes and visualizing them as coherent business models could expose connections amongst existing business systems and associated technologies, and prioritized business strategies. The objective of this business driver was to determine how new IT systems should support and realize business goals.

Although no deliverables or milestones were identified immediately, the executive sponsor anticipated that successfully establishing the BAP and performing associated activities would produce a blueprint for operating and transforming the enterprise within the foreseeable future. Key elements of the desired blueprint of the BAP were identified as:

- Clearly defined business goals, objectives, and initiatives, primarily directed towards influencing enterprise-planning steps in the IT architecture.
- A prioritized set of business processes that could define activities, steps, and information flows between processes, to carry out key business objectives.
- Business services that could identify what value one organization may provide to another – including both internal and external services.
- Business rules, regulations, government mandates, standards, and policies to be complied with.
- Performance metrics to define success factors for the business and IT coalition.

The BAP life cycle has four distinct stages as shown in Figure 11.2. These intertwined stages of the BAP were cascaded appropriately to achieve the innate operational goals of the organization:

- **Stage 1: Building the Practice** – stage for creation and orientation.
- **Stage 2: Enabling the Practice** – stage for socialization of BAP processes and principles.
- **Stage 3: Managing the Practice** – stage of formal collaboration and compliance.
- **Stage 4: Realizing the Practice (Benefits)** – stage of assessment and governance.

In Stage 1, a set of guiding principles are introduced to initiate the practice and then two business units are being prepared to start using the processes and principles

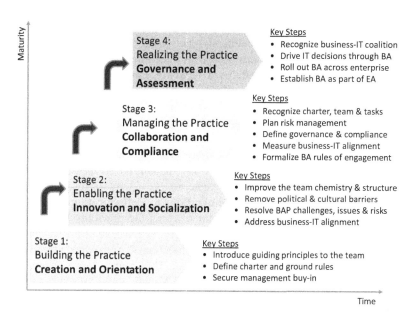

FIGURE 11.2   Four stages of the BAP life cycle.

fostered in the BAP.[10] These principles are modified and refined these principles during Stage 2. The processes and guiding principles of the practice are socialized in an innovative way with the rest of the organization, while paying special attention to aligning the business and IT architectures. In Stage 3, what worked and what didn't inside the selected organizations are determined. We establish the ground rules for formal collaboration among business organizations and the BAP. Finally, in Stage 4, the BA governance body to manage stakeholder expectations, mitigate risks, and assess the effectiveness of the BAP is established. We cultivated a set of best practices to help the business and IT team members deliver tangible business value while improving the performance and productivity of the enterprise. Most common business transformation challenges encountered by the business and IT teams during the past few years were related to information sharing or exchange. Some of these could significantly impact achieving the mission or goals of the BAP.

CHALLENGES, ISSUES, AND CONCERNS

A number of the challenges encountered while embarking upon the BAP initiative were common business transformation ones. However, some were deterrents to the inception of the BAP. The executive sponsor charged the BAP team to resolve the following challenges, issues, risks, and concerns while charting the right road map for the BAP:

- **IT Strategy and Architecture were No Longer in Tune with Current Business Drivers, Strategies or Requirements** – due to acquisitions and business expansion decisions, the business drivers of the EHS unit changed from delivering and often integrating packaged and commercial off-the-shelf (COTS) enterprise healthcare solutions to providing integrated and open standard-based services to support the entire federal HIE.

- **Tightly Coupled, Isolated, or Disparate Processes and Inefficient Information Sharing Across Multiple Organizations** – these were the result of applying isolated efforts to support different business clients with custom application development and management services. For the CDS and HI business units, the issues and concerns were identifying reusable IT assets, application components, and business services that could be assembled and managed efficiently to address the similar business needs of the multiple federal agencies that they cater to.
- **Unwillingness of Business Organizations to Collaborate in Developing Common or Shared Services** – intensifying the previous challenge, the CDS and HI organizations failed to identify the reusable IT assets, application components, and business services mentioned, as they had no common understanding of each other's operations. They had no prior channels of communication or collaboration in place. It made the BAP's job of establishing a common ground for "shared responsibility" very difficult.
- **Higher Cost and Lower Efficiency of Services Supporting Business Operations** – the lack of consistent standards or a cohesive approach to developing information, application, and technology architectures in the PHA business unit put the interoperability of secure clinical and administrative data services to the test. The acquisition of a new security technology–based organization didn't help, as it didn't have any specific security standard(s) in place.

Some of these above-mentioned challenges, issues, and concerns were complex and had no easy resolution. In general, however, most were reviewed periodically to identify their criticality and to seek external help from expert consultants if necessary.

ESTABLISHING THE BAP: STAGE BY STAGE

STAGE 1: BUILDING THE PRACTICE

A readiness assessment and a survey of stakeholders ensured management buy-in for creating the BAP. Representatives from business and IT leadership, the two initially selected business units, the EA and three architecture domains, the program management office (PMO), and operations support organizations were identified as the primary stakeholders of the practice. These individuals participated in activities relevant to establishing a comprehensive approach for developing the BAP and associated governance. However, the key challenge for the team was the lack of pertinent skills and experience within the BA team. Also, the IT organization had no prior experience in developing medical domain-based web services or associated standards for HIE or EHR. The newly acquired training organization extended its organizational development services in all stages of the BAP life cycle to conduct skill gap analyses and also to help professionals involved learn and gain domain knowledge, as well as build adequate advanced BA expertise across the enterprise, for knowledge transfer and mentoring during future stages.

Key steps considered for creating the BAP are presented in Figure 11.2. Some of these steps are very similar to ones that may be considered when building any architecture practice. So what made these efforts so unique? It was evident that the guiding principles cultivated helped in driving the maturity of the BAP. Following is a synopsis of the principles that are being considered and their key impact in building the BAP:

- **Define the Scope of** BA – limiting the scope to supporting only two key business units provided an opportunity for practice members to focus on initial wins. It allowed time for interaction and to be more effective and productive while learning and sharing. It also provided the opportunity for practice members to make the objectives of the BA relevant to these two divisions and their common business goals.
- **Set Up an Integrated and Unified Business-IT Front** – the key to BAP success is to ensure business participation. The focus was directed towards building the BAP as a collaborative environment and prepared the team to be consensus-driven, proactive, and responsive. It allowed the team to make the processes and principles of the architecture easy to follow and comply with.
- **Explore the Relationship to EA** – creating a practice to support the strategic and tactical goals of the enterprise enabled us to explore, establish, and expose the relationship of the BA to the EA early in this stage of the practice life cycle. It helped us shape the organizational structure and charter of this practice. It also facilitated setting up the expectations from other business units.
- **Visualize the "Big Picture" Representation of the Business** – creating a "big picture" view of the business with conceptual architecture models helped us analyze the existing business processes to identify and prioritize service candidates that generate requirements for SOA and Business Process Management (BPM) initiatives. It also enabled us to set the stage for developing the potential blueprint of an enterprise-level business architecture (EBA).
- **Develop Key Performance Indicators (KPIs) for the Practice** – it is essential to create a set of performance indicators to measure the progress in building any practice. With all the acquisitions that happened in the past few years, it was not always easy to obtain buy-in. Measuring progress helped us determine and monitor the performance, efficiency, and productivity needs for consolidated IT assets, and secure management buy-in early for future funding. It allowed the team to make the architecture actionable from the beginning.
- **Identify Candidate Business Functions or Components for Transformation** – Critical business processes are identified and reviewed in this stage. Our intention here was to locate redundant, tightly coupled, or disparate business processes or functions to help improve information sharing as well as collaboration among business units and functions.

For the candidate business units, a number of challenges, issues, risks, and concerns are isolated.

- **Pave the Way for Business and IT Alignment** – engaging both business and IT leaders, managers, and architects helped influence the alignment of current business and IT strategies. Key business drivers are leveraged to guide, plan, and formalize the transition plan for the future enterprise. Also, a number of IT assets are identified that could be shared across multiple business functions and optimized as appropriate.

Initially, it was difficult for the executive sponsor to convince other executives to buy into her idea to develop a coherent and comprehensive enterprise-wide BAP, as it was perceived as taking a step back to create a BAP for refining the enterprise IT strategy. Utilizing the principles mentioned above, an architecture practice was established that would influence the two participating business units and stimulate subsequent enterprise-level initiatives. However, the question still remained: "How can the power of BA be leveraged to enable business-IT alignment?"

STAGE 2: ENABLING THE PRACTICE

Many business and IT leaders jointly contributed significant time and effort in guiding the team from the inception of the BAP. They were instrumental in setting ground rules for delivering the right business value and gaining the trust and confidence of other executives. Using "big picture" business models, the dependencies were exposed, deficiencies, and redundancies between business functions and services in the two business units. This allowed other units to estimate the level of effort needed to use the BAP. However, a few resistances or barriers still existed during this stage:

- Many team members lacked healthcare IT–related business domain skills, and since the industry was still emerging, it was difficult to hire experts on time and within budget.
- The BAP life cycle process and methodology were still new and yet to mature, making it difficult to establish the BAP value proposition adequately and quantitatively. To counter this, evolving industry trends are continuously evaluated, BA best practices leveraged, and thus collectively incorporated significant values.
- Many business associates were either reluctant to accept the change or too busy in dealing with their tactical operations-related challenges – in spite of the commitment made by the training organization to deliver educational learning, executive briefings, and working sessions to cultivate the benefits of the BA.
- The existing EA practice team had taken only an advisory role in technology selection and did not adequately instill the risk management plan or policy compliance and governance reviews.

Each of the above-mentioned barriers or adverse situations made it essential for us to chart a well-planned course in increasing the organizational maturity of the practice by performing the tasks shown in Figure 11.2. A few specific KPIs were developed based on BA requirements that were important for senior management and were essential to us driving enterprise-wide business and IT alignment. Furthermore, this enabled the BAP team to measure, monitor, and manage progress while enforcing corrective actions as necessary.

In order to address all the tasks in Stage 2 and associated supporting activities, the following steps were specifically considered:

- **Leveraging a Comprehensive People-Process-Technology Paradigm** – primarily to establish a consistent and practical approach in order to increase organizational maturity. So as to improve the team chemistry and structure, it was planned to assign the right mix of health IT domain and architecture experts; and to conduct several educational sessions to build knowledge capital across participating business units. It was decided to adopt TOGAF and Zachman's EA methodology along with the Federal Segment Architecture Methodology (FSAM) to augment our BA methodology. A Rational Unified Process (RUP) and Unified Modeling Language (UML) notation-based approach was selected for the BA modeling and creating the "big picture" view of the BA.
- **Revisiting the Charter of the Practice** – essentially to cultivate a few basic rules of engagement with a proposed responsibility and accountability matrix (often defined as a RASCI matrix in the industry) and decided to review the charter and the ground rules defined in the previous stage. An innovative and collaborative "think big and start small" mind-set was devised, in addition to iterative and incremental ways to align the enterprise business blueprint with relevant strategic and tactical business and IT objectives. The initial version of the charter (developed in Stage 1) focused on ensuring consensus on the creation, evolution and adoption of comprehensive business-centric blueprints or models for the two business organizations involved. The charter was revisited to facilitate innovation and collaboration across the enterprise, making sure that the enterprise business blueprint was aligned with relevant strategic and tactical business as well as IT objectives, including:
  a. Strategic planning, budget process, and capital investments planning; and
  b. Business operations and associated operational constraints or issues regarding cost containment efforts and workforce planning.
- **Enforcing Core Principles, Strategies, and Guidelines** – ideally to execute a plan of action to formally introduce the BAP to the enterprise and also to evaluate the impact of this practice on the first two associated organizations. Practical observations and lessons learned were captured and shared the information with all business units and stakeholders appropriately. The BAP was formally introduced to the enterprise and, at the same time, the opportunity was extended to the team involved in evaluating the impact of the practice on the first two business units as a pilot implementation. The plan was to capture the observations and lessons learned,

and share the information with the entire enterprise and all stakeholders. The primary focus for the activities here was to establish:

a. The key objectives of the practice and a set of metrics to measure its effectiveness;
b. The roles and responsibilities of the participating organizations and individual team members;
c. A consistent BA assurance process; and
d. Comprehensive BA governance, risk management, and architecture compliance review procedures.

Most activities performed at this stage were aimed at assessing and improving the maturity of the BAP continuously. It was explored whether the BA team was forward thinking enough to recognize and act on the impact of the key tenets of BA. Furthermore, the processes were investigated to determine how the BAP could help the business and IT functional units chart a road map for delivering a transformational Health-Is-US enterprise.

STAGE 3: MANAGING THE PRACTICE

During the first two phases, our primary focus was directed towards getting the first two business divisions ready to roll out the BAP. The practice charter was formulated with a specific set of principles and guidelines in mind. A straw man working model was developed for the BAP with primary roles, responsibilities, and accountabilities of the business units and associates involved. During this third stage, the focus was extended to managing the knowledge capital, reviewing and refining the guiding principles, and measuring the progress of the practice. As shown in Figure 11.3, a systematic approach was introduced to make the BAP work effectively. This consisted of four iterative and incremental steps, building on the specifics of the current state of the BAP. These steps were performed to evaluate the completeness of BA artifacts periodically. Additionally, three concurrent activities were carried out and directed towards achieving the future prospects of the BAP.

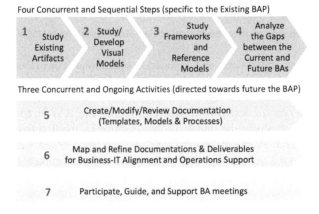

FIGURE 11.3   Making the BAP work effectively.

In Figure 11.3, the steps and activities for making the BAP work effectively are presented. The following three specific steps were most significant:

1. **Check the consistency of templates for BA artifacts** such as documents, modeling guidelines, and inspection or walkthrough procedures. This step helped us standardize the process for business units to engage the BAP efficiently. As needed, the templates were reviewed and modified before publishing them in the corporate process asset library (PAL).

2. **Prepare visual models for the missing areas of** BA to cover business processes in disparate and silo business units and identify the broken links in business processes. This step supported us identifying broken links in business processes, and in establishing a conduit for collaboration amongst participating business and IT functions.

3. **Inculcate changes in both strategic and tactical levels of architecture-related activities** for the modification of the business strategy, in line with evolving changes in business processes and for the alignment of existing and acquired resources. This step also helped us improve the capabilities of business operations by streamlining some processes mentioned above.

Each of these steps offered a specific and measurable value proposition for the BA blueprint. It was useful to manage the effort to build a consensus on understanding of BA for all parties involved, during this stage. A set of common standards were adopted and architectural frameworks (i.e., TOGAF, FSAM, and Zachmann's Architecture Framework) were considered to substantiate the blueprint. The most important aspects of performing these steps in this stage were to relate the elements of the BA blueprint to business strategies, and then to determine the links between business processes and the specific goals of these strategies. The foundation for the risk management and governance plan created and substantiated in the previous stage with a set of comprehensive and quantifiable measurement parameters, including desired KPIs. An independent team was formed to identify the needs for new BA templates, as well as guidelines that must be followed in order to incorporate available standards, mandates, and regulations from various healthcare-related government agencies. This team published such templates in the corporate PAL and also coordinated, collaborated, and worked with business units to identify new template or guideline needs specific to their business focus.

STAGE 4: REALIZING THE PRACTICE

At this stage of the BAP life cycle, it was expected to establish the BAP as an operational and effective practice able to reap the benefits promised at inception. The governance structure of the BAP created a virtual team, since it involved members from both business and IT divisions. The team members, as part of this virtual organization, shared core responsibilities as well as accountabilities and collectively performed the following tasks:

a. Establishing a transparent and collaborative environment across business and IT organizations;

    b. Enabling business sponsors and stakeholders make well-informed IT decisions;

    c. Extending the span of the BAP across the entire enterprise organically; and

    d. Subsequently, establishing the position of the BA as an integral part of the EA and business Strategy.

Our approach here was in alignment with the value stream concept discussed by Whittle and Myrick.[11] As presented by these authors, "a value stream is an end to end collection of activities that creates a result for a customer." A number of basic value streams were identified through our concurrent activities in all four stages and realized the benefits of them using the following principles:

- Aligning business processes or components identified as part of the BAP to business strategy, vision, and objectives or potential business operation goals, and tracking them to improve business system performance and efficiency.
- Making continuous and consistent process improvements using industry standards, recognized architectural frameworks, and full life cycle process maturity models, along with a consistent measurement program.
- Applying governance and risk management processes to reconcile the capability of the BAP in collaborating, coordinating, and delivering business value, with periodic assessments of the BA's value proposition.
- Employing a measurement program to monitor and manage the progress of the BAP during each stage in achieving its goals and objectives, and also to succeed in meeting the expectations of sponsors, customers, and stakeholders.

In this section, a comprehensive account of the steps and activities performed by the BAP team at Health-Is-US has been presented in four stages. As part of the BAP team, involved team also captured a series of observations and lessons learned while performing the activities associated with these stages. As presented in the commentary of the stages, most of these thoughts are specifically related to our experience with the BAP; but they can be leveraged to realize the direct benefits of a BAP at any enterprise.

REALITIES OF THE BAP: FROM THE TRENCHES

At this point, a few other observations from the trenches are introduced in brief. In reality, these lessons learned are from the activities carried out in conjunction with the BAP. Ongoing sourcing initiatives, trading and technology partner collaborations, and proactive compliance efforts for corporate and government specific mandates and regulations are a few of these activities or tasks.

PRACTICAL OBSERVATIONS AND LESSONS LEARNED

As the BAP evolved, so did the interactions between the BAP and rest of the enterprise initiatives or projects. Here a short list of observations and the lessons learned is being shared across the organization that were captured while addressing some key challenges:

- **Lack of clarity in business strategy** made readying the enterprise to adopt or embrace the concepts of the BAP, its processes, principles, and charter difficult to achieve. It also affected the way the BAP engaged business units as well as other IT initiatives. The attention was focused on identifying the key elements of the business strategy and used them to drive clearly the processes and activities involved in the BAP.
- **Lack of understanding of the BAP's role** made collaborative interactions between the BAP and business units, as well as other enterprise-level initiatives, complicated. The team reached out to the office of the CIO to formalize the roles, responsibilities, and rules of engagement in driving the associated strategies, processes, and formalities when engaging the BAP.
- **The organizational structure and the mix of the team members** changed frequently during the initial stages, until a balance of healthcare domain expertise and experienced architects was established. The team involved recognized, during the early stages, that to establish an effective BAP, it was as imperative to have business domain expertise as to have architecture related experience. A balanced team proved to be essential in establishing a truly efficient practice.
- **Impacts from BAP activities were significant for a business unit** as a number of its key business areas transformed to support multiple patient-centric medical systems in the CDS organization. However, various healthcare delivery systems acquired in recent years helped the BAP recognize business processes associated with clinical information systems and decision support solutions. Subsequently it helped develop the "big picture" visual model of the BA. The outcome empowered the BAP to enhance associated business processes with clinical information systems and decision support solutions.

ACTIONS TAKEN

Based on the observations and lessons learned, the BAP team proposed setting a number of ground rules for establishing interactions with the BAP:

1. Recognize the expectations of the business sponsor(s) in order to obtain the buy-in and, in most cases, identify and prioritize the right requirements for the BAP to consider. This action led us to explore opportunities to improve BAP activities and also to establish a clear "big picture" that could be extended across the entire Health-Is-US enterprise.
2. Identify the true cost benefits and find out how the BAP directly relates to the financial objectives of the enterprise. This helped us support business sponsors better in their decision-making process.
3. Review how business values of the BA can be measured, managed, and monitored. This action helped us recognize how to improve performance, productivity, and the quality of business service or solution delivery, as goals of the BAP.
4. Define the roles and responsibilities of each member of the BAP team and associated business and IT teams. This allowed us to attribute appropriate

accountability, responsibility, and ownership to the right team member
while optimizing resource allocation.

5. Capture requirements for compliance with industry and government regulations, policies, and procedures. This made Health-Is-US more Agile in
dealing with most mandates and legal compliance issues and helped the
BAP deal with specific security and privacy issues.

6. Agree upon periodic reviews with the governance body and the stakeholders. This helped us define the goals and objectives of the BAP and map its
progress to meet enterprise-wide business goals, for the business sponsor
and other executives involved.

7. Build and manage a set of ground rules that are correlated to the direct contribution of the BAP to business and IT alignment and operational support.
This enabled us to manage the relationship of the BAP with other business
and IT functions in a more consistent way.

The team submits that most of these actions and steps were specific to the situation of
Health-Is-US – individual practitioners may have to revisit the significance of each
step in terms of his or her own enterprise business goals. However, the team strongly
believes that these actions are effective in setting the charter and rules of engagement
for any BAP.

BEST PRACTICES IN BAP

The team also recognizes that most of the best practices cultivated in this case study
may not be equally applicable to all BAP initiatives. However, it strongly believes that it
is essential to capitalize on them nonetheless. A list of best practices are submitted here:

- **Start with a Business Focus and Keep it that Way** – business strategy and
objectives propelled the creation of the BAP. Today, the BAP has been sup-
porting and influencing all aspects of architectural domains and business
operations, making it essential to maintaining the business focus across the
BAP life cycle.
- **Put Together a Balanced Team** – leveraging existing resources with
expertise in business and architecture domains equally is important for the
BAP. A team with this balance helped us develop the most effective BA.
- **Ready an Enterprise in Stages (Iteratively and Incrementally)** – the
BAP adopted a "think ahead to the big picture, yet start with the small"
mantra from the beginning. It enabled us to create a set of metrics that
measure the value of the BA. Subsequently, the set of metrics has been
modified to capture and monitor the progress of the practice for the entire
enterprise.
- **Keep Business and IT Organizations Engaged at All Levels** – the BAP
acted as the liaison between the business and IT teams. The value proposition for the BAP extended from capitalizing on the guidance of business
strategy to encapsulating business processes to transforming BA elements
into business solutions.

- **Manage and Maintain Executive Sponsorship** – the primary focus of the BAP shifted from guiding IT strategy formulation to driving business solution deployment. However, it is important to secure funding throughout the life cycle of the BAP. The executive sponsors were briefed periodically at each stage.
- **Governance is Essential, Not "Nice to Have"** – the BAP evolved over the stages of its life cycle. However, incorporating governance principles and processes made a significant impact in the success of the practice. It was critical to apply governance and risk management processes that were pragmatic yet practical. These processes instilled a lightweight approach to managing the expectations of sponsors, customers, and stakeholders.

GOVERNANCE, RISK MANAGEMENT, AND COMPLIANCE

A formal and effective governance process usually supports continuous and consistent improvements of the BAP by employing a set of regular and quantifiable metrics and a well-planned measurement program. From the ongoing experience in the field, it is recognized that an effective and fully operational BAP must address challenges that arise from lack of funding, sponsorship, and quantified business and IT alignment, as well as also specific concerns and issues related to the impact of the BAP on other IT initiatives.

In order to bring it all together, it is crucial to apply governance and risk management processes that are pragmatic in approach. The concurrent activities in all four stages of the Health-Is-US BAP initiative helped us define a holistic framework encompassing governance, risk management, and compliance factors incrementally and iteratively. The outcome of the activities from all four stages instilled a lightweight approach for managing the expectations of sponsors, customers, and stakeholders.

During the course of all four stages in the life cycle of the Health-Is-US BAP, the team developed a simple, three-tier, organizationally virtual governance body, as shown in Figure 11.4, to address the major challenges, issues, and risks of the BAP. First and foremost, the framework ensured that the BAP team engaged stakeholders at all levels.

FIGURE 11.4 Basic elements of BA governance.

In Tier 1, the Business Strategy Council included C-Level executives as well as executives from the business units – specifically their operations and compliance functional teams. This body provided executive sponsorship, reviewed and approved changes to business strategy, and also prioritized BA initiatives.

In Tier 2, the leader of the EA team chaired the BA Council and encouraged the participation of all business and IT key functional leaders, including security, infrastructure, and data services team representatives. This body reviewed all changes to the BA and proposed as well as monitored architecturally significant BA initiatives. The BA Council also reviewed presentations and directed effective BA implementation throughout the enterprise by applying standards and architecture principles consistently.

In Tier 3, Health-Is-US had four major BA Stakeholder Committees collaborate and interact with their shared governance, risk management, and compliance issues. Each BA Stakeholder Committee included representatives from key business unit IT projects or programs under its own oversight and jurisdiction. Normally, a BAP team member acted as a chairperson or primary representative in such meetings. These committees gathered periodically in joint sessions and reviewed all major challenges, issues, and concerns. They also identified changes or actions that had to be taken to improve achieving the goals and objectives of the BAP. The committees collectively discussed most significant BA initiatives tracked within their own, individual purview, and shared lessons learned from such initiatives.

GENERAL COMMENTS AND RECOMMENDATIONS

In the initial stages of establishing the BAP, the scope and the team mix are very important. However, subsequently, organizational fiefdoms have to be overcome to identify and focus on the transformation of key business functions and their enterprise-level objectives. Further maturity requires robust business-IT collaboration that is driven within a well-thought-out governance structure and with clearly defined metrics from a well-orchestrated measurement program. As BA methodology, frameworks, and standards continue to emerge today, it is important that BAP team members and sponsors understand that the tools and focus areas ought to differ in each stage of the life cycle.

BAP team members and sponsors must understand the significance of the governance model in each stage of the life cycle. Business units drive and prioritize business process transformation (reengineering or improvement) initiatives. Hence, the BAP should capture and articulate its impact on application, information, and technology architectures to maximize the benefits for business process transformation. The BAP makes the EA more driven and governed by business rather than IT. It instills a fundamental shift in the roles and responsibilities for the EA. Hence, it is important that the roles and responsibilities be clearly defined and the accountabilities be well understood by the professionals involved.

The team has captured, cultivated, and socialized a set of best practices from all four stages – listed in the previous section. The BAP presented in this case study is currently operational and supports the entire enterprise at Health-Is-US. The BAP team also continuously modifies and refines best practices along with the processes and principles adopted in the BAP.

Participants in Activities for BA P Life Cycle Stages

BAP Lifecycle Stages	Business Sponsor	Business Stakeholder(s)	Business User(s)	Business Strategy Council	BA Council	BA Stakeholders Committee(s)	Business Architecture	IT Architecture	Information Architecture	Application Architecture	Technology Architecture	Application Development	Application Integration	Program Management	Operational Support	Business Portfolio Manager
1. Building the Practice	A	R	C	C	R	C	A	S	I	I	I	I	I	I	I	I
2. Establishing the Practice	C	C	C	I	R	S	A	S	S	S	S	C	C	S	I	I
3. Managing the Practice	S	S	I	I	R	S	A	C	S	S	S	S	S	S	S	S
4. Realizing the Practice	R	S	C	C	R	S	A	C	R	R	R	S	S	S	S	R

LEGEND

R (Responsible) - delegated to take an action (on behalf of the practice)
A (Accountable) - accountable for governance, approval, ownership, and authority to delegate action as well take an action
S (Support) - supportive role, which means the party should review and provide additional information
C (Consulting) - consultative role which means the party should be consulted
I (Informing) - information notification role and the party should be informed

FIGURE 11.5 A RASCI matrix to drive BAP stages.

The team used the RASCI matrix presented in Figure 11.5 to establish a common understanding of the roles and responsibilities for the participants involved in various stages of the BAP life cycle.

This RASCI matrix provides only a cursory snapshot of the involvement of various team members, stakeholders, and business sponsors and users. In this matrix, the team has focused on the participants and their roles and responsibilities at a very high level under five categories of – (R) responsible; (A) accountable; (S) supportive; (C) consultative; and (I) informative.

While the industry practice is to choose one responsible and one single accountable party (or individual) for each stage – the team has identified multiple parties in each stage of the BAP initiative. The team strongly urges that professionals involved in developing an enterprise-level BAP recognize and leverage accountability, robust governance, and closely monitored metrics efficiently to succeed in their BAP initiative. Furthermore, business leadership must ensure that maturity is achieved and maintained throughout the life cycle of the practice.

FUTURE PROSPECTS OF THE BAP

While there is no crystal ball to predict the future of the BAP, one can envision the potential future prospects for it. A set of relevant thoughts and suggestions can be categorized in three areas – (1) BAP as a business function; (2) BAP as a driving force behind the future Agile enterprise; and (3) emerging BAP standards that support common goals for business units.

- **BAP as a Business Function** – the BAP will finally be recognized as a business discipline, with value streams or chains, business models, strategic planning, and operational efficiencies. It will directly impact business decision-making. It will include IT, business, and organization architectures. In the short-term, as suggested in this book, the governance of the BAP will be increasingly business driven and top-management heavy. Gradually, the BAP will be called upon more in the business decision-making process, as it deals with business logic, technology, operation, and strategy. As the concepts of the practice mature, it will be important to map the strategy to components and drive an enterprise transformation portfolio that directly impact investments, as well as to take strategic and tactical decisions that drive operational efficiency. Eventually, a BAP will be increasingly required by stakeholders, owners, and investors to provide the blueprint of business operations; to describe IT assets; to provide proof of regulatory compliance, map costs, and profits on various operations; and to align business and IT strategies. The BAP will become a regulatory feature for publicly listed companies, as well as the public sector.
- **BAP Driving the Future Agile Enterprise** – BAP will drive towards designing business to achieve desired outcomes. This will help professionals converge strategy and associated technology to drive business results. Mergers, acquisitions, and outsourcing activities will drive the growth of BAP (ITO/BPO, SaaS, and ASP) and create nimble and Agile enterprises.

BAP will leverage enabler technologies like Cloud Computing and data virtualization to drive towards utility models that provide an on-demand backbone for an Agile enterprise. In fast changing market conditions with intense global competition, BAP will take business strategy and requirements to directly drive the operational constructs that will leverage on-demand, architecturally coherent, cost effective, and "ready when needed" utility models.

- **Emerging BAP Standards to Support Common Business Goals** – BA frameworks will emerge to define a common standard and approach for the business world. For example, BAP will drive SOA as the target architecture and technology, rather than an invocation of shared services. The lack of BA standards has been a challenge that will continue to hurt in the short-term, but as businesses realize the value and as best practices emerge further and gravitate towards common approach, it will be more accepted across the business and IT community. Today, emerging standards are already being accepted more broadly. Also, BAP is already leveraging several standard frameworks that are currently being stretched to suit BA needs. Multiple standards and commonly available frameworks can provide support to a BAP, depending on the background and skill levels of the team members. Consistent and cohesive tools and standards will certainly emerge as the field matures.

NOTES

1 Hazra, T. K., and Kumar, S. "Establishing Business Architecture as a Practice – A Case Study." *Executive Report*, Vol. 15, No. 1, Cutter Consortium, 2012.
2 https://www.omg.org/bawg/ accessed 1 April, 2020.
3 Spewak, S. H., & Hill, S. C., (1993), *Enterprise Architecture Planning – Developing a Blueprint for Data, Applications, and Technology*, (QED Publishing Group), Boston, MA.
4 Whittle, R. "Enterprise Integration with Business Architecture, Executive Report – Business Enterprise Architecture Advisory service." *Cutter Consortium*, Vol. 14, No. 7, 2011.
5 Whittle R., and Myrick C. B., (2004), *Enterprise Business Architecture – The Formal Link Between Strategy and Results*, (CRC Press, LLC), USA, p. 31.
6 Boettger, S. "Achieving Real Value-Add from Your Business-Driven Enterprise Architecture: Realizing the Void." *Executive Report, Enterprise Architecture Advisory Service*, Vol. 13, No. 7, 2010.
7 Whittle, R. "Enterprise Integration with Business Architecture." *Executive Report – Business Enterprise Architecture Advisory Service, Cutter Consortium*, Vol. 14, No. 7, 2011.
8 Ulrich, W. "Business Architecture, Part I – V." *Executive Updates – Enterprise Architecture Advisory Service, Cutter Consortium*, Vol. 14, No. 7–10, and 13, 2011.
9 The case study is real, but the name is hypothetical for obvious reasons.
10 Hazra, T. K. "Aligning business and IT architectures: A seven-step approach." *Negotiating the Path to Business Architecture/IT Architecture Alignment*, Edited by Ulrich W., Cutter IT Journal, December 2008.

Appendix A
Use Cases in EA and Digital Business

SUMMARY

This chapter briefly outlines four practical use cases undertaken by the authors. The identities of the clients are removed for obvious reasons but they reflect real experiences of the lead author. These use cases detail the client, the roles and responsibilities of an Enterprise Architecture (EA) practice, and a summary of the Digital Transformation (DT) initiative. There were numerous challenges, issues, and risks encountered and lessons learned that were represented in the previous chapters of this book. The focus in each of these consulting assignments was to enable the organization to provide and enhance customer value by utilizing EA, Business Architecture, and the processes outlined in this book. These initiatives resulted in considerable benefits for the enterprise and a much better understanding of the value EA can add to the entire organization. The complexities of digital, collaborative business; the reengineering of business processes (especially supply chains); and the need for governance and compliance were all handled through the "EA as a practice" model for these clients.

CASE # 1: BUILDING THE EA AS "ONE ENTERPRISE" ARCHITECTURE

INDUSTRY – INSURANCE

Problem Description – A US-based multibillion dollar company with multiple lines of business, employing about 12,000 people worldwide, 750+ of whom were in IT. The CIO decided to consolidate enterprise-level business applications, while making the delivery of customer-facing business functions highly digitized and personalized.

Challenges, Issues, and Concerns – Most of the IT staff were familiar with the technology, platforms, and operations in different insurance business domains such as policy administration and management, billing, pricing, and underwriting, and they knew how to support their own functional areas or "silos." However, they didn't know how to envision an enterprise-level "big picture" view of the company. Businesses have their own specific IT teams they trust and vendors they procure services from, but the company lacked the senior IT expertise that could lead an enterprise-level effort of this magnitude (more than $300 million dollars was allocated as capital budget), let alone creating a core competency that can be leveraged across the business. The CIO and his direct reports instituted a governance board to evaluate the state of IT organizations inside the company, however, the share services group showed little or no interest in collaborating with the governance team. A major concern for many IT staff is that some of their functions were outsourced to an offshore vendor before the consolidation decision was made, and the CIO instructed that those operations must also be integrated with the enterprise-level initiative.

Recommendations – Enterprise Architecture (EA) metrics should be developed with business requirements, goals, and objectives in mind; all business functions should be engaged from the beginning; and the EA should be founded on a "big picture" concept from the beginning. The EA also needs to provide the base for consolidating the many systems into a holistic solution. Customer value should be measured, through a survey, before and after the digitization and consolidation.

Major Activities Considered – The governance team was initially charged with creating a portfolio of enterprise-level initiatives. The CIO and his team assigned appropriate IT managers and technical leads to collaborate with the corresponding functions and to capture business requirements that would support enterprise-level strategy. Subsequently, an initiative for updating the EA, together with relevant extensions and new builds, was approved.

The EA team started their operations with a charter that planned to support the business case for digitization and the strategy for building a target EA that would enable the desired digitization. They initiated meetings with different business functions to understand their operation, goals, and objectives, and got both business and IT functions engaged to recognize important processes that had to be supported. They prepared a number of documents that described various architectural guidelines, industry best practices, and EA principles to be followed across the enterprise; developed a road map with specific blueprints, milestones, and deliverables while drawing a "big picture'" of the enterprise; and identified a set of EA metrics and subsequently refined them based on the custom needs of the respective functions. The EA team was actively involved with multiple business and IT organizations, as well as offshore teams, to manage EA metrics and align to a "One Enterprise" architecture.

Results Delivered – The governance team is well structured today and has clear oversight of most of the ongoing initiatives across the enterprise; a set of processes were adopted across the enterprise to capture, monitor, and report the EA metrics to the team; periodic review meetings are held by the team to approve funding and look into other critical issues escalated by the EA team; performance levels of the IT functions increased by 11% over a period of 15 months; and recently, the CIO assigned the EA team the task of exploring the possibility of employing the SOA approach in the company.

Observations – The business was not very enthusiastic about the process at first and, in fact, didn't want to be engaged in the EA initiative; the governance team presented the initial version of the "big picture" well enough to get the IT organizations excited; a number of convoluted and manual processes were exposed early in the process to get the attention of business sponsors; multiple data entry points were located to make a strong case for the "reuse" strategy; the EA metrics took a while to be captured and managed well, since there was no previous experience with the measurement and analysis in-house; and the learning process was time consuming and extensive due to a lack of expertise in the EA arena.

Lessons Learned – The awareness program has been educational and has promoted responsibility as well as accountability; both business and IT organizations were motivated to capture the EA metrics and contributed equally to improve their quality; and business-IT alignment played a key role in the adoption of the EA metrics.

CASE # 2: ESTABLISHING AN EA PRACTICE TO INTEGRATE MULTIPLE BUSINESS APPLICATIONS

INDUSTRY – HEALTHCARE

Problem Description – A national healthcare company had recently acquired two other smaller companies to increase their footprint in the managed healthcare arena. Total revenue exceeded $1.25 billion and the total number of employees was 8000, of which 350 were in IT. Most of the current systems at the time were disparate and some needed to be automated or reengineered. A new CIO joined the company after the last acquisition. He planned to consolidate different business applications acquired from the acquisitions.

Challenges, Issues, and Concerns – Direct reportees of the CIO faced the challenge of combining the technology base of each individual company into a single EA; the level of experience of the IT employees of the acquired companies was disparate from the latest technologies – many of them were COBOL programmers and had not been exposed to middleware, client-server, or J2EE technologies; and the knowledge and experience of the EA was almost nonexistent – the company had just hired four senior level enterprise architects and one senior IT strategy leader to create the EA from scratch. Another major concern was that there was no inventory of the business applications the company had at the time.

Recommendations – Use a phased approach to build the EA practice; allow the EA metrics to evolve over time, with the use of EA guiding principles, best practices, and industry standards; engage business teams from the beginning to form a truly effective EA practice; and account for time and effort spent to learn during the enterprise integration process.

Major Activities Considered – An awareness program was institutionalized to educate all IT personnel, executives, and business teams; the EA team started to inventory existing systems and solicited the help of all IT teams to collect business requirements and identify redundant systems; a set of guidelines, best practices, and technology standards were formalized as the EA principles to adopt across the enterprise; a set of EA metrics was agreed on so that various IT and business teams could start their enterprise integration initiatives; and an EA governance team was formalized to report the progress of various projects to executive sponsors and the leadership team.

Results Delivered – The EA team helped IT organizations build multiple application architecture teams while focusing on specific business function areas; the EA team established its position as the strategist and guide for all ongoing projects; a number of business applications were consolidated; and the EA metrics developed to measure progress were refined over a period.

Observations – The business teams got involved early since the EA team recognized their specific requirements; there was heavy dependency on legacy systems across the enterprise; the EA team drew the "big picture" EA and socialized it with all the IT teams; the EA metrics focused on the architectural processes, compliance to the guiding principles, and performance improvement factors; and business processes were automated and reengineered as necessary.

Lessons Learned – The EA team succeeded in adopting an incremental transition path; the use of middleware allowed IT teams to migrate slowly from monolithic to two-tier to multi-tier client-server architectures; the architectural analysis helped the EA evolve, while business requirements were identified, captured, and analyzed; the governance board enforced the measurement and analysis process over multiple phases; and the EA metrics were refined over time, resulting in IT executives using them effectively in decision-making.

CASE 3: SUPPORTING EA MODERNIZATION AND APPLICATION RATIONALIZATION

INDUSTRY – FINANCIAL SERVICES

Problem Description – An internationally recognized multibillion dollar systems integration company, with a large client in the middle of a years-long initiative to integrate and modernize various financial accounting and payment systems. The company had 30,000+ employees worldwide – 1100 of them in IT – all with varied interdisciplinary skills. The client was modifying its business processes to improve the quality of financial services available to end users. The senior executive in charge of the contract planned to modernize the EA and rationalize several applications to streamline certain business processes that impact the quality of current service offerings and that would make a difference for future systems.

Challenges, Issues, and Concerns – The client had no resources with relevant experience or skills in EA; most of the applications in place were packaged solutions, customized over the years by outside consultants; no documents existed that described the interfaces (if any) between different applications; business domain experts were too busy to offer their vision of a future target solution; there were a number of redundant applications, some of which supported a small community of users who accessed those systems frequently; and the business organizations supporting those users were resistant to any changes in the applications. The primary challenge of the executive involved was first to develop a blueprint that included all the applications and which captured both existing business functions and new requirements for supporting existing and future users. His major concern was how to promote enterprise-level architectural processes, standards, frameworks, and best practices to the client since they had no prior experience with that.

Recommendations – Use an iterative and incremental approach for the EA modernization – a consistent awareness program is key; provide the inexperienced client teams a "big picture" blueprint so they could follow the transformation and accept changes; the EA metrics needed to evolve and mature over a period of time; and engage the business teams early to reduce associated risks significantly.

Major Activities Considered – A small but efficient EA team was formed to promote awareness of enterprise-level integration technologies to all IT and business professionals. The EA team started by interacting with all teams and creating a blueprint that captured all "as-is" operations and that documented future "to-be'" possibilities and requirements. A number of industry-leading best practices on modernizing legacy systems were adopted and guidelines for their use were published in the company's shared drive; a number of requests were made to client executives to restructure their functions to better support the blueprint for future operations; a few redundant systems were retired without disrupting any user support; a set of EA metrics was identified; and different IT organizations were assigned to gather relevant data.

Results Delivered – A number of business functions were modernized and more resources were available to support the applications delivering them; IT teams were more motivated as they continued to learn about the latest advanced technologies; the EA team adopted an architectural framework well known in the industry; the business teams became more involved and engaged than earlier; the performance level improved 8% over the past year – as the EA metrics continued to measure it and customer satisfaction; the governance team had their first review meeting; the client extended the contract by a year; and a customer survey showed a much higher satisfaction rating than expected.

Observations – Business teams found the reengineering and automation efforts attractive as they reduced the effort requited to support daily operations but there were still more business reengineering activities needed to make the functions completely customer facing. A portal-development effort commenced to enhance customer service while integrating current service offerings into a single access point; the EA metrics continued to evolve as the governance team was formalizing its charter; and three legacy systems were replaced with one new multi-tier, J2EE-based system.

Lessons Learned – The transition plan for modernizing existing business functions was designed based on impact on business goals, which helped engage business teams early; the contractor used its own experience restructuring a large organization for the client, making identifying parameters for the EA metrics easier; the awareness program helped the client's IT teams recognize business needs and connect with new technologies, best practices, and industry standards; and performance measures became a key component of EA metrics for the client.

The practitioners involved in these three projects have used most of the seven steps mentioned earlier. It was not possible to provide equal importance to each of the steps. Some of the questions listed with these steps are used extensively to drive the initiatives. While using these steps, it is worth mentioning that practitioners must also consider other associated factors and challenges that may be unique to their situation.

CASE 4: MEASURING THE SUCCESS OF OFFSHORING PROJECTS

INDUSTRY – CONSULTING

Problem Description – This use case is different to the previous three as it includes activities undertaken by an EA practice as part of an assignment to evaluate the success of a large US-based firm outsourcing operations to a vendor offering First Level Support (Infrastructure). A third-party independent consulting company with extensive experience in measuring the success of offshoring projects was invited to assess the client situation, organize EA-based metrics and measures, and comment on the results.

Challenges, Issues, and Concerns – We were to identify key performance indicators, determine if there were any gaps between desired business goals and expectations, and appraise the overall success of the current operation. The assessment had the additional challenge of looking at costs associated with cross-cultural differences, diversity, different working behaviors, etc., and then identifying if these or any other unexpected factors would result in extra costs.

Recommendation – We recommended a three-phased approach to help the company evaluate its outsourcing activities. Our EA practice designed this to deliver value at each stage, to maximize benefits to our client from the beginning and at every step, regardless of how many of the steps they chose to pursue. The three phases identified three specific focus areas:

1. Identifying key performance indicators (KPIs),
2. Determining gaps in desired business goals and expectations (of the involved client organization), and
3. Appraising the success of the initiative.

MAJOR ACTIVITIES

In the following section, we provide – for each phase – a synopsis of the objectives and a detailed work breakdown structure.

Phase I: Establishing, Assessing, and Reviewing KPIs

The cornerstone of success is establishing a set of key parameters that can pragmatically measure the incremental level of progress over time. For the client's current offshoring initiative, it was essential to recognize existing KPIs and rigorously review them. Following this, it would be necessary to verify and validate their significance to the objectives and goals of the initiative. Subsequently, it was imperative that we documented these KPIs along with possible critical success factors evident in the initiative. Primary tasks, deliverables, and the level of efforts (in hours) for this phase were estimated and recorded in the establishment of the KPIs.

Phase 2: Conducting Gap Analysis and Presenting Benchmarks

Once the KPIs were identified and formally accepted by the organization, it was imperative to perform a comprehensive investigation of the "as-is" and "to-be" situations of the infrastructure and associated services, to determine the level of success in the offshoring initiative. The primary objective of this phase was to perform a rigorous gap analysis, investigate various relevant parameters, and measure their direct and indirect impact with respect to the benchmarks and industry trends.

Phase 3: Performing Success Evaluation and Offering Recommendations
During this final phase of the engagement, the appraisal of the initiative is performed, taking into consideration the KPIs and independently developed evaluation criteria. The primary intention was to deliver an independent assessment report, as well as recommendations to improve the prospect of success in the client's current and future offshoring initiatives. Most of the appraisal activities were conducted on-site and the appraisal report was submitted to the engagement sponsor. The consulting engagement delivered the following benefits to the organization:

- A strategic and yet pragmatic and consistent approach to optimizing cost control for the ongoing and future offshore outsourcing initiatives
- Highly quantifiable and repeatable metrics to measure and monitor the return on technological investments and resource utilization across the boundaries of organization, assuring the values of cultural shift in the paradigm of sourcing
- A road map for achieving the sustainable value of offshoring, including reduced management time, improved process of governing offshore projects, and enhanced customer satisfaction levels
- A highly effective impact analysis that can be utilized in identifying and resolving critical risks in the ongoing and future organization offshore projects.

Observations – Measurements and metrics played a crucial role in the relationship between the client and the outsourcing partner. Firstly, the metrics provided the senior leadership of our client enough justification for their outsourcing effort. Secondly, the metrics proved the value of the outsourcing partner, which, in turn, strengthened the relationship. Cultural nuances were better understood across the physical and cultural divide, which opened up doors for further engagement of other partners on both sides. We found that the EA practice experience was highly beneficial in carrying out a metrics and measurement program because it was focused and, as discussed in the Business Architecture Practice chapter (Chapter 11), balanced both the business and the technology sides.

Index

Printed in the United States
by Baker & Taylor Publisher Services